W9-BSK-672

MAKE COINS MORE PROFITABLE FOR YOU THAN FOR THE DEALER!

Do you know why a 1909-S V.D.B. Lincoln cent is worth more than the much rarer 1876 nickel three-cent piece? How to guarantee that a coin's condition is what the seller says it is? What to pay for a 1913 Buffalo nickel? What today's value is for a 1963 proof set that originally cost $2.10? Why "cleaning" is a dirty word for serious collectors?

Top authority Scott A. Travers makes sure you know the bottom line on U.S. coins—their condition, their scarcity, and *the price they bring right now!* You can feel confident when you buy and satisfied when you sell because you have at hand the best coin book in America—

THE INSIDER'S GUIDE TO U.S. COIN VALUES 2003

Also by Scott A. Travers

The Coin Collector's Survival Manual
How to Make Money in Coins Right Now
The Investor's Guide to Coin Trading
One-Minute Coin Expert
Travers' Rare Coin Investment Strategy
Scott Travers' Top 88 Coins Over $100

The
INSIDER'S GUIDE
to
U.S. COIN VALUES
2003

SCOTT A. TRAVERS

A Dell Book

Published by
Dell Publishing
a division of
Random House, Inc.
New York, New York

Dell books may be purchased for business or promotional use or for special sales. For information please write to: Special Markets Department, Random House, Inc., New York, New York.

Dell® and its colophon are registered trademarks of Random House, Inc.

ISBN: 0-440-23754-8

Printed in the United States of America

Published simultaneously in Canada

December 2002
10 9 8 7 6 5 4 3 2 1
OPM

Table of Contents

ACKNOWLEDGMENTS
viii

PREFACE
xi

THE 1933 DOUBLE EAGLE GOLD COIN
xiii

AMERICA'S STATE QUARTER PROGRAM
xix

Chapter One
THE LURE OF COINS
1

Chapter Two
FIGURING OUT WHAT IT'S WORTH
9

Chapter Three
MAKING THE GRADE IN COINS
18

Chapter Four
U.S. COIN VALUES
28

Half Cents
Large Cents
Flying Eagle Cents
Indian Head Cents
Lincoln Cents
Two-Cent Pieces
Silver Three-Cent Pieces
Nickel Three-Cent Pieces
Half Dimes
Shield Nickels
Liberty Head Nickels
Buffalo Nickels
Jefferson Nickels
Draped Bust Dimes
Capped Bust Dimes
Seated Liberty Dimes
Barber Dimes
"Mercury" Dimes
Roosevelt Dimes
Twenty-Cent Pieces
Draped Bust Quarter Dollars
Capped Bust Quarter Dollars
Seated Liberty Quarter Dollars
Barber Quarter Dollars
Standing Liberty Quarter Dollars
Washington Quarter Dollars
Flowing Hair Half Dollars
Draped Bust Half Dollars
Capped Bust Half Dollars
Seated Liberty Half Dollars
Barber Half Dollars
Walking Liberty Half Dollars
Franklin Half Dollars
Kennedy Half Dollars
Flowing Hair Silver Dollars

Contents

Draped Bust Silver Dollars
Gobrecht Silver Dollars
Seated Liberty Silver Dollars
Morgan Silver Dollars
Peace Silver Dollars
Trade Dollars
Eisenhower Dollars
Anthony Dollars
Sacagawea Dollars
Gold Dollars
$2.50 Gold Pieces
$3 Gold Pieces
$4 Gold Pieces
$5 Gold Pieces
$10 Gold Pieces
$20 Gold Pieces
Commemoratives
American Eagle Bullion Coins
Modern Proof Sets
Special Mint Sets
Type Coins

Appendix A
COIN PERIODICALS
199

Appendix B
COIN SPECIFICATIONS
201

Appendix C
WHERE TO LOOK FOR MINT MARKS
219

ACKNOWLEDGMENTS

I especially appreciate the support, advice, and in some instances the pricing data and information provided to me by a number of persons. The following list is, I believe, all-encompassing; however, I apologize if I have omitted anyone.

John Albanese, David T. Alexander, Charles Anastasio, Dennis Baker, Jack Beymer, Steve Blum, Q. David Bowers, Jeanne Cavelos, William L. Corsa Sr., John W. Dannreuther, Steve Deeds, Thomas K. DeLorey, Silvano DiGenova, Cathy Dumont, John Flicker, Leo Frese, Michael Fuljenz, David L. Ganz, Klaus W. Geipel, Larry Gentile Sr., Salvatore Germano, David Hall, David C. Harper, Brian Hendelson, John Highfill, Robert L. Hughes, Steve Ivy, Kathleen Jayes, Robert W. Julian, Christine Karstedt, Chester L. Krause, David W. Lange, Julian Leidman, Kevin J. Lipton, Denis W. Loring, Dwight Manley, Steve Mayer, Raymond N. Merena, James L. Miller, Lee S. Minshull, John Pack, Martin Paul, Ed Reiter, Maurice Rosen, Michael Keith Ruben, Margo Russell, Mark Salzberg, Greg Samorajski, Florence Schook, Hugh Sconyers, Rich Sear, Vincent Sgro, Larry Shepherd, Michael W. Sherman, Rick Snow, Harvey G. Stack, Rick Sundman, Armen Vartian, Brian Wagner, Mark Yaffe, and Keith M. Zaner.

Bowers and Merena Galleries provided invaluable assistance by supplying excellent photographs for every single coin pictured in this book. The company's talented photographer, Cathy Dumont, spent countless days poring through its files to compile the clear, crisp photos. They greatly enhance this book, and I'm grateful both to her and to the firm.

John Albanese, founder of the Numismatic Guaranty Corporation of America (NGC), provided invaluable assistance in the compilation of values for Barber dimes, quarters and half dollars. Albanese is a preeminent authority on this segment of the coin market. He selflessly devoted many hours to this project, drawing upon both his in-depth book knowledge of these series and his many years of practical experience as a trader.

Jack Beymer, a longtime coin dealer from Santa Rosa, California, graciously agreed to assist me in compiling the prices for U.S. copper coins for the last edition. This is an area in which Beymer is a leading authority and one of the nation's most important dealers. His guidance on the prices was invaluable, and I'm pleased and proud to have had such an expert's services available to me in this project. Denis W. Loring updated these prices for this edition.

Michael R. Fuljenz of Universal Coin & Bullion in Beaumont, Texas, updated the values for gold eagles through double eagles. He is one of the nation's highest-profile and most esteemed gold coin authorities. His contributions, like the metal itself, glitter.

John W. Highfill, a highly esteemed coin dealer and author from Broken Arrow, Oklahoma, was a pillar of strength in the compilation of prices for silver dollars. Highfill is an expert without peer in this segment of the coin market. Among his many accomplishments, he is the founder of the National Silver Dollar Roundtable and the author of *The Comprehensive U.S. Silver Dollar Encyclopedia,* a massive and magnificent book on this popular subject.

Robert L. Hughes, who has handled virtually all of the rarities listed in this book, provided invaluable assistance in filling the dashes with actual values in cases of coins that were previously believed to be too infrequently traded to have their values listed.

Norman W. Pullen of Portland, Maine, a coin dealer whose knowledge is deep as well as broad, furnished particular expertise on the pricing of small cents. His guidance, based on decades as an authoritative market-maker in this area, was immensely helpful and reinforces my confidence in the accuracy of the prices.

Maurice Rosen of Plainview, New York, is not only a major dealer in his own right but also a peerless coin market analyst. His award-winning newsletter, *The Rosen Numismatic Advisory,* has an uncanny knack not only for spotting trends but also for predicting them. Rosen's brilliance shines through in this book in the sections on early silver coins, where he provided tremendous assistance.

Deborah G. Rosenthal is one of the brightest contract lawyers I know and a longstanding friend for many years. She was instrumental in reviewing the language of my agreement with Dell that helped to make the 2003 edition—and editions for years to come—a working reality.

Michael Keith Ruben of Hilton Head, South Carolina, is one of the busiest and savviest coin traders in the business. Ruben probably handles more "super-grade" coins—coins in extremely high levels of preservation—than any other dealer in the world. He generously shared his vast knowledge by helping me prepare and refine the prices for Seated Liberty coinage.

Larry Shepherd is arguably the greatest authority on U.S. commemorative coins, having assembled the finest 144-piece commemorative set. In 1998, he personally oversaw the compilation of prices for commemorative coins. Sal Germano updated those prices for this edition.

The United States Mint Public Information Office assisted me in compiling mintage figures.

> **R. W. Julian, a renowned numismatic scholar, is accorded special thanks and recognition for his superb and outstanding work on the mintage figures in this book.**

PREFACE

If you're like most people, you've probably found a penny lying in the street. Maybe you've even come across a nickel or a dime—or really hit the big time and picked up a stray half dollar.

Did it ever occur to you that coins like these might be worth a lot of money? The odds are against it, of course; most of the "lucky pennies" that turn up at our feet are as common as three-leaf clovers, and so are most of the coins we get in our pocket change. But every now and then, Lady Luck flashes an extra-special smile and directs our attention to a truly exceptional coin—one that's worth a premium of hundreds or thousands of dollars to collectors. And it happens a lot more often than you might think.

That coin may not appear on the sidewalk or the street; instead, you may discover it in a long-forgotten cigar box or tucked away in the drawer of an old, unused dresser in your attic. When it does turn up, however, you'll need a reliable way to determine how much it's worth. *The Insider's Guide to U.S. Coin Values* gives you that information in simple and accurate form, making it far more likely you'll receive a fair price for that special coin when you go to sell it.

Sometimes, the stakes can be staggering. I know of one coin dealer who had a rare coin worth $25,000 in his pocket while riding in a New York City taxicab, but when he got out of the cab the coin was missing. He offered a reward of many thousands of dollars for its return. If you had been fortunate enough to find it, you could have earned yourself a small fortune. And once you've read this book, you'll have a big advantage in knowing what to look for and what the coins you find are really worth.

People who buy or sell coins have traditionally faced three primary risks. The first of these has been an acquisition risk— the risk that they might buy something for $1,000 and then learn it was worth only $100. The second has been a marketplace risk—the risk that they might buy something for $1,000 that was really worth $1,000, but that it might go down in value later because of market conditions. The third has been a sale risk—the risk that if they went to sell a coin worth $1,000, a dealer might take advantage of their ignorance and give them a great deal less.

The Insider's Guide to U.S. Coin Values will be especially helpful to you in minimizing the sale risk. The information contained in these pages will give you the knowledge you need to keep from being the victim of a rip-off.

Recently, someone I know found a coin worth $200 in his pocket change. He took it to a coin shop near his home and the dealer offered him $10. Someone else I know had some valuable old 25-cent pieces that had been in her family for many years. These coins were valued at $2,000 each—but when she took them to a local dealer, he offered her $10 each. There are many honest dealers, but a few bad apples can spoil things for everyone, and you should be prepared to recognize and avoid them.

Armed with the facts and figures in *The Insider's Guide to U.S. Coin Values*, you'll never fall prey to unscrupulous buyers such as these. Knowledge is power, and this book will enable you to always deal from strength when buying or selling coins.

Read on. And happy hunting!

—Scott A. Travers
Scott Travers Rare Coin Galleries Inc.
Box 1711, F.D.R. Station
New York, N.Y. 10150-1711
1-212-535-9135
e-mail: travers@pocketchangelottery.com
Internet: www.pocketchangelottery.com
December 2002

THE 1933 DOUBLE EAGLE GOLD COIN

By ROBERT W. JULIAN

The year 2002 may be recalled in the future as the year in which the fabled 1933 Saint-Gaudens double eagle, or $20 gold piece, was sold at public auction for millions of dollars.

As early as 1937, examples of this coin were openly bought and sold, with more than one prominent collector displaying such a coin at national conventions of the American Numismatic Association and local shows. One advertisement, which appeared in *The Numismatist* of February 1943, offered to buy various rare dates of double eagles—including the 1933—but specified that the pieces had to be uncirculated; the dealer obviously believed that circulated specimens existed.

In January 1944, Stack's, the well-known New York coin firm, announced that it would be holding a public auction on Feb. 18–19 and that the "rare 1933" double eagle, from the collection of Col. James W. Flanagan of Toronto, would be included. For various reasons, the sale was delayed and rescheduled for March 23–25, but at this point the Treasury stepped in and seized the Flanagan coin, saying that it was illegal to own a double eagle of this date. The Treasury further announced that all outstanding specimens were subject to confiscation.

Over the next several years the government showed that this was no idle threat, acting through the Secret Service to seize several specimens, all of which were melted. In a July 1947 court action, Tennessee numismatist L. G. Barnard sued to recover his coin but the judge ruled, according to Mint Director Nellie Tayloe Ross, that "the Government was entitled to the possession of the 1933 Double Eagle in question on the theory that the Double Eagle was never issued as currency but that it was and always has been recognized as a rare coin and as such, having been illegally removed from the Treasury, the Government is entitled to possession of the coin." Other collectors whose coins were seized included Colonel Flanagan, C.M. Williams, James Stack, T. James Clarke, F.C.C. Boyd, James F. Bell and Max Bernstein. As late as 1952, one more piece was voluntarily surrendered by famed numismatist Louis Eliasberg of Baltimore. There is little doubt that this was difficult for Eliasberg to do, as he was well on his way to having the most complete collection of United States coins ever formed, an extraordinary accomplishment unlikely ever to be duplicated.

There has been general criticism from the numismatic community over these actions, as there are many U.S. coins, such as the patently illegal 1913 Liberty Head nickel and the Trade dollars of 1884–1885, which have never been seized by the government. One of the minor numismatic mysteries of the 20th century is why this coin, above all others, was singled out for official displeasure. One source at the Mint recently claimed that the investigation was brought about by an inquiry from a newspaper reporter—but this seems odd, considering that coin auctions were virtually never reported in the mass media in those days; the war then raging in Europe and the Pacific was far more important. Moreover, the number of active collectors able to afford a 1933 double eagle probably was quite small; coin collecting as a truly national hobby did not take root until after 1945.

It is worth noting that the Bureau of the Mint received numerous letters over the years from citizens inquiring about the 1913 Liberty Head nickel, a well-publicized rarity. But in contrast to the thorough investigation and seizures of 1933 double eagles that began in 1944, the government from the 1920s onward simply did nothing about the five known 1913 Liberty nickels and sent noncommittal responses to the letters—an interesting commentary in itself for the mindset of government officials then and now.

The coinage of double eagles in 1933 had begun on March 15, with a delivery of 25,000 pieces. This came after President Franklin D. Roosevelt had declared the Bank Holiday—in an effort to stop panic runs on the banking system by the simple expedient of closing every bank—but before the presidential order of April 5 which required citizens to turn in all gold, except for a sum of up to $100 which they were allowed to keep.

There appears to be a widespread belief among historians that gold could not be used publicly after the Bank Holiday ended on March 9, but this is not true—and both the Mint and the Federal Reserve System, as well as ordinary banks, were allowed to pay out gold until April 5, 1933. (The last 45,500 double eagles of that year were delivered by the coiner of the Philadelphia Mint on May 19, making a total of 445,500 for the year.) At the very end of 1933, there was another executive order which mandated that all gold be turned in to the government, with the exception of recognized collector coins.

More than a decade later, one 1933 double eagle was legally exported to King Farouk of Egypt. In early February 1944, the Egyptian legation in Washington received this coin from flamboyant Texas dealer B. Max Mehl and, in line with wartime regulations, submitted the coin to the Treasury for the purpose of obtaining the necessary export license. The Treasury, in turn, consulted the curator of the Smithsonian collection, who agreed that the coin was a recognized rarity and therefore could be exported to Egypt.

Once the formalities were completed in the first week of March 1944, the specimen was sent by air mail to Cairo. (A few days later, the Secret Service began its lengthy involvement with 1933 double eagles by seizing the Flanagan coin before it could be sold by Stack's at the March public auction.) The Farouk coin remained in the king's massive collection until the 1952 coup d'etat, led by Col. Gamal Abdul Nasser, that drove him into exile. His coin holdings were quickly seized by the new government and auctioned off in a landmark sale that began in late February 1954 and lasted for several days. The 1933 double eagle, originally part of lot No. 185, was withdrawn just before the sale, at the request of the United States government, but its whereabouts remained a mystery for several decades. The U.S. Treasury requested its return from the Egyptian authorities, but the attempt was apparently half-hearted and nothing was accomplished. The highly volatile political situation in that area, which persists to this day, may well have influenced U.S. inaction.

In early 1996, English coin dealer Stephen Fenton brought what is said to be the Farouk specimen into the United States with the intention of selling it privately. However, the Secret Service learned of the coin's presence in this country and seized it. The owner and prospective buyer were both arrested and charged with possessing stolen property, charges which were eventually dropped for lack of evidence. The coin, however, remained in the possession of the government and a civil suit was instituted shortly afterward to recover it permanently for the Treasury.

Several years of legal maneuvering followed, and in September 2000 the two sides began negotiations toward a settlement. In January 2001, an out-of-court settlement was in fact reached. The only portions of this agreement made public specified that the coin would be sold at public auction and that the net proceeds would be split between the U.S. Mint and Stephen Fenton. In early 2002, it was announced that the sale would be held jointly by Stack's and Sotheby's on July 30 in New York City. Pre-sale estimates were in the $4 million to $6 million range. The coin sold for a record $7,590,020. At press time, October 2002, however, the coin's terms of sale had apparently not been finalized.

This coin very nearly became a casualty of a terrorist action, as it was kept for a considerable length of time in a Secret Service office vault in one of the Twin Towers in New York City. Luckily, it was removed several months prior to September 11.

There are rumors that other 1933 double eagles exist in European collections, but nothing has been confirmed publicly; it is of course possible that one or more lie hidden in American collections as well. Those interested in viewing a genuine coin may do so by visiting the National Numismatic Collection at the Smithsonian Institution in Washington, D.C.

Robert W. Julian is an acclaimed numismatic scholar and researcher. In preparing this article, he used material gathered in part while conducting research for some of the principals involved in the dispute over the Farouk specimen of the 1933 double eagle. His work was used to bring about the sale of the coin. Julian has done extensive research in the Archives of the United States Mint and written numerous articles based upon his findings. He was inducted into the American Numismatic Association's Hall of Fame in 1998.

AMERICA'S STATE QUARTER PROGRAM

By DAVID L. GANZ
Past president, American Numismatic Association

America's 50-State Quarter Program has Kermit as its national spokes-frog, and is based on an idea so special that the U.S. government has claimed a trademark on the name and concept.

Over the next six years, and possibly more, the U.S. Mint will manufacture billions of circulating commemorative coins in 50 different designs from now through the year 2008.

The idea is deceptively simple: coins with certain common elements, bound together by a common theme of statehood, being produced in abundance and placed into circulation. Collector coins follow.

Each of these coins bears the national motto "IN GOD WE TRUST," the Latin phrase "E Pluribus Unum" (an expression of national unity meaning "Out of many, one"), the word "Liberty," a statement of denomination, and the inscription, "United States of America."

All of them will have George Washington's portrait on the obverse (or "heads" side), modified by Mint designer-engraver William Cousins, but basically the same as the one that has appeared on the U.S. quarter dollar since 1932. But all will have distinctive reverse designs that, one by one, will showcase each state in the Union—and, by the end of the program (which could very well extend beyond 2008), they may well be joined by additional Washington quarters honoring the District of Columbia and

American territories such as Guam, American Samoa, Northern Marianas, Virgin Islands, and Puerto Rico.

This 50-state program completes the task that the traditional—and original—U.S. commemorative coin program (from 1892 to 1954) began but did not see to fruition: honoring important anniversaries connected with all 50 states.

Earlier programs celebrated milestones for 15 states and territories, including a 75th-anniversary jubilee (California), centennials (Alabama, Arkansas, Illinois, Iowa, Maine, Missouri, Texas, and Wisconsin), sesquicentennials (Hawaii and Vermont), and tercentenaries (Connecticut, Delaware, Maryland, and Rhode Island).

Termination of that program in 1954, for reasons that had little to do with the themes being celebrated, probably prevented its extension to all of the states—but that program involved silver half dollars, for the most part, rather than base-metal quarters. And those coins were issued for sale at a premium, rather than to circulate at face value.

Under the present program, the Mint intends to produce five brand-new quarter dollars annually—at the rate of one roughly every 10 weeks—for at least a 10-year period (coins for the District of Columbia and America's territories probably will be issued in the 11th year).

Initially, the concept was for each coin to be minted in quantities of about 800 million pieces, divided between the two mints at Philadelphia and Denver. About 2.5 million proof pieces were expected from San Francisco. All 50 states will be honored in the order in which they entered the Union, starting with Delaware (1st) and ending with Hawaii (50th).

By the end of the third state's participation, the demand had grown so considerably that it is highly likely that at least 1.4 billion coins (spread among the two mints) will be typical production runs—and demand is so intense that there are shortages developing together with a secondary market for uncirculated coins plucked from circulation.

Here's the complete order of the circulating statehood coins that can be anticipated from 1999 to 2008, all to be struck at the main U.S. mint in Philadelphia and the branch mint in Denver:

Year 1999

1. Delaware
2. Pennsylvania
3. New Jersey
4. Georgia
5. Connecticut

Year 2000

6. Massachusetts
7. Maryland
8. South Carolina
9. New Hampshire
10. Virginia

Year 2001

11. New York
12. North Carolina
13. Rhode Island
14. Vermont
15. Kentucky

Year 2002

16. Tennessee
17. Ohio
18. Louisiana
19. Indiana
20. Mississippi

Year 2003

21. Illinois
22. Alabama

23. Maine
24. Missouri
25. Arkansas

Year 2004

26. Michigan
27. Florida
28. Texas
29. Iowa
30. Wisconsin

Year 2005

31. California
32. Minnesota
33. Oregon
34. Kansas
35. West Virginia

Year 2006

36. Nevada
37. Nebraska
38. Colorado
39. North Dakota
40. South Dakota

Year 2007

41. Montana
42. Washington
43. Idaho
44. Wyoming
45. Utah

Year 2008

46. Oklahoma
47. New Mexico
48. Arizona
49. Alaska
50. Hawaii

Possible for Year 2009

51. District of Columbia
52. Puerto Rico
53. American Samoa
54. Guam
55. U.S. Virgin Islands
56. Northern Marianas

The 50-state coinage is a long way from what was originally contemplated—and, for that matter, even proposed—by the Citizens Commemorative Coin Advisory Committee, a federal appointive panel that advises the government on such matters.

At its very first meeting in Washington, D.C., on December 14, 1993, I made a formal recommendation that the CCCAC take its mandate from Congress seriously, explore the idea of circulating commemoratives and make an affirmative recommendation favoring such a proposal in its annual report to Congress.

In the beginning, the cause was lonely. The statutory chairman of the panel, Philip N. Diehl of the U.S. Mint, was joined in questioning the viability of the proposal by four other members: Tom Shockley III, Reed Hawn, Elsie Sterling Howard, and Elvira Clain-Stefanelli. Only Charles Atherton, a statutory appointee from the federal Commision of Fine Arts, and Dan Hoffman, a young numismatist from South Carolina, initially spoke in favor.

Ultimately, the CCCAC members came around—and by the time the panel filed its First Annual Report to Congress in December 1994, it formally recommended that a circulating, legal-tender commemorative should become part of U.S. coinage.

On the legislative side, the key supporter of the plan was Rep. Michael Castle, R-Del., then-chairman of the House coinage subcommittee. It was his proposal, H.R. 3793—legislation directing the Mint to strike 50 different coins, one for each state, over the next 10 years—that got the ball rolling when he introduced it on July 11, 1996.

That was almost exactly the one-year anniversary of a hearing held before the Subcommittee on Domestic and International Monetary Policy of the House Banking and Financial Services Committee, a subcommittee Castle chaired at the time and which has charge of all coinage matters.

At the hearing, on July 12, 1995, Castle picked up on the remarks of one expert witness, New York City coin dealer Harvey G. Stack, suggesting a commemorative program honoring the 13 original colonies—just as Canada had commemorated each of its 12 provinces and territories on special coins in 1992, the 125th anniversary of Canadian confederation.

By the midpoint of the hearing, Castle remarked that all coins "seem to have a constituency, just like Delaware will become the first State issue" of the circulating commemorative program. This put the cart before the horse, for even though this one key legislator was there, the rest of Congress and a recalcitrant bureaucracy had to be persuaded that the proposal made sense and was viable.

Castle's 1996 legislation took the concept from the July 1995 hearing to its logical conclusion: a continuity program of five coins per year, issued over a 10-year period. Silver versions also would be produced for sale to collectors.

Initial estimates suggested that the Mint would produce 1.25 billion quarters a year, divided equally among five different designs (or about 250 million apiece)—a number sufficient to meet standard commercial demand. Actually, the proposal calculated that about 800 million statehood quarters would stay in circulation each year, while about 425 million pieces could be expected to be withdrawn by collectors and other interested people.

What eventually emerged was a proposal that would have the mints produce a total of between 8 million and 10 million coins per day for a 10-week period, or about 750 million coins, which the Federal Reserve would place in circulation.

That plan underestimated the pent-up demand. Today, the U.S. Mint estimates that over 125 million Americans are collecting the State quarters, sufficient interest to warrant hundreds of newspaper articles, and at least one book that I've written, *The Official Guide to America's State Quarters,* which Random House's House of Collectibles imprint published in late 2000.

The profit to the government in year one of the State Quarters program has aggregated over $1 billion in pure profit (based on production of 4.4 billion quarters, consisting of 2.225 billion at the Philadelphia Mint and 2.205 billion at the Denver Mint).

This turns out to be more than the Mint has made on all of its commemorative coin programs intended primarily for collectors. (Seigniorage is the amount by which the face value of a coin exceeds the costs of producing and distributing that coin. In the case of base-metal coinage, it represents a substantial profit for the government.)

Although the program seems in retrospect to have been almost inevitable, it faced intense opposition initially within the Mint and the Treasury Department as a whole, based in large part on bureaucratic inertia. These same forces had conspired to oppose other circulating commemorative coin proposals that had taken place at various times since the 1930s. In all but two instances— the Washington quarter of 1932 and the Bicentennial coins of 1975–76—they successfully blocked the efforts.

Treasury bureaucrats also had succeeded in quashing a number of proposals for noncirculating commemorative coins from 1929 to 1954—and after that year, they had obtained executive and legislative approval to ban all further commemoratives as being disruptive to commerce. I talk a lot about this in my book *The Official Guide to U.S. Commemorative Coins* (Bonus Books, 1999).

Commemorative coins were issued again starting in 1982—but by the early 1990s, commemorative coinage had come to be identified again with abuses and excesses. It was being produced by governments around the world largely for the profit of a few private organizations lucky enough to have the connections necessary to secure and promote such programs.

Congress recognized that there was a huge problem, and attempted to fix it with the U.S. Mint Reauthorization & Reform Act of 1992, which created the Citizens Commemorative Coin Advisory Committee to report to Congress on proposed solutions. I was fortunate enough to be appointed to the initial coin advisory panel in 1993 by Treasury Secretary Lloyd Bentsen. At the time, I was president of the American Numismatic Association (ANA), the national coin club.

At the panel's very first meeting in December 1993, I said that if there was only one thing I hoped to accomplish during my tenure, it would be for the committee to endorse issuance of a circulating commemorative coin.

Philip Diehl, then executive deputy director of the Mint (and later Mint director), said at the time that he was not certain this fell within the committee's purview, since its sole statutory mandate was to designate people, places, and things for a five-year program of commemorative coins and submit a report to Congress explaining its recommendations. I disagreed.

Diehl, who later embraced the concept wholeheartedly—over his staff's opposition—was patient in listening to my arguments as to why circulating coins should be part of the committee's mandate. In the time-honored Washington tradition, he asked that a report be submitted on this matter. Committee members had no staff, no research assistance, and were unpaid—so this had every possibility of being a "kiss-off."

Nonetheless, I prepared a 5,000-word "Report to the Citizens Commemorative Coin Advisory Committee on Circulating Coins," which was delivered to all members of the committee and the Mint staff. A formal oral presentation was scheduled, and though I prefer not to use a prepared text, I presented a 750-word summary to the committee on February 22, 1994. (You can read the entire report on the state quarter link on the website for my book *The Official Guidebook to America's State Quarters,* www.AmericasStateQuarters.com).

I continued to advocate this at each meeting throughout the year. In mid-1998, Philip Diehl, reflecting on all this in an interview with Kari Stone, then managing editor of *COINage* magazine, called me "Johnny One-Note" on that subject. He was right. Like John Adams two centuries earlier, while separation from England was being debated in Independence Hall, I made myself thoroughly obnoxious in favor of one cause: circulating commemorative coinage.

In a December 11, 1998 letter to David Harper, the editor of *Numismatic News,* Diehl offered a fuller and rather more complimentary appraisal of my role:

> From my vantage point, the lion's share of the credit for making the 50 states program a reality goes to David Ganz, for his persistence as an advocate, and Congressman Michael Castle for championing the proposal through Congress. David gradually persuaded me of the merits of the proposal, and we at the Mint, in turn, convinced Treasury and the Hill it was doable. There are other claimants, to be sure, but the hobby owes a debt of gratitude to Congressman Castle and Mr. Ganz.

In September 1994, as the committee met to consider its annual report, I drafted a proposed chapter that was faxed to each member, strongly advocating that we propose a circulating commemorative coin. Significantly, the memo focused on the quarter.

There was considerable internal argument among the Mint staff, and among the citizen members, as to whether to take a position on circulating coins and, if so, how strong a position. From my perspective, I had decided that this was the issue for which I was prepared to fall on my sword. I announced that I was prepared to issue a formal dissenting opinion to the CCCAC Annual Report and to its recommendations if the committee did not formally endorse a circulating coin.

My persistence paid off. Four paragraphs in the committee's

November 1994 annual report are devoted to the theme that the CCCAC "endorses issuance by the Mint of a circulating commemorative coin." It states: "Coinage is a tangible way to touch the lives of every American. Circulating coinage promotes our national ideals, builds awareness and pride in our history, and informs millions of foreign visitors who use U.S. coins."

By the time of the July 1995 hearings, several more meetings of the Citizens Advisory Committee had been held, and at each there was continuing discussion on the topic. Diehl soon became a more active proponent—to the point where, by 1996, he had taken the lead and rose to the occasion when Castle jumped on the bandwagon for statehood commemoratives.

But America's 50-state commemorative coin program, even after being endorsed enthusiastically by the House coinage subcommittee, the Citizens Commemorative Coin Advisory Committee, and the director of the Mint, still was almost thwarted before it began. A combination of bureaucratic resistance to change, opposition from members of Congress who recalled decades of Treasury Department recalcitrance, and a lack of momentum nearly kept the program from reaching reality.

Altogether, three separate laws had to be passed before the circulating commemorative program could be achieved.

First of these three laws was Public Law 104-329, enacted October 24, 1996, which created a host of noncirculating commemorative coins, restructured the CCCAC and called for a study of the circulating coin proposal.

In point of fact, that study was intended by its proponents to kill the measure—for after the CCCAC endorsed the proposal formally, opposition to it arose high in the Treasury Department among political appointees near the top. They were determined to derail the 50-state project, arguing that if there wasn't a market for the product, or if the Mint couldn't successfully produce it, the move would be the wrong one for the government to back.

The Treasury secretary was given the option of going ahead directly with the program without any study, but he chose to conduct one anyway—a course of indifference that could well have aborted the program in its entirety.

In stepped Congressman Castle. On December 1, 1997, Congress passed another measure, P.L. 105-124, directing that the program proceed. And when it became clear that there were difficulties in designing the coins because existing law required the placement of statutory inscriptions on one side rather than the other, Castle secured more legislative relief: Public Law 105-215, enacted on May 29, 1998, which allows statutory verbiage previously required on the obverse to be moved to the reverse, and vice versa, as long as it is incorporated into the design.

The idea for a 1997 study of the proposal, after Congress already had indicated definite enthusiasm, came as the 50-state commemorative coin proposal seemed to be on a fast track. Its mandate to the Treasury: Report by August 1, 1997—and, if affirmative, start production by January 1, 1999. With the first-strike ceremony now having taken place at Philadelphia, and the start-up of production under way, we know the outcome of the story. It was less clear in late 1996, after Congress moved to slow down the freight train bearing the 50-state commemorative coin program.

The all-important public study of the utility of circulating commemorative coins, undertaken on behalf of the Treasury Department by the Big-8 accounting firm of Coopers & Lybrand, was released by the Treasury on May 30, 1997, and sent to Capitol Hill on June 10.

Its key finding, based on a statistically sound survey and focus group, was emphatic: Only 11 percent of those surveyed opposed a 50-state commemorative coin program. Even more significantly, 75 percent of those polled declared that they would be "almost certain" to start collecting the series, or minimally there was a "good possibility" that they would do so.

Each 50-state coin that is collected and removed from circulation represents a 22-cent profit for the government, meaning that hundreds of millions of dollars in seigniorage profit is likely to accrue in a program of 10 years or more.

Still, the Treasury dithered. With the decision hanging in the balance, Castle sprang into action, putting together a letter that went from the Speaker of the House, Newt Gingrich; the majority leader, Dick Armey; the Republican whip, Tom DeLay; the chairman of the House Banking Committee, James A. S. Leach, and himself to Treasury Secretary Robert Rubin, asking for the change in our change.

Rubin finally responded, giving his mandate for change. His instructions to the nation's governors, sent to them less than a month after President Clinton signed the legislation, made clear that the designs were to be tasteful, and that there was to be no portraiture of any living person involved.

America's grand experiment with 50 different circulating commemorative quarters, one for each state in the Union, was launched at the Philadelphia Mint on December 7, 1998, in a ceremony headed by Mint Director Diehl and U.S. Treasurer Mary Ellen Withrow, joined by Delaware's Congressman Castle and Governor Thomas Carper.

On the first coin in the series, issued at the outset of 1999, Delaware chose to honor Caesar Rodney, a Revolutionary War patriot who made a historic 80-mile horseback ride from Dover to Philadelphia in July 1776. Rodney arrived there in time to cast a decisive vote at the Continental Congress in favor of American independence.

Governor Carper made the point in his brief remarks to the assembled first-strike crowd that more than 1,500 Delawareans participated in an in-state design competition. Interestingly, he revealed, slightly more than half of these involved submitted designs, or design concepts, through the state's website on the Internet.

Since that time, there have been many new issues—averaging one every 10 weeks—some of which had first-strike ceremonies at the Philadelphia Mint, and all of which have been well received by the public. In fact, the secondary market has developed so rapidly that it has astonished all comers.

There have been many mint errors produced—not surprising given the high rate of turnaround and number of designs in a year. Prices for regular issues have jumped for Delaware (averaging

$1.75 a coin in mid-2001), Pennsylvania (a $2.25 coin in MS-63 in August 2001), and other coins are also selling above face.

If the coin is in MS-66 or better condition, it carries real premium dollars—hundreds of dollars, it turns out—based on supply and demand.

America's statehood coins have also built up cottage industries supplying boards in the shape of the continental United States for storage and display of the coins, and dozens of promotions the nation over to accommodate the desire to collect these neat coins.

Mintage figures remain unreliable and imprecise for the series—in part because the Mint no longer counts individual coins, but instead relies on weight in the name of expediency. With a profit of $1 billion riding on it, no one much cares whether Georgia had 451.188 million coins from Philadelphia or 452 million pieces.

What is clear is that even with high mintages, premium quality Gem Mint State issues are in scarce supply, and their future could well have a life of their own—and in the process, influence the coin market for all other items into the long-term future.

David L. Ganz is a New York City attorney and author of *Official Guide to U.S. Commemorative Coins: The Quarters Book All Collectors Want and Need* (Bonus Books, $13.95) and the award-winning *Official Guidebook to America's State Quarters* (House of Collectibles/Random House, 2000).

Chapter One

THE LURE OF COINS

Coins have kindled people's imagination and aroused their collecting instincts ever since the first crude examples were struck in Asia Minor more than five hundred years before the birth of Christ.

Coins are handheld works of art . . . miniature milestones along the march of time. Many times, they're stores of precious metal. Rare coins are worth far more than face value (the value stamped on their surface)—and far more than just their metal content—as collectibles. They can even be an exceptional investment. And, best of all, collecting them can be tremendous fun.

In a sense, collecting coins is like digging up buried treasure. The treasure isn't hidden underground, and finding it doesn't require a secret map, but still there's a sense of adventure, an air of excitement—and ultimately a thrill of discovery—in locating needed coins to complete a set (a group of similar coins containing one example from every different date and every different mint that struck the coins). For those who buy wisely and well, there's also an ultimate payoff, for collecting rare coins, like tracking buried treasure, has the potential to be a richly rewarding pursuit.

No longer the private preserve of wealthy princes, coin collecting today is among the most popular spare-time diversions in the world. Millions of Americans collect coins on a regular basis, and many others dabble in the field.

Most confine their collecting to U.S. coinage, but many use a broader frame of reference in terms of both history and geography, collecting coins from earlier ages—all the way back to ancient times—and from hundreds of other countries around the globe.

In recent years, the far-flung base of traditional collectors has been broadened substantially by newcomers who think of themselves not as pure hobbyists but rather as collector/investors. For them, the profit motive is important—and rare coins' profit performance has been excellent when they are held over time.

Frequently, people who enter the rare coin market as investors find the field's lure irresistible and cross over the line to become pure collectors. This gives them an opportunity to enjoy the best of both worlds—the fun of a fascinating hobby and the profit of a fine investment, too.

Although the instinct to save and savor coins is as old as coinage itself, coin collecting didn't reach the masses until the twentieth century. Prior to that, it was largely an indulgence of the nobility and scholars—people with time and money to devote to such a pursuit. As recently as the early 1900s, major U.S. coin shows seldom attracted more than a few hundred participants, and the major activity wasn't the buying and selling of coins, but rather the exhibiting of collections.

The democratization of coin collecting got under way in earnest in the 1920s and '30s. During that period, Americans were starting to find themselves with more leisure time (some of it enforced, during the 1930s, by the Great Depression). What's more, the United States Mint was turning out dozens of commemorative coins, which piqued people's interest and drew many thousands into the hobby.

Special holders for storing and displaying coins started to appear around that time, along with guidebooks listing the coins' value—and those set up a framework that made collecting easier for the many new devotees.

During the next few decades, rare coins evolved from a drawing-room diversion into a field with true mass appeal and a massive collector base.

THE LURE OF COINS

The coin market's growth was hastened by developments at the Mint. In the 1950s, for instance, many new collectors became involved with coins by buying annual proof sets—sets of specimen coins—from Uncle Sam. The Mint resumed production of these in 1950, following an eight-year lapse, and by the end of the decade, sales had mushroomed from fewer than 52,000 sets in 1950 to more than 1.1 million in 1959.

In 1960, the growth became a full-fledged boom, largely on the strength of a single new "mint-error" coin. The coin in question was the so-called "small-date" cent. In the spring of 1960, sharp-eyed collectors noticed that there were two major varieties of current-year Lincoln cents, one of which had a perceptibly smaller date. It soon became apparent that the "small-date" variety was scarce—especially the version struck at the nation's main mint in Philadelphia. A nationwide scavenger hunt ensued, and coins became the object of widespread coverage in the media. That, in turn, drew many new participants to the hunt and to coin collecting, as well.

Just four years later, in 1964, the Mint introduced a new half dollar honoring President John F. Kennedy following his assassination—and that, too, stirred widespread interest. In 1965, the rising cost of silver forced the Mint to issue a new kind of dime and quarter: "sandwich-type" coinage made from copper and nickel, with no precious metal at all. The half dollar kept a reduced amount of silver until 1971, when it, too, became fiat money—money whose acceptance is based on public trust in the government, not on its own intrinsic worth. The dawn of clad coinage wasn't a happy time for collectors, but it did focus new attention on the rare coin field—and that, in turn, attracted more recruits.

The 1970s witnessed continued growth, and also a new direction in the marketing of coins. For the first time, many dealers were reaching beyond traditional collectors to lure noncollectors, especially wealthy professionals, into purchasing rare coins as an investment. Instead of building collections, buyers were now assembling portfolios.

Again, the federal government played a pivotal role in

stimulating interest in coins. First came the sale of surplus silver dollars by the General Services Administration. Most of these dollars were low-mintage coins from the Carson City Mint, and their release to the market in a series of ballyhooed sales did much to raise public consciousness of rare coins in general and Morgan silver dollars in particular.

In 1974, the government gave coins another big, though indirect, boost by lifting the long-standing ban on U.S. citizens' right to buy, sell, and own gold bullion. That sparked new interest in bullion-type coins such as South Africa's Krugerrand, and the interest carried over into numismatic coinage, or collectible coins, as well.

Coin prices rose throughout the 1970s—steadily at first, then dramatically. In 1972, for the very first time, a single coin changed hands for $100,000. The sale was a private transaction and the coin was an 1804 silver dollar.

By 1979, that seemed puny. As the decade neared a close, in November '79, a Brasher doubloon—a gold piece minted privately in 1787 by New York City jeweler Ephraim Brasher—was gaveled down for a stratospheric $725,000 at an auction of rare coins from the famous Garrett Collection.

For nearly a decade, that remained the highest price ever paid for any single coin at a public auction. The record was finally broken in July 1989, when an 1804 silver dollar brought $990,000, missing the million-dollar mark by just a single bid.

In 1990, a rare U.S. gold coin was sold in a private transaction for more than $1.5 million. The coin was a 1907 double eagle, or $20 gold piece, designed by famed sculptor Augustus Saint-Gaudens. While all Saint-Gaudens double eagles are considered to be magnificent works of coinage art, this one was distinguished by both its exquisite sharpness of detail (it's said to have "extremely high relief") and its virtually flawless condition.

In 1996, for the very first time, a U.S. coin changed hands at public auction for more than a million dollars. The coin was a 1913 Liberty Head nickel—one of only five examples known—and it broke the barrier by a wide margin, selling for nearly $1.5 million.

(In 2001, this same nickel was sold at auction for $1.84 million.) The very next year, that record was exceeded when an 1804 silver dollar brought more than $1.8 million. Both coins came from the same collection, formed half a century earlier by a Baltimore banker named Louis E. Eliasberg Sr. In August 1999, a Proof-68 1804 dollar brought $4.14 million at public auction. I was one of the underbidders.

Low mintage and high condition are the two main ingredients buyers seek in a coin, and these combine with supply and demand to determine its market value. While rarity is important, the stress in recent years has been on quality. Investors covet nothing but the best, and are willing to pay for it. Consequently, coins command far higher premiums in pristine mint condition than in grades only slightly lower. There are even degrees of pristineness: the Mint-State range has 11 different grades, with premiums rising steeply as a coin ascends the scale.

Coins are now graded on a scale of 1 to 70, with 1 representing a coin that is barely identifiable as to its type and 70 signifying a coin that is absolutely perfect. The use of numbers to designate grades is a practice of relatively recent origin. In the past, collectors used words instead, describing coins as "uncirculated," "fine," and "good," for example. These were less precise, but were adequate for the needs of a less sophisticated marketplace. The numbers now in use do correspond to descriptive words. For instance, coins graded 60 to 70 are said to be Mint State.

To assure that buyers and sellers get coins that have been accurately graded, independent third-party grading services have come into being. These companies, operated and staffed by knowledgeable, reputable experts, have effectively removed the risk that coins may be overgraded and therefore overpriced on the basis of grade.

The "grading revolution" began in 1986 with the establishment of the Professional Coin Grading Service (PCGS). The following year, a second major grading service—the Numismatic Guaranty Corporation of America (NGC)—opened its doors.

These companies provide unbiased opinions regarding the

THE LURE OF COINS

grade, or state of preservation, of coins that are submitted for their review. They then encapsulate each coin in a ionically sealed, tamper-resistant hard plastic holder (or a "slab"), along with a paper insert indicating its date, type, and grade.

In 1990, the nonprofit American Numismatic Association sold ANACS, its certification service, to Amos Press, Inc., of Sidney, Ohio. When the new ANACS began operations, the coins it certified were not traded as fluidly as those certified by NGC and PCGS. Over time, ANACS's standards became about on par with the standards of NGC and PCGS.

Together, PCGS and NGC have certified millions of coins. They also have made a valuable contribution to the marketplace by issuing regular "population" or "census" reports telling how many coins of each type and date they have certified in each different grade. These have become valuable reference tools in determining rarity and value. Other grading services have also been founded. One respected entry is the Independent Coin Grading Company (ICG), based in Colorado.

Fun and profit can and do overlap in the rare coin field. Consider the case of New York City lawyer Harold Bareford, a man who approached rare coins as a pure collector but whose acquisitions proved to be a marvelous investment.

Bareford began acquiring coins just before World War II and remained an active buyer for several decades. He seldom paid more than a few hundred dollars, but he bought with great care, insisting on the ultimate in quality.

In all, he spent about $40,000 assembling sets of U.S. coins struck from gold and silver. Shortly after his death in 1978, the coins were sold at auction and brought a combined total of $3.1 million. One coin—a specimen-quality 1827 dime—had cost Bareford $20 in 1947. Not much more than three decades later, it brought his estate an eye-popping $29,000.

Bareford's insistence on quality was the key: he always demanded the best at a time when other collectors were content to settle for less. And during the years when he was buying coins, prices were laughably low by current standards.

THE LURE OF COINS

Can similar huge profits still be achieved by people buying rare coins today? Only time will tell, but Harold Bareford's story has a rather intriguing footnote: Bareford stopped buying U.S. coins in 1955, years before the market began to really boom.

He thought they were getting too expensive.

Chapter Two

FIGURING OUT WHAT IT'S WORTH

What's it worth?

That's the first question most people ask when they see an old or unusual-looking coin. They take it for granted that something so intriguing must be worth a lot of money.

Many times, they're right—but not necessarily for the reason they believe. Coins don't gain added value simply because they're old; you can buy Roman coins from the time of Julius Caesar for just a few dollars apiece. Nor does odd appearance always command a premium; a great many coins with dramatic minting mistakes, although they may be terrific conversation pieces, bring very little as collectibles.

THREE KEYS TO VALUE

Three basic factors determine just how much a coin is worth—or, on the other hand, how much it isn't worth. The first of these is the grade of the coin—its level of preservation. The second is the coin's collector base—the number of collectors who covet it enough to pay a bonus price for it. The third is the coin's availability—the number of examples that exist.

The grade of a coin is the most important factor, and because it is so crucial I'll be dealing with this subject in much greater detail in the next chapter. I do want to give you some basic guidelines now, though, on how a coin's grade and value are intertwined.

When asked to describe their coins, the uninitiated often like to say they're in "good condition." They're using that expression in a general sense, of course, but to knowledgeable collectors the term "good condition" has a very specific meaning—and that meaning is just the opposite of what most laypersons think. Among the established grade levels, Good is one of the lowest, not the highest: it signifies a coin that has passed through a great many hands and undergone heavy wear but still possesses all the basic elements needed to identify its design.

As I explained in Chapter One, experts grade U.S. coins on a scale of 1 to 70, with 1 representing a coin that can barely be identified and 70 denoting a coin that is sheer perfection. The coins that enjoy the greatest demand and bring the biggest premiums are those that have never passed from hand to hand; these are said to be in "uncirculated" condition and identified by grades within an eleven-number Mint State range. This range is at the top of the 1-through-70 spectrum, covering the numbers from 60 to 70.

Perfection is highly prized by many coin collectors and investors. They will pay a great deal more for a Mint State coin than they will for a similar coin that is worn ever so slightly—even when that wear is all but undetectable without the use of powerful magnification. What's more, they will frequently pay several times as much for one Mint State coin than they will for a second Mint State coin just one or two numbers lower on the grading scale.

Prices rise sharply in grades above Mint State-65 (MS-65, for short). As coins approach the perfection denoted by the grade of 70, their prices very often approach the stratosphere. You may find, for example, that a coin with a value of $500 in MS-65 condition is worth ten times as much in MS-67—and one hundred times as much in MS-69. This difference reflects the fact that hardly any exist in the highest grades. People who collect these coins are willing to pay top dollar for top quality not only because the coins are breathtakingly beautiful in these very high levels of preservation, but also because they're flat-out rare.

PROOF COINS

"Proof" coins are graded similarly to regular coins but separately. A proof is a specimen coin—one that has been struck two or more times to give it greater sharpness of detail. The same numerical scale is used in grading proofs, but instead of being labeled, say, Mint State-65, a proof would be given a grade of Proof-65.

The process of minting proof coins is really quite simple. Think of what would happen if you pressed a rubber stamp onto a piece of paper, then pressed it down again in the very same spot. After you did this the second time, the impression on the paper would be sharper, deeper, and darker. Likewise, the multiple striking brings out every nuance of a proof coin's design in razor-sharp detail.

Proof coins won't appear in your everyday pocket change. But you might very well encounter such a coin—or a whole set of proof coins—among your family's keepsakes in the drawer or cigar box that I mentioned in this book's Preface. Every year the United States Mint puts together proof sets containing proof examples of all five current U.S. coins: the Lincoln cent, Jefferson nickel, Roosevelt dime, Washington quarter, and Kennedy half dollar. It sells these sets to collectors for a premium—currently $12.50 per set. For further information on how to order such sets, write to: The United States Mint, P.O. Box 13576, Philadelphia, PA 19162–0011.

SUPPLY AND DEMAND

Some coins are more popular than others. Lincoln cents, for instance, have always held great appeal to a broad cross section of collectors. Obscure and obsolete coins have far fewer followers; the Lincoln Cent Fan Club is enormous, for example, compared to the number of hobbyists actively pursuing three-cent pieces and twenty-cent pieces, two coin series the United States abandoned in the late 1800s.

Popularity, or unpopularity, has enormous implications for the value of a coin. What it boils down to is the age-old law of supply and demand: the greater the demand for a given supply of coins, the higher the price will be—and popularity is, of course, just another name for demand.

Consider the case of the 1909-S V.D.B. Lincoln cent. This is a famous coin minted in San Francisco in 1909, the year Lincoln cents first appeared, and bearing the initials of Victor David Brenner, the artist who designed the coin. The San Francisco Mint produced 484,000 examples of this coin, so it hardly qualifies as a great rarity. Yet, there are literally millions of collectors who would love to own one. As a result, this coin is worth several hundred dollars even in well-worn condition.

Now consider the case of the 1876 nickel three-cent piece (a coin with the same metallic composition as our present-day Jefferson nickel but a face value, or denomination, of only three cents). The Mint produced only 162,000 examples of this coin— barely a third as many as the number of 1909-S V.D.B. Lincoln cents. Furthermore, this coin is older by thirty-three years. Yet, it's only worth 10 to 20 dollars in worn condition. The explanation is simple: The number of collectors pursuing this coin is significantly smaller than the number of pieces available.

The third and final determinant of the value of a coin is the flip side of demand: the coin's supply.

In general, you can gauge the number of coins available by checking the number minted in the first place. The United States Mint has a long-standing policy of disclosing mintage figures, and *The Insider's Guide to U.S. Coin Values* furnishes those figures for each and every date that each and every U.S. coin was made. You'll find them conveniently located right beside the listings of year-by-year market values.

There are instances, however, where unusual circumstances led to the loss or destruction of large numbers of coins after the Mint produced them. Many silver dollars from the turn-of-the-century era were melted, for example, when the government needed silver for other uses. So were many gold coins left in federal vaults, or surrendered by the public, when the nation suspended gold coinage in 1933. More recently, untold millions of modern silver coins wound up in the melting pot when silver rose in value to $50 an ounce at the start of the 1980s. In that case, the coins were melted because they had more value as metal than as money.

In recent years, buyers and sellers have gained a major new tool in their effort to assess the available supply of certain coins. Companies known as "grading services," which evaluate rare coins, have issued periodic reports detailing the number of coins their personnel have graded—type by type, date by date, and grade by grade. These "population" and "census" reports provide important guidance to what is known as "condition rarity"—a circumstance where coins, however high their mintages and however available they may be in lower grades, are scarce and even rare in very high grades.

MINT MARKS

Supply and demand—and consequently value—can be influenced greatly by the presence or absence of one or more tiny letters on a coin. These letters are known as "mint marks," and they designate the mint where the coin was produced.

In 1792, when the United States Mint came into being, there was just one mint facility, a modest mint building in Philadelphia. As the nation and its coinage needs grew, Congress began to authorize branch mints in other locations around the country, chosen for their advantageous geographic locations or sometimes their proximity to sources of the precious metal needed in making coins. The San Francisco Mint was opened, for example, following the California Gold Rush.

During much of U.S. history, the branch mints' coinage output has been substantially smaller than that of the mother mint in Philadelphia. Thus, if a mint mark appears on a coin, the chances are good that the mintage (or number made) may be relatively low, enhancing that coin's value to collectors.

Until recent years, the Philadelphia Mint didn't place a mint mark on its coins. Coins from that mint could be recognized instead by the absence of any such mark. Since 1980, the Philadelphia Mint has stamped the letter "P" on all the coins it makes except the cent.

At present, there are three U.S. branch mints. Their locations, and the mint marks of their coins, are as follows: Denver (D); San Francisco (S); and West Point, New York (W). In earlier years, there also were branch mints in Charlotte, North Carolina (C); Carson City, Nevada (CC); Dahlonega, Georgia (D); and New Orleans (O). Although the mint mark "D" appears on coins produced in both Dahlonega and Denver, no confusion exists because those mints were active in different eras. The Dahlonega Mint was closed in 1861, and the Denver Mint didn't begin operations until 1906.

For a detailed list of where mint marks appear on various coins, see Appendix C.

COMMEMORATIVE COINS

In addition to making regular-issue coins for use in the nation's commerce, the United States Mint also has produced a wide variety of commemorative coins. These are special coins authorized by Congress to recognize important people, places, and events. Centennials of statehood, anniversaries of battles, and the staging of Olympic Games have been among the subjects honored on these coins. Normally, they are minted in just a single year and in limited quantities; however, in some cases, production has continued for as long as thirteen years. Rather than being placed in circulation, these coins are offered for sale at a premium.

U.S. commemorative coins are divided into two general groups: those from the "traditional" period, from 1892 to 1954, and those from the "modern" era, which got under way in 1982. Issuance of commemoratives was suspended from 1954 to 1982 because of opposition by the Treasury Department.

As with regular-issue coinage, the value of commemoratives depends upon the coins' level of preservation and the workings of supply and demand. A number of the traditional commemoratives command impressive premiums, especially in very high grades. However, the modern issues haven't yet shown great market strength. Most have been sold by the Mint at relatively high initial prices, and then had difficulty sustaining those price levels. Abundant supply has held prices down in the resale market: mintages of the modern commemoratives have been consistently higher than those of their traditional counterparts.

Typically, U.S. commemoratives not only pay tribute to the subjects they portray but also raise funds for some related cause. The 1986 Statue of Liberty coins, for instance, marked the centennial of that national shrine and also helped generate money to finance its repair and restoration. Since 1982, legislation authorizing commemoratives has spelled out how much of a "surcharge" should be added to benefit the designated cause.

BULLION COINS

In 1986 the Mint began producing a series of special coins called American Eagles. These are what is known as "bullion coins"—precious-metal coins whose price goes up or down, depending on fluctuations in the value of the metal they contain. They are made not to be spent, but rather to be sold as stores of precious metal.

American Eagles are issued in platinum, gold, and silver. The platinum and gold coins both come in four different sizes: a one-ounce piece plus fractional coins with precious-metal contents of $\frac{1}{2}$, $\frac{1}{4}$, and $\frac{1}{10}$ of an ounce, respectively. There is just one silver coin, and it weighs an ounce. All these coins carry denominations well below the bullion value of their gold or silver. The one-ounce gold American Eagle, for instance, has a face value of $50—less than one-sixth what an ounce of gold is worth at this writing. The silver American Eagle has a face value of $1, but its metal value would be more than five times that much.

The platinum American Eagles made their first appearance in 1977, and the one-ounce version has a face value of $100—only about one-fourth what an ounce of platinum is worth as this is written.

To make the American Eagles more appealing to collectors, the Mint chose designs based partially on classics of the past. The "heads" side of each of the four gold coins carries the portrait of Miss Liberty designed by famous sculptor Augustus Saint-Gaudens for the U.S. double eagle, or $20 gold piece, minted from 1907 to 1933. The heads side of the silver American Eagle duplicates the Walking Liberty design that graced the half dollar from 1916 to 1947. New designs appear on the bullion coins' reverses.

The platinum coins depict the Statue of Liberty—a portrait not based on a previous coin design.

In addition to the regular American Eagles, the Mint also makes proof versions every year for sale at an added premium as collectibles.

GETTING THE BEST OFFER

Clearly, the bottom line when you go to sell a coin is to get the highest price you possibly can. To do this, you need to be aware of the factors that affect overall values in the coin market and the steps that you can take to minimize your risk and maximize your return.

Keep in mind that coins, like any other commodities, can vary in value greatly as time goes by and market conditions change. Inflation, for example, tends to push coin values up; much like precious metals, coins are excellent hedges against a shrinking dollar, and many people turn to them for shelter in inflationary times. Recessions, on the other hand, tend to cause coin prices to decline. When times are tough and people can barely afford life's necessities, they're far less likely to spend their limited funds on "extras" such as coins.

Coin market cycles, and the interrelationship of coins and the economy, are examined in greater detail in two of my earlier books, *One-Minute Coin Expert* and *The Coin Collector's Survival Manual.* Those who would like to learn more about these fascinating subjects will find both of these books well worth reading.

The price you get for a coin can also depend, to a very great extent, on the circumstances surrounding the sales transaction itself. You're likely to receive a substantially higher offer if, for example, the dealer you approach perceives you as a knowledgeable collector, or at least an informed amateur, rather than a hapless babe in the woods.

Typically, coin dealers' offers fall into a number of readily identifiable categories. To show you what I mean, here are three examples:

The low-ball offer. A low-ball offer isn't the same as a rip-off; the offer is low, but the dealer isn't trying to get the coin for just a tiny fraction of its value. Let's say you have a coin that the dealer would sell for $1,000 to a knowledgeable consumer. He could pay you $700 or even $800 and still turn a normal profit, but instead he makes you an offer of $300. If you were knowledgeable, you could probably get him to upgrade the offer by holding out for more—especially if he had a potential buyer in mind. The lesson here is clear. Knowledge is power—the kind of power measured in cold, hard cash.

The fair-market wholesale offer. This is the kind of offer a dealer would make to another dealer, or possibly to a collector who was reasonably familiar with the value of the coin. If you were in no hurry to sell your coin, you also could receive a fair-market wholesale price by consigning it to a reputable coin auction firm for sale at a public auction.

Fair market value. When a dealer offers you "fair market value" for a coin, what he's really offering is a price somewhere between fair-market wholesale value and fair-market retail value. He'll still make a decent profit when he resells it, but not quite as much as he would have made if he had paid you a strictly wholesale price. Fair market value is the price that is arrived at when both the buyer and seller are ready and willing to consummate a deal, both of them are knowledgeable regarding the coin's market value, and neither of them is under special pressure to make the deal.

The price listings used in this book are based upon fair market value.

Chapter Three

MAKING THE GRADE IN COINS

Coins are made to be spent. But collectors prefer coins that have never been spent at all—coins that are still as shiny and sharp as the day they left the mint—and they're willing to pay big premiums to obtain them.

"Quality" is a very important word in coin collecting today, and a very important word for you, as well, if you have any plans to buy or sell coins in today's marketplace. Buying the best will cost you more money, but you'll get more money back when you go to sell, and chances are, those high-quality coins will hold their value better in the meantime. Conversely, if you're thinking of selling any coins you already own, you'll find potential buyers placing heavy stress on the coins' condition.

The condition or "grade" of a coin—its level of preservation—has become a primary key in determining how much that coin is worth. A brand-new coin, one in what is called Mint State or "uncirculated" condition, is often worth many times as much as another coin of the same type and date that has passed from hand to hand. What's more, there are nuances of "newness." Coins aren't looked upon as simply "new" or "used": experts now recognize no fewer than eleven different grade levels within the Mint State range, and a shift of just one or two levels can mean a difference of many thousands of dollars in the value of a coin.

RECOGNIZED GRADING STANDARDS

The coin market's preoccupation with quality has led to the establishment of industrywide standards for grading coins. These standards were promulgated in 1977 by the American Numismatic Association (ANA), the world's largest organization of coin collectors, and have come to be accepted and observed throughout the marketplace.

The system set up by the ANA rates coins on a scale of 1 to 70, with the numbers ascending as the level of quality rises. A coin graded 1 can barely be identified; if it were a Lincoln cent, for instance, you could tell that's what it was, but little more. A coin graded 70 would be positively perfect in every respect: a coin with no nicks, no flaws, no scratches, and no imperfections of any kind. It also wouldn't have the slightest bit of friction on its highest points from having been touched or passed from hand to hand.

"Uncirculated" becomes "circulated" if just two tiny letters are removed. It's similarly easy to transform a Mint State coin into something a little less than that—and a lot less valuable. Suppose you had a coin worth $5,000 to collectors because of its virtual perfection—a coin that looked as new as the day it left the mint because it had never been spent and its owners had never mishandled it even once. If you were to take a sweat-soaked finger and wipe it lightly over that coin, it wouldn't be considered Mint State anymore; experts would downgrade it all the way to About Uncirculated, a grade that corresponds to the number 58—perhaps 10 points lower on the scale. The real damage would show up on your ledger sheet, for the value of that coin might now be just a few hundred dollars—and possibly even less.

Even the slightest mishandling can damage a coin irreparably. And once a coin passes from hand to hand, the most exposed parts of the metal begin to wear down, causing the loss of detail— detail that can never be replaced.

The grade assigned to each coin includes not only a number but also a word description. That perfect coin, for instance, would be designated Mint State-70. If it were a proof, or specimen coin, its grade would be Proof-70. Proofs are graded separately from regular coins (also known as "business strikes"), but the same 1-to-70 scale is used.

The ANA may have standardized grading with its 1-to-70 scale, but it didn't invent the concept of using specific terms to describe a coin's condition. Long before the present system evolved, dealers and collectors were utilizing such adjectives as "good," "fine," "choice," and "gem" to characterize their coins. These adjectives provided a convenient kind of shorthand for long-distance buyers and sellers—mail-order coin dealers, for example. They could carry out transactions by telephone or mail with reasonable confidence because there was general agreement on the meaning of the basic grading terms. This type of confidence is important in the rare coin business, for coins by their nature lend themselves well to long-distance sales. Coins are small, extremely portable, and often quite valuable, so deals involving very high values can be carried out easily through the mail, using registered mail to protect against possible loss.

THE ELEMENTS OF GRADING

A number of different elements help to determine the grade of a coin. It's beyond the scope of this book to examine these elements in detail, but a brief discussion will give you a general idea of what's involved. For a much fuller treatment, I recommend that you read my companion book *One-Minute Coin Expert*.

When a professional numismatist—usually a coin dealer—looks at a coin, he focuses on several different factors, and all of these have a bearing on how he grades the coin. He checks, of course, to see if there is wear—and, if so, how much. He also looks for obvious imperfections such as cuts, scratches, or nicks: Smooth *surfaces* enhance a coin's appearance and its grade. With a Mint State coin, in particular, the expert puts great emphasis on the *strike*—the sharpness of detail imparted to the coin when it was made. He also takes into account the *luster* of the coin—the way it reflects light. Finally, he considers everything all together by gauging the coin's *eye appeal.* Sometimes a coin may seem to have much to recommend it in each of the individual categories but somehow comes up short when viewed as a whole.

THE MOST IMPORTANT GRADES

There may be 70 numbers on the ANA grading scale, but not all those numbers are created equal. The 11 grades at the top of the scale, those between 60 and 70, constitute the Mint State range, and this is where the action is in today's coin market. This is where we see the overwhelming majority of important coin transactions—those involving substantial amounts of money. This is also the area where accurate grading is most crucial and where the greatest potential exists for disputes and costly mistakes.

Mint State coins cannot have any wear; by definition, a coin cannot be uncirculated if it has entered circulation—that is to say, been passed from hand to hand—and suffered even the slightest loss of detail. Mint State coins can have flaws, but any such imperfections must have occurred at the mint. For example, they can have "bag marks" from coming into contact with other coins at the mint. They still would be considered Mint State coins, but the marks would reduce their grade.

In practice, few coins qualify for designation as Mint State-70. This is really more of a theoretical grade, a utopian goal that is constantly pursued but seldom attained. MS-69 and MS-68 are attainable, but only with great difficulty. To qualify for one of these grades, a coin must be free of all but the tiniest flaws.

Here are some of the most important grades in the current marketplace:

• **MS-67.** A coin in this grade can have one or two small defects that are visible under 5-power magnification. However, these would not be apparent to the naked eye and the coin would seem practically perfect upon first being viewed.

• **MS-65.** While clearly not perfect, a coin in this grade is still highly desirable. In fact, coins graded MS-65 fall just short of what is called "super-grade" status. They possess great appeal but are held back by a single minor blemish.

• **MS-63.** A coin in this grade is still desirable, but even the naked eye can detect some flaws. There may be an obvious bag mark, for example, or spots on the surface of the coin.

• **MS-60.** A coin graded MS-60 is uncirculated—but just barely. It hasn't been passed from hand to hand, so technically it doesn't have any wear. But it does have very obvious mint-made imperfections. These may include scratches, nicks, and even large gashes in prominent locations.

• **About Uncirculated.** This is the grading level just below the Mint State range. It has three main components: AU-58, AU-55, and AU-50. Coins graded AU-58 may have considerable eye appeal; in fact, they may be more attractive at first glance than many Mint State coins. However, closer scrutiny will reveal slight wear on the highest points. These coins have passed through people's hands—but only through a few.

• **Extremely Fine.** Next in line, as we move down the scale, are coins graded EF-45 and EF-40. These coins have light wear on their highest points, but overall they're still detailed and attractive.

• **Very Fine.** Coins graded VF-30 and VF-20 are moderately worn, but all their major features remain sharp.

• **Fine.** A coin graded Fine-12 has passed through many hands and emerged with moderate to heavy wear. However, the wear is even and all the major features are still clearly discernible.

• **Very Good.** When we reach the grade of VG-8, we're obviously approaching the bottom of the scale. A coin in this grade is well worn. Its design remains clear, but it's flat and lacks details.

- **Good.** It soon becomes evident that this is not what the uninitiated have in mind when they say that their coins are "in good condition." Far from being desirable, G-4 coins are heavily worn. The design and inscriptions are still discernible; however, they're faint here and there.

- **About Good.** For all practical purposes, AG-3 is the lowest collectible grade—and most collectors shun it except in the case of scarce-date coins. On an AG-3 coin, the design remains visible only in outline and parts of the date and inscriptions are worn smooth.

For in-depth information on coin grading, I recommend that you read *Official Guide to Coin Grading and Counterfeit Detection* by the Professional Coin Grading Service (House of Collectibles, $29.95).

CLEANING COINS

Uninformed individuals mistakenly believe that dark, dull, or damaged coins can be magically restored to something approaching their original brilliance through the application of baking soda and elbow grease. This is a disastrous misconception.

Never clean a coin. Far from enhancing the value of a coin, cleaning almost always diminishes—or destroys—whatever appeal that coin might have held for collectors. A coin that has been cleaned may look bright and shiny to the untrained eye, but under a magnifying glass its surfaces will reveal unsightly scratches. The friction involved in cleaning a coin wears down the metal on its surface. This actually lowers the grade of the coin. What's more, many collectors find cleaned coins repugnant and flatly refuse to put them in their collections.

There are ways of cleaning coins that minimize the damage; museums, for example, have experts who are skilled in removing foreign substances from coins. For everyone else, however, the message is clear. When it comes to your coins, "cleaning" is a very dirty word.

GRADING SERVICES

The so-called "good old days" may stir our sense of nostalgia, but the old days weren't always all that good. Consider what used to happen when people had valuable coins to sell.

There wasn't any system in place in those days to offer people guidance on how much their coins were worth. Experienced collectors knew where to turn; besides being knowledgeable themselves about coins, they also knew which coin dealers could be counted upon to render honest appraisals. But those unschooled in the ways of the coin world had no such protection. They ended up taking their coins to local coin shops and putting themselves, quite literally, at the dealers' mercy. And all too often, those dealers weren't merciful: they offered ridiculously low sums for coins that were actually rare and valuable, then, after buying the coins, turned around and sold them for huge profits.

Today, there is a safety net for consumers—meaning you! Companies known as grading services provide impartial opinions on the grades of rare coins that are sent in to them for review. They don't come right out and say what your coins are worth, but since a coin's value is determined by its grade, it's a very simple matter to figure out the value once you know the grade. Those of you who dabble in the stock market are undoubtedly familiar with Moody's Investor Services, a company that offers independent ratings of stocks. The grading services play a similar role today in the coin market: they offer independent third-party opinions on the grades of the coins they examine, based upon the 1-to-70 scale.

Three top grading services are the Numismatic Guaranty Corporation of America (NGC), the Professional Coin Grading Service (PCGS), and ANACS. For a fee of approximately $25 per coin, these companies will examine your coins, assign appropriate grades, then encapsulate each coin in a hard plastic holder along with an insert stating the grade. Coins in these holders are said to be "certified coins." They enjoy wide acceptance in the marketplace, and this will facilitate sale of your coins for fair market prices.

When you think of it, $25 is a small price to pay for the peace of

MAKING THE GRADE IN COINS

mind and protection you receive. As you can see from reading through this book, it's not at all impossible that you may have a coin worth many thousands of dollars. If you walk into a coin shop without first having that coin certified, you're likely to receive a low-ball offer—and possibly even a rip-off offer. Once you get it certified, you'll know what it's worth and you can then deal from a position of strength in seeking a buyer. Furthermore, its status as a certified coin will make it much easier to sell.

NGC does not accept direct submissions of coins from the public. PCGS accepts such submissions; write or call for details. Both services maintain networks of authorized submission centers. The centers will advise you on how to submit your coins. For information and lists of authorized centers, write to NGC and PCGS as follows:

Numismatic Guaranty Corporation of America Inc.
Box 4776
Sarasota, FL 34230-4776

Professional Coin Grading Service
P.O. Box 9458
Newport Beach, CA 92658-9458

ANACS accepts coins from the public for encapsulation and takes an admirable educational approach to coin grading. That service will encapsulate coins that have been cleaned or damaged and will place an explanatory statement with the grade. This is one reason ANACS is popular with knowledgeable and informed collectors. For information on how to submit coins to that service, write:

ANACS
Amos Certification Service, Inc.
P.O. Box 182141
Columbus, OH 43218-2141

Wherever possible, the prices quoted in Chapter Four of this book represent fair market values for certified coins of the dates and mints listed—coins graded by NGC, PCGS, or ANACS. These are far and away the most accurate statements of real market value—the prices at which coins actually change hands in the current marketplace.

In cases where insufficient numbers of certain coins have been certified to establish firm price levels, the prices represent fair market values for uncertified coins. These are the prices at which those coins would change hands in a transaction between two people who are reasonably knowledgeable of the facts, are willing participants, and are under no special compulsion to consummate the transaction.

Mintage figures—the quantities produced by the mint—are shown alongside the listing of each coin's date, grade, and value. To further assist you, I have included a number of high-quality photographs to illustrate the major coin types and varieties. These will help you identify each of your coins. All of these photographs were obtained on a courtesy basis from Bowers and Merena Galleries Inc., Box 1224, Wolfeboro, NH 03894–1224.

I'm confident that this book will enable you to determine how much your coins are worth. I'm sure it will also help you obtain a fair price if you choose to sell them. More than this, however, I firmly believe that after reading this book, you will be richer not only in dollars and cents but also in knowledge. And that's the best kind of wealth that money can buy.

PRICE PERFORMANCE STATISTICS

Statistics can be highly useful. They also can be abused. For that reason, you always should be wary when confronted with statistics touting rare coins' investment performance and potential.

There isn't any question that over the long term, truly rare coins that are free from imperfections and wear have appreciated in value handsomely—even spectacularly. Over shorter terms, however, coins encounter ups and downs just like any other investment you might make. Thus, it would be misleading to take a fairly short time span—a year or two, for instance—and argue that just because coins did very well (or very poorly) during that period, they were likely to perform similarly in the future.

MAKING THE GRADE IN COINS

Consider what happened in 1990 and 1991. The coin market, like many other parts of the U.S. economy, experienced widespread setbacks during that two-year period. Some rare coins lost more than half their value. But things began to turn around during the early part of 1992, and prices rebounded dramatically. If someone drew up a chart showing coins' performance from 1989 through 1991, the downward-pointing arrows would alarm the most cockeyed optimist. Yet in the long-term scheme of things, that was just a narrow—and not at all typical—band in the market's performance. And it certainly didn't serve as an accurate barometer of what lay ahead, even in the very near term.

It would be extremely difficult to fashion an accurate chart of coin price performance over, say, a period of fifty years. The reason is that over the long haul, major changes have taken place in how rare coins are graded—how buyers and sellers assess those coins' level of preservation.

It would certainly be possible to go back fifty years and come up with statistics on how much certain coins were selling for at that time, then compare those figures with the prices of similar coins forty years ago, thirty years ago, and so on. But all those figures wouldn't be very meaningful unless the grade was constant for each and every coin being charted. In other words, the "uncirculated" coin from fifty years ago would have to correspond exactly to the Mint State coin of today. In practice, grading standards have changed significantly even within the last fifteen years, much less the last fifty.

The truest test of coins' price performance is to see how well (or how poorly) coin buyers have done after holding their acquisitions for many years. Those who purchased desirable material years ago at market-related prices—prices that were fair at the time of the transaction—have fared quite well indeed. I know of numerous cases where people assembled collections for just a few thousand dollars several decades ago and sold them in recent years for enormous profits. Some of these people ended up close to being millionaires. On the other hand, people who purchased coins that weren't as desirable may have very little to show for those acquisitions, even after holding them many years.

Chapter Four

U.S. COIN VALUES

(NOTE: All photographs in this chapter were provided by Bowers and Merena Galleries Inc., with special assistance furnished by company photographer Cathy Dumont.)

IMPORTANT NOTE: Values for Mint State and Proof copper coins are for specimens which exhibit both *red* and *brown* color, except where indicated.

URGENT INFORMATION ON MINTAGE FIGURES

In the earliest days of the U.S. Mint, officials went out of their way to publicize the number of coins being struck, as it proved to the new nation that the institution was fulfilling its task. It was commonplace to find, for example, large eastern newspapers reporting the monthly coinage figures from the Philadelphia Mint.

Three branch mints were opened in 1838, followed by others at irregular intervals, but the general procedure was the same as in the earlier days. There was, however, a major change in 1857 when the government changed the fiscal year to end on June 30 and required the mint service to follow suit. Because of this change, mintage figures were now given out to the public on a fiscal-year basis, and calendar-year figures were not published. In 1887, Mint director James P. Kimball, responding to numerous collector inquiries, ordered that the missing calendar-year figures for 1857–1886 be compiled and published for all to see. This was done, but a few errors crept in that were generally corrected by numismatic researchers in the 1960s, using materials in the National Archives. After 1887, the Mint Bureau published both calendar- and fiscal-year figures so that there was no longer any confusion.

The Mint did not generally publish proof mintage figures, and the records for such pieces do not exist for years prior to 1858. In the 1940s, the Mint Bureau finally published the relevant figures beginning with 1864; earlier years were later filled in by researchers. Due to a quirk in record keeping, minor proof statistics do not exist before 1878, but are well documented after that time.

In the twentieth century, the Mint Bureau was usually quite open with mintage figures. Until the early 1960s, numismatic publications normally reported coinage production figures on a monthly and yearly basis. The coin shortage of the 1960s ushered in a new era, however, and Mint officials began to release only annual totals (though this has been relaxed somewhat in recent years for the regular—noncommemorative—coinage).

The number of coins struck by the different United States mints for regular issues and commemorative coins is not completely available from the Mint office at press time despite repeated requests from researchers, numismatic periodicals, and general-interest publications for these facts. *In several cases, it has been necessary to use parentheses to indicate that the Mint has furnished sales figures rather than the number actually struck.* **In a few cases, no figures of any kind have been made available.**

Following are fair market values for U.S. coins issued from 1792 to the present. The coins are arranged from the smallest-value denomination (the half cent) through the highest (the $20 gold piece), with commemoratives and American Eagle bullion coins listed separately.

The values are provided in several different grades, or levels of preservation; the better the condition of a coin, the higher its value will be. In some cases, you will find only two or three grades listed for certain coins. It may be that these coins are normally encountered only in those grades; other times, they may have no special value except in the very highest grades.

You will find a number of listings for "overdates." These are coins on which one or more of the numbers in the date are engraved over other numbers. This was a common occurrence in the U.S. Mint's early years, when dies from prior years were reused—and the new dates were cut over the old ones—in order to save money. Dies are the pieces of metal used to stamp coins; you might think of them as being like the cookie cutters used to press designs into cookies.

The italicized numbers after the dates of certain coins denote the number of proofs—or specimen coins—that were struck in that year at that mint.

HALF CENTS (1793–1857)

Liberty Cap Portrait (1793–1797)

Portrait Facing Left (1793)

	Mintage	Good 4	Fine-12	EF-40
1793	35,334	$1,600	$4,250	$12,000

Portrait Facing Right (1794–1797)

	Mintage	Good-4	Fine-12	EF-40
1794	81,600	$240	$700	$2,300
1795	139,690	220	525	1,750
1796 combined total	1,390			
1796 with pole		5,500	12,500	32,000
1796 without pole		13,500	27,000	—
1797 combined total	127,840			
1797 plain edge		240	575	1,950
1797 lettered edge		550	2,000	8,500

Draped Bust Portrait (1800–1808)

	Mintage	Good-4	Fine-12	EF-40
1800	202,908	$25.00	$60.00	$300
1802 combined total	20,266			
1802/0 overdate with same reverse as 1800		7,500	22,500	—
1802/0 with new reverse.		275	1,100	8,000
1803	92,000	30.00	60.00	350
1804 combined total	1,055,312			
1804 with "spiked" chin		25.00	50.00	300
1804, all others.		22.50	45.00	225
1805 combined total	814,464			
1805 with small 5 and stems .		275	1,100	—
1805, all others.		27.50	55.00	220
1806 combined total	356,000			
1806 with small 6 and stems .		110	375	1,900
1806, all others.		27.50	55.00	220
1807	476,000	30.00	60.00	240
1808 combined total	400,000			
1808 regular date.		30.00	65.00	275
1808/7 overdate		80.00	240	1,500

Classic Head Portrait (1809–1836)

	Mintage	Good-4	Fine-12	EF-40	Proof-63
1809 combined total	1,154,572				
1809 regular date		$22.50	$37.50	$100	
1809/6 overdate		24.00	40.00	110	
1810	215,000	25.00	52.50	250	
1811	63,140	100	325	2,100	
1825	63,000	24.00	40.00	100	
1826	234,000	20.00	35.00	95.00	
1828 combined total	606,000				
1828 with 13 stars		20.00	32.50	85.00	
1828 with 12 stars		22.50	37.50	100	
1829	487,000	20.00	32.50	85.00	
1831 original	2,200	—	—	6,000	
1831 restrike with large berries (proof only).....	unknown	—	—	—	$7,000
1831 restrike with small berries (proof only).....	unknown	—	—	—	11,000
1832	51,000	25.00	32.50	75.00	
1833	103,000	25.00	32.50	75.00	
1834	141,000	25.00	32.50	75.00	
1835	398,000	24.00	31.00	72.50	
1836 original (proof only)............	unknown	—	—	—	5,000
1836 restrike (proof only)............	unknown	—	—	—	6,000

Coronet Portrait (1840–1857)

	Mintage	Good-4	Fine-12	EF-40	Proof-63
1840–1848 original (proof only)............... *unknown*		—	—	—	$4,850
1840–1848 restrike (proof only)............... *unknown*		—	—	—	3,700
1849 large date...........	39,364	$30.00	$52.50	$100	
1849 small date original (proof only)........... *unknown*		—	—	—	3,800
1849 small date restrike (proof only)........... *unknown*		—	—	—	3,900
1850	39,812	32.50	55.00	110	
1851	147,672	27.50	50.00	90.00	
1852 restrike (proof only).. *unknown*		—	—	—	3,900
1853	129,694	27.50	50.00	90.00	
1854	55,358	30.00	52.50	100	
1855	56,500	30.00	52.50	100	
1856	40,430	32.50	55.00	110	
1857	35,180	35.00	57.50	120	

LARGE CENTS (1793–1857)

Flowing Hair Portrait (1793)

Chain on Reverse (1793)

	Mintage	Good-4	Fine-12	EF-40
1793 combined total	36,103			
1793 with AMERICA spelled out .		$2,400	$5,250	$19,500
1793 with AMERICA abbreviated AMERI		2,750	8,000	25,000

Wreath on Reverse (1793)

	Mintage	Good-4	Fine-12	EF-40
1793 combined total	63,353			
1793 with vine and bars on edge		$900	$2,250	$8,250
1793 lettered edge		950	2,400	9,000
1793 with strawberry leaves above the date	4 known	—		(unknown in higher grades)

Liberty Cap Portrait (1793–1796)

	Mintage	Good-4	Fine-12	EF-40
1793	11,056	$1,600	$3,750	$27,500
1794 combined total	918,521			
1794 with same head as 1793 . . .		275	1,750	11,500
1794 with new head		150	450	2,250
1794 with stars on the reverse . .		6,500	19,500	85,000
1795 lettered edge	37,000	150	450	2,250
1795 plain edge	501,500	125	375	1,750
1795 Jefferson head		4,500	13,500	—
1796	109,825	150	450	2,250

Draped Bust Portrait (1796–1807)

	Mintage	Good-4	Fine-12	EF-40
1796 combined total	363,375			
1796 with same reverse as 1794 .		$125	$375	$2,250
1796 with regular 1796 reverse . .		120	360	2,750
1796 with same reverse as 1797 .		115	345	1,650
1796 with LIBERTY spelled LIHERTY		135	425	10,000
1797 combined total	897,510			
1797 with gripped edge		60.00	275	1,650

	Mintage	Good-4	Fine-12	EF-40
1797 plain edge		65.00	290	1,750
1797 with new reverse and stems on wreath		55.00	220	1,350
1797 with new reverse and no stems		85.00	255	3,000
1798 combined total	1,841,745			
1798 with old hair style		32.50	150	1,200
1798 with new hair style		32.50	150	1,000
1798 with same reverse as 1796		65.00	300	2,900
1798/7 overdate		75.00	325	2,800
1799 regular date (mintage included with 1798)		1,000	4,000	
1799/8 overdate (mintage included with 1798)		1,100	4,250	
1800 combined total	2,822,175			
1800 regular date		30.00	120	750
1800/1798 overdate with old hair style		32.50	130	1,800
1800, 80/79 overdate with new hair style		30.00	120	875
1801 combined total	1,362,837			
1801 with regular reverse		32.50	130	875
1801 with fraction 1/000		32.50	130	950
1801 with fraction 1/100 over 1/000		35.00	150	1,350
1801 with 3 errors (1/000, only one stem and IINITED instead of UNITED)		60.00	400	4,000
1802 combined total	3,435,100			
1802 with regular reverse		32.50	120	750
1802 with no stems on wreath ..		32.50	120	800
1802 with fraction 1/000		35.00	140	825
1803 combined total	3,228,191			
1803 small date		32.50	120	750
1803 large date with small fraction		2,400	7,250	
1803 large date with large fraction		60.00	240	2,750
1803 with no stems on wreath ..		32.50	120	850
1803 with fraction 1/100 over 1/000		32.50	120	850
1804 (mintage included with 1803)		350	1,400	6,000
1805	941,116	32.50	120	850
1806	348,000	35.00	140	1,000

	Mintage	Good-4	Fine-12	EF-40
1807 combined total	829,221			
1807 with small fraction		32.50	130	925
1807 with large fraction		30.00	120	800
1807/6 overdate with small 7 . . .		1,750	6,000	24,500
1807/6 overdate with large 7		32.50	120	825

Classic Head Portrait (1808–1814)

	Mintage	Good-4	Fine-12	EF-40
1808	1,007,000	$37.50	$140	$900
1809	222,867	75.00	300	1,825
1810 combined total	1,458,500			
1810 regular date		32.50	120	800
1810/09 overdate		32.50	120	800
1811 combined total	218,025			
1811 regular date		60.00	240	1,750
1811/0 overdate		65.00	250	2,100
1812	1,075,500	32.50	120	800
1813	418,000	45.00	160	1,100
1814	357,830	32.50	120	975

Coronet Portrait (1816–1857)

	Mintage	Good-4	Fine-12	EF-40	AU-55	MS-63
1816	2,820,982	$9.50	$22.00	$100	$225	$400
1817 combined total	3,948,400					
1817 with 13 stars		9.50	22.00	100	200	400
1817 with 15 stars		12.50	27.50	150	300	800
1818	3,167,000	9.50	22.00	100	200	375
1819 combined total	2,671,000					
1819 regular date		9.50	22.00	100	200	375
1819/8 overdate		11.00	24.00	110	250	400
1820 combined total	4,407,550					
1820 regular date		9.50	20.00	110	240	375
1820/19 overdate		11.00	24.00	120	275	400
1821	389,000	17.50	47.50	375	1,750	—
1822	2,072,339	9.50	22.00	125	325	550
1823 combined total	68,061					
1823 regular date		27.50	110	1,000	4,000	—
1823/2 overdate		25.00	100	850	2,500	—
1824 combined total	1,193,939					
1824 regular date		9.50	22.00	250	1,250	2,350
1824/2 overdate		15.00	45.00	500	1,750	—
1825	1,461,100	9.50	22.00	125	375	800
1826 combined total	1,517,425					
1826 regular date		9.50	22.00	110	350	700
1826/5 overdate		15.00	45.00	225	900	1,800
1827	2,357,732	9.50	22.00	100	200	350
1828 combined total	2,260,624					
1828 small date		10.00	22.50	47.50	375	800
1828 large date		9.50	22.00	45.00	350	775
1829 combined total	1,414,500					
1829 with medium letters		11.00	24.00	150	2,250	—
1829 with large letters		9.50	22.00	100	200	350
1830 combined total	1,711,500					
1830 with medium letters		17.50	52.50	275	2,500	—
1830 with large letters		9.50	22.00	100	200	350
1831	3,359,260	9.50	22.00	100	200	350

	Mintage	Good-4	Fine-12	EF-40	AU-55	MS-63
1832	2,362,000	9.50	22.00	100	200	350
1833	2,739,000	9.50	22.00	100	200	350
1834 combined total	1,855,100					
1834 with small 8, large stars and medium letters		9.50	22.00	100	200	350
1834 with large 8, small stars and medium letters		9.50	22.00	100	200	350
1834 with large 8, large stars and medium letters		75.00	200	600	3,000	—
1834 with large 8, large stars and large letters		10.00	25.00	110	500	—
1835 combined total	3,878,400					
1835 with same head as 1834 ...		10.00	22.50	120	240	400
1835 with same head as 1836 ...		9.50	22.00	110	220	425
1836	2,111,000	9.50	22.00	100	200	375
1837	5,558,300	9.00	20.00	100	200	350
1838	6,370,200	9.00	20.00	100	200	350
1839 combined total	3,128,661					
1839 with regular head		9.50	22.00	100	200	375
1839 with "silly" head		11.00	24.00	120	400	1,100
1839 with "booby" head		9.50	22.50	100	300	850
1839/6 overdate		120	480	2,750	12,500	—
1840 combined total	2,462,700					
1840 regular date		9.00	12.00	65.00	125	325
1840 with small 18 over large 18		9.50	15.00	90.00	200	375
1841	1,597,367	9.00	12.00	65.00	130	350
1842	2,383,390	9.00	12.00	65.00	125	300
1843 combined total	2,425,342					
1843 with small head and small letters		9.00	12.00	65.00	125	300
1843 with small head and large letters		11.00	27.50	120	400	800
1843 with large head and large letters		9.00	17.50	75.00	130	350
1844 combined total	2,398,752					
1844 regular date		8.50	11.00	65.00	125	300
1844/81 error		11.00	27.50	150	450	—
1845	3,894,804	8.50	11.00	65.00	125	300
1846 combined total	4,120,800					
1846 regular date		8.50	11.00	60.00	120	285
1846 small date		8.00	10.50	57.50	110	280
1847 combined total	6,183,669					
1847 regular date		8.00	10.50	57.50	110	280
1847 with 7 over small 7		11.00	22.50	90.00	250	

	Mintage	Good-4	Fine-12	EF-40	AU-55	MS-63
1848	6,415,799	7.50	10.00	75.00	125	300
1849	4,178,500	7.50	10.00	75.00	125	300
1850	4,426,844	7.50	10.00	57.50	110	300
1851 combined total	9,889,707					
1851 regular date		7.50	10.00	52.50	110	300
1851/81 error		11.00	20.00	90.00	180	375
1852	5,063,094	7.50	10.00	52.50	100	275
1853	6,641,131	7.50	10.00	52.50	100	275
1854	4,236,156	7.50	10.00	52.50	100	275
1855 combined total	1,574,829					
1855 with slanting 5 and knob on ear		8.50	15.00	60.00	110	285
1855, all other		7.50	10.00	52.50	100	275
1856	2,690,463	7.50	10.00	52.50	100	275
1857 combined total	333,456					
1857 small date		22.50	45.00	65.00	125	300
1857 large date		20.00	40.00	60.00	120	325

FLYING EAGLE CENTS (1856–1858)

	Mintage	Good-4	Fine-12	EF-40	AU-55	MS-63	MS-65	Proof-65
1856 pattern	1,000	$4,000	$4,250	$5,500	$6,000	$12,500	$75,000	$27,500
1857	17,450,000	12.50	17.50	67.50	135	350	4,200	22,000
1858 combined total	24,600,000							
1858 with small letters		12.50	17.50	67.50	135	350	4,200	22,000
1858 with large letters		12.50	17.50	67.50	135	350	4,200	22,000
1858/7 overdate		100	150	425	950	5,000		

INDIAN HEAD CENTS (1859–1909)

Copper-Nickel Composition (1859–1864)

Wreath on Reverse Without Shield (1859)

	Mintage	Good-4	Fine-12	EF-40	AU-55	MS-63	MS-65	Proof-65
1859 ...... *800*	36,400,000	$7.50	$10.00	$75.00	$150	$285	$2,800	$6,700

Wreath and Shield on Reverse (1860–1909)

	Mintage	Good-4	Fine-12	EF-40	AU-55	MS-63	MS-65	Proof-65
1860 ..... *1,000*	20,566,000	$6.00	$9.00	$27.50	$55.00	$150	$950	$4,500
1861 ..... *1,000*	10,100,000	12.50	22.50	65.00	100	170	1,000	6,500
1862 ..... *550*	28,075,000	5.00	7.50	25.00	52.50	150	975	3,000
1863 ..... *460*	49,840,000	4.00	6.00	22.50	45.00	150	980	3,200
1864 ..... *370*	13,740,000	11.00	21.00	32.50	65.00	165	900	3,200

Bronze Composition (1864–1909)

	Mintage	Good-4	Fine-12	EF-40	AU-55	MS-63	MS-65	Proof-65
1864 combined total	39,233,714							
1864 with no L *150*		$6.00	$9.00	$25.00	$37.50	$120	$500	$900

	Mintage	Good-4	Fine-12	EF-40	AU-55	MS-63	MS-65	Proof-65
1864 with L on headdress 20		30.00	57.50	120	180	350	1,375	100,000
1865 ..... 500	35,429,286	5.00	7.50	27.50	37.50	110	400	800
1866 ..... 725	9,826,500	27.50	37.50	90.00	120	200	600	800
1867 ..... 625	9,821,000	27.50	37.50	90.00	120	200	600	850
1868 ..... 600	10,266,500	27.50	37.50	90.00	120	200	600	850
1869 combined total	6,420,000							
1869 regular date 600		32.50	110	240	300	400	875	875
1869/9 overdate		100	200	400	600	1,000	2,500	
1870 ..... 1,000	5,275,000	27.50	120	240	300	400	800	800
1871 ..... 960	3,929,500	30.00	125	250	300	400	800	875
1872 ..... 950	4,042,000	50.00	150	300	350	475	5,000	900
1873 combined total	11,676,500							
1873 with closed 3 .... 1,100		12.00	27.50	75.00	100	300	650	700
1873 with open 3		12.00	25.00	45.00	60.00	175	450	
1873 with double letters on LIBERTY		150	800	2,000	5,800	19,500	75,000	
1874 ..... 700	14,187,500	12.00	20.00	60.00	80.00	150	450	700
1875 ..... 700	13,528,000	12.00	20.00	60.00	80.00	150	450	700
1876 ..... 1,150	7,944,000	17.50	35.00	80.00	110	225	500	750
1877 ..... 900	852,500	250	450	1,000	1,900	4,000	8,000	6,500
1878 ..... 2,350	5,799,850	20.00	37.50	90.00	120	240	600	550
1879 ..... 3,200	16,231,200	4.00	7.50	25.00	32.50	75.00	400	550
1880 ..... 3,955	38,964,955	3.00	4.50	15.00	25.00	65.00	375	550
1881 ..... 3,575	39,211,575	3.00	4.50	15.00	25.00	65.00	375	550
1882 ..... 3,100	38,581,100	3.00	4.50	15.00	25.00	65.00	375	550
1883 ..... 6,609	45,598,109	3.00	4.50	15.00	25.00	65.00	375	550
1884 ..... 3,942	23,261,742	3.25	5.00	17.50	27.50	70.00	365	550
1885 ..... 3,790	11,765,384	3.75	10.00	30.00	40.00	90.00	375	550
1886 ..... 4,290	17,654,290	3.50	8.00	35.00	47.50	95.00	400	550
1887 ..... 2,960	45,226,483	1.50	3.00	12.50	20.00	65.00	260	550
1888 combined total	37,494,414							
1888 regular date .... 4,582 ..		1.50	3.00	12.50	20.00	65.00	260	550
1888/7 overdate		1,200	5,000	20,000	23,000	35,000	—	
1889 ..... 3,336	48,869,361	1.50	2.50	11.00	20.00	65.00	260	550
1890 ..... 2,740	57,182,854	1.50	2.50	11.00	17.50	65.00	260	550
1891 ..... 2,350	47,072,350	1.50	2.50	11.00	17.50	65.00	260	550
1892 ..... 2,745	37,649,832	1.50	2.50	11.00	17.50	65.00	260	550
1893 ..... 2,195	46,642,195	1.50	2.50	11.00	17.50	65.00	260	550
1894 ..... 2,632	16,752,132	2.25	4.50	17.50	27.50	100	300	550
1895 ..... 2,062	38,343,636	1.00	2.00	10.00	17.50	60.00	250	550
1896 ..... 1,862	39,057,293	1.00	2.00	10.00	16.00	60.00	250	550
1897 ..... 1,938	50,466,330	1.00	2.00	10.00	16.00	60.00	250	550
1898 ..... 1,795	49,823,079	1.00	2.00	10.00	16.00	60.00	250	550

	Mintage	Good-4	Fine-12	EF-40	AU-55	MS-63	MS-65	Proof-65
1899 ......*2,031*	53,600,031	1.00	2.00	10.00	16.00	60.00	250	550
1900 ......*2,262*	66,833,764	.85	1.75	7.50	15.00	55.00	240	550
1901 ......*1,985*	79,611,143	.85	1.75	7.50	15.00	55.00	240	550
1902 ......*2,018*	87,376,722	.75	1.50	6.00	12.50	55.00	240	550
1903 ......*1,790*	85,094,493	.75	1.50	6.00	12.50	55.00	240	550
1904 ......*1,817*	61,328,015	.75	1.50	6.00	12.50	55.00	240	550
1905 ......*2,152*	80,719,163	.75	1.50	6.00	12.50	55.00	240	550
1906 ......*1,725*	96,022,255	.75	1.50	6.00	12.50	55.00	240	550
1907 ......*1,475*	108,138,618	.75	1.50	6.00	12.50	55.00	240	550
1908 ......*1,620*	32,327,987	.80	1.60	6.75	13.50	57.50	245	550
1908-S	1,115,000	22.50	30.00	70.00	100	225	800	
1909 ......*2,175*	14,370,645	1.00	2.00	10.00	20.00	60.00	225	550
1909-S	309,000	140	165	250	400	525	1,375	

LINCOLN CENTS (1909–PRESENT)

Wheat-Ears Reverse (1909–1958)

Bronze Composition (1909–1942)

	Mintage	Good-4	Fine-12	EF-40	AU-55	MS-63	MS-65	Proof-65
1909 with initials								
V.D.B. on back *420*	27,994,580	$2.00	$2.50	$3.75	$5.25	$15.00	$50.00	$7,500
1909-S V.D.B.	484,000	375	450	525	690	750	1,600	
1909 without								
initials ....*2,198* ..	72,700,420	.60	.80	2.00	4.50	22.50	48.00	800
1909-S	1,825,000	42.50	50.00	90.00	125	195	300	
1910 ......*2,405*	146,798,813	.15	.30	1.80	3.50	22.50	100	700
1910-S	6,045,000	7.50	9.00	22.50	40.00	120	210	
1911 ......*1,733*	101,176,054	.20	.50	4.00	6.00	32.50	200	700
1911-D	12,672,000	3.75	5.75	27.50	42.50	95.00	375	
1911-S	4,026,000	17.50	20.00	35.00	50.00	220	950	
1912 ......*2,145*	68,150,915	.30	1.50	9.00	15.00	35.00	200	950
1912-D	10,411,000	4.25	6.75	37.50	47.50	150	850	
1912-S	4,431,000	11.00	14.00	37.50	47.50	150	1,000	
1913 ......*2,848*	76,529,504	.25	.90	7.50	10.00	37.50	250	700
1913-D	15,804,000	2.25	3.75	20.00	37.50	150	875	

LINCOLN CENTS (1909–PRESENT)

	Mintage	Good-4	Fine-12	EF-40	AU-55	MS-63	MS-65	Proof-65
1913-S	6,101,000	6.50	8.50	22.50	45.00	210	1,100	
1914 ..... *1,365*	75,237,067	.25	1.20	8.00	12.50	75.00	300	700
1914-D	1,193,000	80.00	120	400	725	1,500	6,000	
1914-S	4,137,000	9.50	12.50	35.00	57.50	360	3,000	
1915 ..... *1,150*	29,090,970	1.00	3.50	35.00	50.00	120	400	700
1915-D	22,050,000	.85	1.75	9.00	17.50	110	425	
1915-S	4,833,000	7.00	8.50	27.50	40.00	195	1,150	
1916 ..... *1,050*	131,832,627	.15	.40	2.00	3.50	27.50	175	700
1916-D	35,956,000	.20	.90	7.50	22.50	100	800	
1916-S	22,510,000	.85	1.65	8.00	25.00	120	1,100	
1917	196,429,785	.15	.30	2.00	4.00	27.50	100	
1917-D	55,120,000	.30	.85	7.00	20.00	120	650	
1917	32,620,000	.30	.90	7.25	25.00	130	1,000	
1918	288,104,634	.15	.30	2.00	4.50	27.50	175	
1918-D	47,830,000	.25	.75	6.00	12.50	110	800	
1918-S	34,680,000	.35	.80	6.50	14.00	130	1,300	
1919	392,021,000	.15	.30	1.75	3.25	22.50	150	
1919-D	57,154,000	.25	.50	5.00	8.50	85.00	525	
1919-S	139,760,000	.20	.40	2.25	3.50	75.00	750	
1920	310,165,000	.10	.25	1.75	3.25	20.00	150	
1920-D	49,280,000	.20	.65	6.00	11.00	90.00	550	
1920-S	46,220,000	.20	.45	3.50	12.00	110	1,000	
1921	39,157,000	.25	.65	4.50	10.00	75.00	300	
1921-S	15,274,000	.75	1.50	12.50	42.50	250	1,250	
1922-D combined total	7,160,000							
1922-D		5.25	7.50	17.50	40.00	120	400	
1922 Plain (without D)		325	400	1,400	2,800	28,000	100,000	
1923	74,723,000	.20	.40	3.00	6.00	22.50	200	
1923-S	8,700,000	1.60	3.25	20.00	65.00	375	2,100	
1924	75,178,000	.15	.35	4.00	6.50	45.00	200	
1924-D	2,520,000	10.00	12.50	47.50	95.00	375	1,250	
1924-S	11,696,000	.80	1.60	15.00	30.00	190	1,500	
1925	139,949,000	.10	.25	2.00	3.50	20.00	100	
1925-D	22,580,000	.30	.60	6.50	10.00	90.00	500	
1925-S	26,380,000	.25	.40	6.00	9.00	130	2,200	
1926	157,088,000	.10	.25	2.00	3.25	17.50	100	
1926-D	28,020,000	.30	.55	5.00	8.50	80.00	600	
1926-S	4,550,000	3.25	4.25	12.50	45.00	190	2,750	
1927	144,440,000	.10	.25	1.75	3.00	17.50	100	
1927-D	27,170,000	.25	.45	3.00	8.00	70.00	350	
1927-S	14,276,000	.50	1.25	7.50	15.00	130	1,200	
1928	134,116,000	.10	.25	1.75	3.00	17.50	100	
1928-D	31,170,000	.25	.40	2.50	5.00	52.50	200	
1928-S	17,266,000	.35	.65	3.75	7.50	110	500	
1929	185,262,000	.10	.25	1.75	3.25	14.00	100	

LINCOLN CENTS (1909–PRESENT)

	Mintage	Good-4	Fine-12	EF-40	AU-55	MS-63	MS-65	Proof-65
1929-D	41,730,000	.15	.30	1.75	3.50	30.00	160	
1929-S	50,148,000	.15	.30	1.75	3.25	17.50	150	
1930	157,415,000	.10	.25	1.20	2.00	10.00	50.00	
1930-D	40,100,000	.15	.30	1.50	3.50	27.50	100	
1930-S	24,286,000	.20	.35	1.50	3.00	12.50	90.00	
1931	19,396,000	.40	.60	2.00	4.00	37.50	140	
1931-D	4,480,000	2.50	3.25	7.25	22.50	90.00	325	
1931-S	866,000	32.50	37.50	42.50	50.00	90.00	200	
1932	9,062,000	1.50	2.25	3.00	7.50	30.00	100	
1932-D	10,500,000	.75	1.25	3.00	7.50	32.50	100	
1933	14,360,000	.90	1.35	3.25	7.50	30.00	100	
1933-D	6,200,000	1.80	2.25	4.50	9.00	35.00	110	

(NOTE: Mint State and Proof values are for Lincoln cents 1934 to present exhibiting full red color.)

	Mintage	Fine-12	EF-40	AU-55	MS-60	MS-63	MS-65	Proof-65
1934	219,080,000	$.15	$.50	$1.00	$2.50	$5.00	$25.00	
1934-D	28,446,000	.25	1.00	7.50	17.50	27.50	85.00	
1935	245,388,000	.15	.50	.85	1.50	2.50	20.00	
1935-D	47,000,000	.15	.50	1.25	2.50	5.00	30.00	
1935-S	38,702,000	.25	1.00	5.00	7.50	12.50	125	
1936 5,569	309,632,000	.10	.50	.85	1.50	3.00	25.00	$1,100
1936-D	40,620,000	.15	.50	1.00	1.75	3.25	25.00	
1936-S	29,130,000	.20	.60	1.25	2.00	3.50	27.00	
1937 9,320	309,170,000	.10	.40	.75	1.25	2.25	10.00	200
1937-D	50,430,000	.15	.45	.85	2.00	3.00	12.00	
1937-S	34,500,000	.15	.45	.85	1.75	3.25	9.50	
1938 14,734	156,682,000	.10	.30	.75	1.50	2.50	6.25	110
1938-D	20,010,000	.20	.50	1.00	2.25	3.50	8.50	
1938-S	15,180,000	.30	.60	1.10	2.40	3.75	30.00	
1939 13,520	316,466,000	.10	.25	.50	.75	1.25	6.00	100
1939-D	15,160,000	.45	.75	1.50	2.50	3.50	11.00	
1939-S	52,070,000	.15	.35	.75	1.25	1.75	15.00	
1940 15,872	586,810,000	.10	.20	.35	.70	1.10	8.00	100
1940-D	81,390,000	.10	.20	.40	.75	1.25	4.50	
1940-S	112,940,000	.10	.20	.50	.80	1.35	6.00	
1941 21,100	887,018,000	—	.15	.25	.65	1.00	3.50	100
1941-D	128,700,000	—	.15	.75	2.00	2.75	7.50	
1941-S	92,360,000	—	.15	.90	2.25	3.00	20.00	
1942 32,600	657,796,000	—	.10	.20	.50	.75	2.50	105
1942-D	206,698,000	—	.10	.25	.60	.90	3.50	
1942-S	85,590,000	—	.15	.90	3.50	5.25	50.00	

Zinc-Coated Steel Composition (1943)

	Mintage	Fine-12	EF-40	AU-55	MS-60	MS-63	MS-65	Proof-65
1943	684,628,670	$.10	$.25	$.50	$.75	$1.00	$3.50	
1943-D	217,660,000	.10	.25	.50	.85	1.50	10.00	
1943-S	191,550,000	.15	.45	.75	1.25	2.25	15.00	

Bronze* Composition (1943 Mint Error)

	Mintage	Fine-12	EF-40	AU-55	MS-60	MS-63	MS-65	Proof-65
1943	14	$38,000	$52,000	$94,000	$112,500	—	—	
1943-D	2	—	—	215,000	—	—	—	
1943-S	7	50,000	62,000	97,000	115,000	—	—	

*1943 Bronze ("copper" or brown in color) Lincoln cents are extremely rare, and these listed mintages are merely estimates that are subject to change. Zinc-coated steel ("white" or "silver" in color) cents that were copper plated outside the Mint are not valuable. 1943 cents that appear to be bronze but are attracted to a magnet are zinc-coated steel cents that carry the lower value. In order to command these values, the coin must be authenticated by a third-party grading and authentication service.

Brass Composition (1944–1946)

	Mintage	Fine-12	EF-40	AU-55	MS-60	MS-63	MS-65	Proof-65
1944	1,435,400,000	—	$.10	$.15	$.35	$.60	$1.25	
1944-D combined total	430,578,000							
1944-D regular mint mark		—	.10	.15	.40	.90	1.50	
1944-D/S Variety 1 (more obvious)		75.00	150	225	300	450	1,275	
1944-D/S Variety 2		60.00	120	180	240	360	900	
1944-S	282,760,000	—	.10	.15	.40	.80	1.50	
1945	1,040,515,000	—	.10	.15	.40	.80	1.50	
1945-D	266,268,000	—	.10	.15	.40	.80	1.50	
1945-S	181,770,000	—	.10	.15	.40	.80	1.50	
1946	991,655,000	—	.10	.15	.40	.80	1.50	
1946-D	315,690,000	—	.10	.15	.40	.80	1.50	
1946-S	198,100,000	—	.10	.15	.40	.80	1.50	

Bronze Composition (1947–1962)

	Mintage	Fine-12	EF-40	AU-55	MS-60	MS-63	MS-65	Proof-65
1947	190,555,000	—	$.10	$.15	$.40	$.80	$1.50	
1947-D	194,750,000	—	.10	.15	.40	.80	1.50	
1947-S	99,000,000	—	.10	.15	.40	.85	1.60	
1948	317,570,000	—	.10	.15	.40	.80	1.50	
1948-D	172,637,500	—	.10	.15	.40	.80	1.50	
1948-S	81,735,000	—	.10	.15	.40	.85	1.75	
1949	217,775,000	—	.10	.15	.40	.75	1.50	
1949-D	153,132,500	—	.10	.15	.40	.75	1.75	
1949-S	64,290,000	—	.15	.20	.75	1.25	4.00	
1950 51,386	272,635,000	—	.10	.15	.40	.85	1.25	$50.00
1950-D	334,950,000	—	.10	.15	.40	.75	1.10	
1950-S	118,505,000	—	.10	.15	.40	.80	1.20	
1951 57,500	284,576,000	—	.10	.15	.40	.90	1.50	40.00
1951-D	625,355,000	—	.10	.15	.25	.60	.90	
1951-S	136,010,000	—	.10	.15	.35	.75	1.75	
1952 81,980	186,775,080	—	.10	.15	.25	.60	.90	29.00
1952-D	746,130,000	—	.10	.15	.25	.60	.75	
1952-S	137,800,004	—	.10	.15	.35	1.00	2.25	
1953 ... 128,800	256,755,000	—	.10	.15	.25	.60	.70	25.00
1953-D	700,515,000	—	.10	.15	.25	.60	.70	
1953-S	181,835,000	—	.10	.15	.25	.75	1.00	
1954 233,300	71,640,050	—	.15	.25	.35	.65	1.25	10.00
1954-D	251,552,500	—	.10	.15	.20	.30	.40	
1954-S	96,190,000	—	.15	.20	.25	.50	.75	
1955 combined total	330,580,000							
1955 regular date ... 378,200		—	.10	.15	.20	.25	.35	12.00
1955 with doubled-die obverse		425	550	700	1,300	1,800	6,500	
1955-D	563,257,500	—	.10	.15	.20	.25	.35	
1955-S	44,610,000	—	.20	.40	.60	.75	1.00	
1956 669,384	420,745,000	—	—	—	.15	.20	.30	2.50
1956-D	1,098,201,100	—	—	—	.15	.20	.30	
1957 ... 1,247,952	282,540,000	—	—	—	.15	.20	.30	2.00
1957-D	1,051,342,000	—	—	—	.15	.20	.30	
1958 875,652	252,525,000	—	—	—	.15	.20	.30	2.25
1958-D	800,953,300	—	—	—	.15	.20	.30	

Lincoln Memorial Reverse (1959–Present)
Bronze Composition (1959–1962)

	Mintage	Fine-12	EF-40	AU-55	MS-60	MS-63	MS-65	Proof-65
1959 ...... *1,149,291*	609,715,000	—	—	—	—	$.10	$.20	$1.50
1959-D	1,279,760,000	—	—	—	—	.10	.20	
1960 combined total ... *1,691,602*	586,405,000							
1960 with large date		—	—	—	—	.10	.20	1.25
1960 with small date		$.50	$.75	$.90	$1.50	2.00	3.00	12.50
1960-D combined total	1,580,884,000							
1960-D with large date		—	—	—	—	.10	.20	
1960-D with small date		.10	.15	.20	.30	.40	.50	
1961 ...... *3,028,244*	753,345,000	—	—	—	—	.10	.15	1.00
1961-D	1,753,266,700	—	—	—	—	.10	.15	
1962 ...... *3,218,019*	606,045,000	—	—	—	—	.10	.15	1.00
1962-D	1,793,148,400	—	—	—	—	.10	.15	

Brass Composition (1963–1982)

	Mintage	Fine-12	EF-40	AU-55	MS-60	MS-63	MS-65	Proof-65
1963 ...... *3,075,645*	754,110,000	—	—	—	—	—	$.10	$1.00
1963-D	1,774,020,400	—	—	—	—	—	.10	
1964 ...... *3,950,762*	2,648,575,000	—	—	—	—	—	.10	1.00
1964-D	3,799,071,500	—	—	—	—	—	.10	
1965	1,497,224,900	—	—	—	—	—	.15	
1966	2,188,147,783	—	—	—	—	—	.15	
1967	3,048,667,100	—	—	—	—	—	.15	
1968	1,707,880,970	—	—	—	—	—	.20	
1968-D	2,886,269,600	—	—	—	—	—	.10	
1968-S *3,041,506*	258,270,001	—	—	—	—	—	.15	1.00
1969	1,136,910,000	—	—	—	—	—	.30	
1969-D	4,002,832,200	—	—	—	—	—	.10	
1969-S combined total ... *2,934,631*	544,375,000	—	—	—	—	—	.15	1.00
1969-S with full doubled-die obverse		—	—	$15,000	—	—	—	
1970	1,898,315,000	—	—	—	—	—	.20	

	Mintage	Fine-12	EF-40	AU-55	MS-60	MS-63	MS-65	Proof-65
1970-D	2,891,438,900	—	—	—	—	—	.10	
1970-S combined								
total ... 2,632,810	690,560,004							
1970-S with small date		$12.50	$17.50	$22.50	32.50	$37.50	65.00	90.00
1970-S with large date		—	—	—	—	—	.15	1.00
1970-S with small date and a								
full doubled-die obverse ...		—	—	—	—	10,500	29,000	
1971	1,919,490,000	—	—	—	—	—	.20	
1971-D	2,911,045,600	—	—	—	—	—	.20	
1971-S 3,220,733	525,133,459	—	—	—	—	—	.15	1.00
1972 combined total	2,933,255,000							
1972 regular date		—	—	—	—	—	.10	
1972 with doubled-die								
obverse		100	120	140	175	200	225	
1972-D	2,665,071,400	—	—	—	—	—	.10	
1972-S 3,260,996	376,939,108	—	—	—	—	—	.15	1.00
1973	3,728,245,000	—	—	—	—	—	.10	
1973-D	3,549,576,588	—	—	—	—	—	.10	
1973-S 2,760,339	317,177,295	—	—	—	—	—	.15	1.00
1974	4,232,140,523	—	—	—	—	—	.10	
1974-D	4,235,098,000	—	—	—	—	—	.10	
1974-S 2,612,568	409,426,660	—	—	—	—	—	.15	1.00
1975	5,451,476,142	—	—	—	—	—	.10	
1975-D	4,505,275,300	—	—	—	—	—	.10	
1975-S (proof only)	2,845,450	—	—	—	—	—	—	3.00
1976	4,674,292,426	—	—	—	—	—	.10	
1976-D	4,221,592,455	—	—	—	—	—	.10	
1976-S (proof only)	4,149,730	—	—	—	—	—	—	1.50
1977	4,469,930,000	—	—	—	—	—	.10	
1977-D	4,194,062,300	—	—	—	—	—	.10	
1977-S (proof only)	3,251,152	—	—	—	—	—	—	1.50
1978	5,558,605,000	—	—	—	—	—	.10	
1978-D	4,280,233,400	—	—	—	—	—	.10	
1978-S (proof only)	3,127,781	—	—	—	—	—	—	2.00
1979	6,018,515,000	—	—	—	—	—	.10	
1979-D	4,139,357,254	—	—	—	—	—	.10	
1979-S combined total								
(proof only)	3,677,175							
1979-S with clogged S		—	—	—	—	—	—	2.00
1979-S with clear S		—	—	—	—	—	—	6.00
1980	7,414,705,000	—	—	—	—	—	.10	
1980-D	5,140,098,660	—	—	—	—	—	.10	
1980-S (proof only)	3,544,806	—	—	—	—	—	—	1.25
1981	7,491,750,000	—	—	—	—	—	.10	
1981-D	5,373,235,677	—	—	—	—	—	.10	

	Mintage	Fine-12	EF-40	AU-55	MS-60	MS-63	MS-65	Proof-65
1981-S (proof only)	4,063,083	—	—	—	—	—	—	1.25
1982 combined total	10,712,525,000							
1982 with small date		—	—	—	—	—	.15	
1982 with large date		—	—	—	—	—	.10	
1982-D with large date		—	—	—	—	—	.10	
1982-S (proof only)	3,857,479	—	—	—	—	—	—	1.50

Copper-Plated Zinc Composition
(1982–Present)

	Mintage	Fine-12	EF-40	AU-55	MS-60	MS-63	MS-65	Proof-65
1982 mintage included in combined total								
1982 with small date		—	—	—	—	—	$.60	
1982 with large date		—	—	—	—	—	.40	
1983 combined total	7,752,355,000							
1983 with regular reverse		—	—	—	—	—	.10	
1983 with doubled-die reverse		$90.00	$105	$125	$150	$180	225	
1983-D	6,467,199,428	—	—	—	—	—	.10	
1983-S (proof only)	3,279,126	—	—	—	—	—	—	3.00
1984 combined total	8,151,079,000							
1984 with regular obverse		—	—	—	—	—	.10	
1984 with doubled-die obverse		40.00	50.00	60.00	75.00	105	140	
1984-D	5,569,238,906	—	—	—	—	—	.10	
1984-S (proof only)	3,065,110	—	—	—	—	—	—	4.00
1985	5,648,489,887	—	—	—	—	—	.10	
1985-D	5,287,399,926	—	—	—	—	—	.10	
1985-S (proof only)	3,362,821	—	—	—	—	—	—	2.75
1986	4,491,395,493	—	—	—	—	—	.10	
1986-D	4,442,866,698	—	—	—	—	—	.10	
1986-S (proof only)	3,010,497	—	—	—	—	—	—	7.00
1987	4,682,466,931	—	—	—	—	—	.10	
1987-D	4,879,389,514	—	—	—	—	—	.10	
1987-S (proof only)	3,792,233	—	—	—	—	—	—	2.75
1988	6,092,810,000	—	—	—	—	—	.10	
1988-D	5,253,740,443	—	—	—	—	—	.10	
1988-S (proof only)	3,262,948	—	—	—	—	—	—	4.00
1989	7,261,535,000	—	—	—	—	—	.10	
1989-D	5,345,467,111	—	—	—	—	—	.10	
1989-S (proof only)	3,215,728	—	—	—	—	—	—	4.00
1990	6,851,765,000	—	—	—	—	—	.10	
1990-D	4,922,894,533	—	—	—	—	—	.10	
1990 without S mint mark (proof only)	3,555	—	—	—	—	—	—	2,900

LINCOLN CENTS (1909–PRESENT)

	Mintage	Fine-12	EF-40	AU-55	MS-60	MS-63	MS-65	Proof-65
1990-S (proof only)	3,296,004	—					—	6.00
1991	5,165,940,000	—	—	—	—	—	.10	
1991-D	4,158,442,076	—	—	—	—	—	.10	
1991-S (proof only)	2,867,787	—	—	—	—	—	—	6.75
1992	4,648,905,000	—	—	—	—	—	.10	
1992-D	4,448,673,300	—	—	—	—	—	.10	
1992-S (proof only)	4,176,544	—	—	—	—	—	—	5.00
1993	5,684,705,000							
1993-D	6,426,650,571							
1993-S (proof only)	3,360,876	—	—	—	—	—	—	5.00
1994	6,502,060,896	—	—	—	—	—	.10	
1994-D	7,132,975,896	—	—	—	—	—	.10	
1994-S (proof only)	3,212,792	—	—	—	—	—	—	5.75
1995 combined total	6,412,481,352	—	—	—	—	.10		
1995 with doubled-die obverse		—	—	5.00	10.00	15.00	30.00	
1995-D	7,129,601,352	—	—	—	—	—	.10	
1995-S (proof only)	2,796,345	—	—	—	—	—	5.75	
1996	6,613,919,215	—	—	—	—	—	.10	
1996-D	6,512,249,215	—	—	—	—	—	.10	
1996-S (proof only)	2,925,305	—	—	—	—	—	—	5.75
1997	4,622,800,000	—	—	—	—	—	.10	
1997-D	4,576,555,000	—	—	—	—	—	.10	
1997-S (proof only)	2,788,020	—	—	—	—	—	—	5.75
1998	5,032,200,000	—	—	—	—	—	.10	
1998-D	5,225,200,000	—	—	—	—	—	.10	
1998-S (proof only)	2,965,503	—	—	—	—	—	—	5.75
1999	5,237,600,000	—	—	—	—	—	.10	
1999-D	6,360,065,000	—	—	—	—	—	.10	
1999-S (proof only)	(2,454,319)*	—	—	—	—	—	—	5.75
2000	5,503,200,000	—	—	—	—	—	.10	
2000-D	8,774,220,000	—	—	—	—	—	.10	
2000-S (proof only)	(3,934,000)*	—	—	—	—	—	—	5.75
2001	4,959,600,000	—	—	—	—	.10		
2001-D	5,374,990,000	—	—	—	—	.10		
2001-S (proof only)	(2,293,200)**	—	—	—	—	—	—	5.75
2002		—	—	—	—	.10		
2002-D		—	—	—	—	.10		
2002-S (proof only)		—	—	—	—	—	—	5.75
2003		—	—	—	—	.10		
2003-D		—	—	—	—	.10		
2003-S (proof only)		—	—	—	—	—	—	5.75

*Through March 31, 2001
**Through May 28, 2002

TWO-CENT PIECES (1864–1873)

	Mintage	Fine-12	EF-40	AU-55	MS-60	MS-63	MS-65	Proof 65
1864 combined total	19,847,400							
1864 with small motto		$52.50	$90.00	$240	$300	$750	$2,300	
1864 with large motto *100*		6.00	10.00	32.50	65.00	140	225	$800
1865 .... *500*	13,639,500	6.00	10.00	32.50	65.00	140	225	800
1866 .... *725*	3,176,275	6.00	10.00	32.50	65.00	140	225	800
1867 .... *625*	2,938,125	6.00	10.00	32.50	65.00	140	225	800
1868 .... *600*	2,803,150	6.50	11.00	35.00	70.00	175	300	900
1869 combined total	1,545,900							
1869 regular date ..... *600* ...		7.50	12.50	37.50	75.00	225	400	900
1869/8 overdate		175	250	400				
1870 .... *1,000*	860,250	9.00	17.50	60.00	90.00	325	500	1,000
1871 .... *960*	720,290	10.00	20.00	75.00	105	350	600	1,000
1872 .... *950*	64,050	70.00	140	350	475	1,050	2,300	1,200
1873 closed 3 (proof only)	*600*	—	—	—	—	—	—	1,000
1873 open 3 (proof only)	*500*	—	—	—	—	—	—	2,000

SILVER THREE-CENT PIECES (1851–1873)

	Mintage	Good-4	Fine-12	EF-40	AU-55	MS-63	MS-65	Proof-65
1851	5,447,400	$11.00	$17.50	$60.00	$110	$225	$1,350	
1851-O	720,000	17.50	32.50	120	200	450	3,250	
1852	18,663,500	11.00	17.50	57.50	115	225	1,350	
1853	11,400,000	11.00	17.50	52.50	115	225	1,350	
1854	671,000	12.50	25.00	100	200	540	5,000	—
1855	139,000	17.50	42.50	160	240	1,050	15,500	$6,000

	Mintage	Good-4	Fine-12	EF-40	AU-55	MS-63	MS-65	Proof-65
1856	1,458,000	11.00	20.00	85.00	175	540	5,000	6,000
1857	1,042,000	11.00	20.00	80.00	190	540	5,000	6,000
1858	1,604,000	11.00	22.50	90.00	180	540	5,000	6,000
1859 800	364,200	11.00	20.00	52.50	110	300	1,050	1,400
1860 1,000	286,000	11.00	20.00	52.50	110	300	1,050	1,400
1861 1,000	497,000	11.00	20.00	52.50	110	300	1,050	1,400
1862 combined total	343,000							
1862 regular date 550		11.00	20.00	52.50	110	300	1,050	1,400
1862/1 overdate		14.00	22.50	70.00	150	350	1,150	
1863 combined total 460	21,000							
1863 regular date		175	250	325	375	750	1,800	1,600
1863/2 overdate		200	275	350	400	800	1,900	1,800
1864 470	12,000	225	300	375	425	850	1,900	1,600
1865 500	8,000	235	325	375	425	900	2,000	1,600
1866 725	22,000	200	275	325	375	900	1,800	1,600
1867 625	4,000	250	325	375	450	875	2,600	1,600
1868 600	3,500	250	325	375	450	1,200	2,800	1,600
1869 combined total 600	4,500							
1869 regular date		250	325	400	475	1,050	2,800	1,600
1869/8 overdate		350	425	500	575	1,300	2,900	1,650
1870 1,000	3,000	250	325	375	450	900	2,000	1,600
1871 960	3,400	250	325	400	475	825	1,800	1,600
1872 950	1,000	275	400	550	650	1,250	2,800	1,600
1873 closed-3 (proof only) 600		—	—	—	—	—	—	2,500

NICKEL THREE-CENT PIECES (1865–1889)

	Mintage	Good-4	Fine-12	EF-40	AU-55	MS-63	MS-65	Proof-65
1865 500	11,381,500	$5.50	$7.50	$15.00	$35.00	$150	$700	$550
1866 725	4,800,275	5.50	7.50	15.00	35.00	150	700	550
1867 625	3,914,375	5.50	7.50	15.00	35.00	150	700	550
1868 600	3,251,400	5.50	7.50	15.00	35.00	150	700	550
1869 600	1,603,400	5.50	7.50	15.00	37.50	150	700	550
1870 1,000	1,334,000	6.00	8.25	17.50	40.00	150	700	550

	Mintage	Good-4	Fine-12	EF-40	AU-55	MS-63	MS-65	Proof-65
1871 . . . . 960	603,040	6.00	8.25	17.50	40.00	200	900	550
1872 . . . . 950	861,050	6.00	8.25	17.50	40.00	175	900	550
1873 closed								
3 . . . . 1,100	388,900	6.00	8.00	17.50	40.00	180	950	550
1873 open 3	783,000	6.00	8.00	17.50	40.00	180	950	550
1874 . . . . 700	789,300	6.00	8.00	17.50	40.00	190	950	550
1875 . . . . 700	227,300	7.50	10.00	22.50	60.00	200	950	550
1876 . . . . 1,150	160,850	10.00	15.00	32.50	90.00	300	950	550
1877 (proof only)	900	—	—	—	—	—	—	2,200
1878 (proof only)	2,350	—	—	—	—	—	—	800
1879 . . . . 3,200	38,000	42.50	57.50	90.00	125	375	900	600
1880 . . . . 3,955	21,000	57.50	75.00	120	160	425	900	600
1881 . . . . 3,575	1,077,000	5.50	7.50	15.00	35.00	150	700	550
1882 . . . . 3,100	22,200	57.50	75.00	110	150	450	900	600
1883 . . . . 6,609	4,000	120	160	240	275	650	1,400	750
1884 . . . . 3,942	1,700	275	350	400	450	700	1,700	750
1885 . . . . 3,790	1,000	325	400	475	550	750	1,600	750
1886 (proof only)	4,290	—	—	—	—	—	—	675
1887 combined								
total 2,960	5,001							
1887 regular date		250	325	400	450	750	900	675
1887/6 overdate (proof only) . .		—	—	—	—	—	—	775
1888 . . . . 4,582	36,501	40.00	50.00	75.00	120	400	900	675
1889 . . . . 3,436	18,125	60.00	75.00	110	140	350	700	675

HALF DIMES (1792)

	Mintage	Good-4	Fine-12	EF-40
1792	1,500	$3,000	$5,000	$10,000

HALF DIMES (1794–1873)

Flowing Hair Portrait (1794–1795)

	Mintage	Good-4	Fine-12	EF-40
1794	7,756	$700	$1,200	$2,500
1795	78,660	525	900	1,800

Draped Bust Portrait with Small Eagle on Reverse (1796–1797)

	Mintage	Good-4	Fine-12	EF-40
1796 combined total	10,230			
1796 regular date		$675	$1,200	$2,500
1796/5 overdate		725	1,325	2,800
1796 with LIBERTY spelled LIKERTY		675	1,250	3,000
1797 combined total	44,527			
1797 with 15 stars		650	1,200	2,500
1797 with 16 stars		675	1,250	2,600
1797 with 13 stars		750	1,500	3,500

Draped Bust Portrait with Heraldic Eagle on Reverse (1800–1805)

	Mintage	Good-4	Fine-12	EF-40
1800 LIBERTY	24,000	$450	$675	$2,000
1800 LIBEKTY	16,000	460	685	2,100
1801	27,760	525	750	2,500
1802	3,060	7,500	17,500	60,000
1803	37,850	500	700	2,300
1805	15,600	625	900	3,000

Capped Bust Portrait (1829–1837)

	Mintage	Good-4	Fine-12	EF-40	AU-55	MS-63
1829	1,230,000	$13.00	$23.00	$95.00	$250	$650
1830	1,240,000	13.00	23.00	95.00	250	650
1831	1,242,700	13.00	23.00	95.00	250	650
1832	965,000	13.00	23.00	100	275	675
1833	1,370,000	13.00	23.00	95.00	250	650
1834	1,480,000	13.00	23.00	95.00	250	650

	Mintage	Good-4	Fine-12	EF-40	AU-55	MS-63
1835	2,760,000	13.00	23.00	95.00	250	650
1836	1,900,000	13.00	23.00	95.00	250	650
1837 combined total	871,000					
1837 with small 5c		24.00	40.00	200	575	2,250
1837 with large 5c		14.00	24.00	100	275	700

Seated Liberty Portrait (1837–1873)
Without Stars on Obverse (1837–1838)

	Mintage	Good-4	Fine-12	EF-40	AU-55	MS-63	MS-65
1837 combined total	1,405,000						
1837 with small date		$20.00	$40.00	$175	$350	$1,250	$3,700
1837 with large date		20.00	40.00	175	350	1,000	3,500
1838-O	70,000	60.00	140	400	750	4,000	30,000

With Stars on Obverse (1838–1859)

	Mintage	Good-4	Fine-12	EF-40	AU-55	MS-63	MS-65
1838 combined total	2,225,000						
1838 with regular stars		$5.00	$10.00	$50.00	$100	$700	$2,000
1838 with small stars		15.00	40.00	150	350	1,000	
1839	1,069,150	5.00	10.00	50.00	100	700	2,000
1839-O	1,034,039	6.00	10.00	60.00	130	1,000	—
1840 without drapery from elbow	1,034,000	5.00	10.00	50.00	100	700	2,000
1840 with drapery from elbow	310,085	15.00	40.00	130	350	800	2,000
1840-O without drapery from elbow	695,000	6.00	14.00	60.00	175	1,300	—
1840-O with drapery from elbow	240,000	20.00	90.00	300	750	4,000	—
1841	1,150,000	5.00	9.00	50.00	90.00	480	1,900
1841-O	815,000	9.00	20.00	90.00	300	1,500	4,000
1842	815,000	5.00	9.00	50.00	90.00	500	1,400
1842-O	350,000	20.00	45.00	225	500	1,100	17,500
1843	1,165,000	5.00	9.00	50.00	80.00	400	1,250
1844	430,000	5.00	9.00	50.00	80.00	400	1,250
1844-O	220,000	50.00	130	800	1,800	—	—
1845	1,564,000	5.00	9.00	50.00	80.00	400	1,250
1846	27,000	150	300	900	2,000	6,000	—
1847	1,274,000	5.00	9.00	50.00	80.00	400	1,250
1848 combined total	668,000						
1848 regular date		5.00	9.00	50.00	80.00	400	1,250
1848 with large date		9.00	22.00	75.00	200	1,300	—

	Mintage	Good-4	Fine-12	EF-40	AU-55	MS-63	MS-65
1848-O	600,000	9.00	20.00	75.00	150	525	1,400
1849 combined total	1,309,000						
1849 with regular date		5.00	9.00	50.00	80.00	400	1,250
1849/6 overdate		7.00	15.00	90.00	150	700	—
1849/8 overdate		9.00	20.00	90.00	170	900	—
1850	955,000	5.00	9.00	50.00	80.00	400	1,250
1850-O	690,000	8.00	15.00	70.00	220	1,800	1,900
1851	781,000	5.00	9.00	50.00	80.00	400	1,250
1851-O	860,000	7.00	17.00	62.50	180	750	3,000
1852	1,000,500	5.00	9.00	50.00	80.00	400	1,250
1852-O	260,000	20.00	50.00	200	300	1,300	—
1853 without arrows	135,000	30	70	250	500	1,000	2,750
1853-O without arrows	160,000	125	240	1,200	3,000	9,000	35,000

With Arrows Beside the Date (1853–1855)

	Mintage	Good-4	Fine-12	EF-40	AU-55	MS-63	MS-65	Proof-65
1853	13,210,020	$6.00	$9.00	$50.00	$90.00	$500	$2,000	
1853-O	2,200,000	8.00	9.00	60.00	90.00	600	4,650	
1854	5,740,000	8.00	9.00	60.00	90.00	600	2,400	
1854-O	1,560,000	6.00	12.00	60.00	100	700	3,900	
1855	1,750,000	6.00	8.00	50.00	90.00	500	2,300	$20,000
1855-O	600,000	12.00	30.00	125	190	1,100	5,250	

Without Arrows Beside the Date (1856–1859)

	Mintage	Good-4	Fine-12	EF-40	AU-55	MS-63	MS-65	Proof-65
1856	4,880,000	$5.00	$9.00	$50.00	$80.00	$200	$1,500	
1856-O	1,100,000	9.00	18.00	80.00	250	1,000	2,000	
1857	7,280,000	5.00	9.00	50.00	80.00	200	1,500	$7,500
1857-O	1,380,000	9.00	15.00	60.00	200	300	1,400	
1858 combined total	3,500,000							
1858 regular date		5.00	9.00	50.00	80.00	200	1,500	5,000
1858 with inverted date underneath		20.00	40.00	150	225	400	1,800	
1858-O	1,660,000	6.00	10.00	60.00	140	400	2,200	
1859 combined total	340,000							
1859 with regular date		7.00	20.00	60.00	110	275	1,900	4,500
1859-O	560,000	8.00	20.00	90.00	200	400	1,900	

With Motto on Obverse (1860–1873)

	Mintage	Good-4	Fine-12	EF-40	AU-55	MS-63	MS-65	Proof-65
1860 .... *1,000*	798,000	$5.00	$7.00	$20.00	$50.00	$300	$1,600	$2,500
1860-O	1,060,000	5.00	8.00	30.00	70.00	400	1,600	
1861 combined total	3,360,000							
1861 regular date .... *1,000* ...		5.00	8.00	20.00	60.00	300	1,400	2,000
1861/0 overdate		20.00	50.00	250	350	—	—	
1862 .... *550*	1,492,000	5.00	8.00	26.00	57.50	320	1,600	1,700
1863 .... *460*	18,460	135	180	375	485	1,150	1,800	1,800
1863-S	100,000	15.00	27.50	80.00	200	1,500	2,900	
1864 .... *470*	48,000	210	350	700	900	1,600	2,600	1,700
1864-S	90,000	40.00	80.00	300	400	900	3,500	
1865 .... *500*	13,000	225	325	640	725	1,500	3,500	1,900
1865-S	120,000	15.00	25.00	125	325	1,825	—	
1866 .... *725*	10,000	225	325	640	725	1,600	3,500	1,900
1866-S	120,000	12.00	30.00	110	300	1,300	5,000	
1867 .... *625*	8,000	325	450	650	800	1,400	—	1,800
1867-S	120,000	15.00	30.00	100	300	1,000	—	
1868 .... *600*	88,600	40.00	60.00	300	400	900	2,900	1,800
1868-S	280,000	6.00	15.00	30.00	90.00	900	—	
1869 .... *600*	208,000	6.00	15.00	30.00	90.00	900	2,100	1,600
1869-S	230,000	7.00	9.00	30.00	90.00	500	—	
1870 .... *1,000*	535,000	6.00	9.00	20.00	50.00	300	1,400	1,800
1870-S	1 known (graded MS-60)							—
1871 .... *960*	1,873,000	6.00	9.00	20.00	50.00	300	1,400	1,700
1871-S	161,000	7.00	35.00	65.00	150	500	3,000	
1872 .... *950*	2,947,000	5.00	10.00	25.00	50.00	300	1,800	1,700
1872-S combined total	837,000							
1872-S with S inside the wreath		5.00	9.00	25.00	60.00	300	1,400	
1872-S with S below the wreath		5.00	9.00	25.00	60.00	300	1,400	
1873 .... *600*	712,000	5.00	9.00	25.00	60.00	300	1,875	1,650
1873-S	324,000	5.00	9.00	25.00	60.00	300	1,400	

NICKELS (1866–Present)

Shield Portrait (1866–1883)

	Mintage	Good-4	Fine-12	EF-40	AU-55	MS-63	MS-65	Proof-65
1866 with rays between the stars *125*	14,742,375	$16.00	$21.00	$90.00	$125	$275	$2,300	$4,500
1867 with rays	2,018,975	16.00	25.00	115	225	275	4,000	80,000
1867 without rays ..... *625* ...	28,880,900	7.50	11.00	22.50	45.00	150	675	3,000
1868 .... *600*	28,816,400	7.50	11.00	20.00	42.50	150	675	1,500
1869 .... *600*	16,394,400	7.50	11.00	25.00	47.50	150	675	1,250
1870 .... *1,000*	4,805,000	8.25	12.50	27.50	52.50	150	675	1,550
1871 .... *960*	560,040	27.50	42.50	90.00	150	225	825	1,250
1872 .... *950*	6,035,050	8.25	12.50	27.50	65.00	150	675	1,000
1873 with closed 3 .... *1,100*	434,950	10.00	25.00	75.00	105	225	825	1,000
1873 with open 3	4,113,950	8.25	12.50	30.00	60.00	150	675	
1874 .... *700*	3,537,300	8.50	13.00	32.50	65.00	150	675	1,200
1875 .... *700*	2,086,300	8.50	15.00	37.50	75.00	175	2,200	1,800
1876 .... *1,150*	2,528,900	8.50	15.00	35.00	70.00	185	725	1,000
1877 (proof only)	900	—	—	—	—	—	—	2,750
1878 (proof only)	2,350	—	—	—	—	—	—	800
1879 .... *3,200*	25,900	235	340	450	525	650	3,000	675
1880 .... *3,955*	16,000	260	325	475	550	3,500	7,500	675
1881 .... *3,575*	68,800	160	240	360	410	550	1,500	675
1882 .... *3,100*	11,472,900	9.00	12.00	27.50	45.00	185	675	675
1883 combined total	1,456,919							
1883 regular date ..... *5,419* ...		9.00	12.00	27.50	47.50	180	675	675
1883/2 overdate		20.00	70.00	140	180	475	3,500	

Liberty Head Portrait (1883–1912)

	Mintage	Good-4	Fine-12	EF-40	AU-55	MS-63	MS-65	Proof-65
1883 without CENTS on reverse ..*5,219*	5,474,300	$2.40	$3.75	$7.50	$12.50	$40.00	$325	$600
1883 with CENTS .....*6,783* ..	16,026,200	7.50	12.50	37.50	62.50	80.00	575	500
1884 ....*3,942*	11,270,000	8.00	15.00	40.00	65.00	150	825	500
1885 ....*3,790*	1,472,700	175	325	575	650	700	4,000	600
1886 ....*4,290*	3,326,000	47.50	120	235	350	500	3,500	600
1887 ....*2,960*	15,260,692	5.50	12.50	30.00	57.50	175	575	500
1888 ....*4,582*	10,715,901	8.00	15.00	40.00	75.00	150	800	500
1889 ....*3,336*	15,878,025	4.50	11.00	30.00	57.50	120	575	500
1890 ....*2,740*	16,256,532	4.50	11.00	30.00	60.00	135	900	500
1891 ....*2,350*	16,832,000	4.00	11.00	30.00	57.50	100	800	500
1892 ....*2,745*	11,696,897	4.00	11.00	30.00	60.00	100	800	500
1893 .... *2,195*	13,368,000	4.00	11.00	30.00	60.00	100	800	500
1894 ....*2,632*	5,410,500	6.00	22.50	65.00	110	170	950	500
1895 ....*2,062*	9,977,822	3.00	10.00	30.00	57.50	100	975	500
1896 ....*1,862*	8,841,058	4.50	11.00	32.50	65.00	110	975	500
1897 .... *1,938*	20,426,797	2.50	5.00	17.50	47.50	90.00	975	500
1898 .... *1,795*	12,530,292	2.00	5.00	17.50	50.00	90.00	575	500
1899 ....*2,031*	26,027,000	1.25	4.50	17.50	42.50	80.00	575	500
1900 ....*2,262*	27,253,733	.75	3.50	15.00	37.50	80.00	575	500
1901 ....*1,985*	26,478,228	.75	3.50	14.00	35.00	80.00	575	500
1902 ....*2,018*	31,487,561	.75	3.50	14.00	35.00	80.00	575	500
1903 ....*1,790*	28,004,935	.75	3.50	14.00	35.00	80.00	575	500
1904 ....*1,817*	21,403,167	.75	3.50	14.00	35.00	80.00	575	500
1905 ....*2,152*	29,825,124	.75	3.50	14.00	35.00	80.00	575	500
1906 ....*1,725*	38,612,000	.75	3.50	14.00	35.00	80.00	575	500
1907 ....*1,475*	39,213,325	.75	3.50	14.00	35.00	80.00	575	500
1908 ....*1,620*	22,684,557	.75	3.50	14.00	35.00	80.00	575	500
1909 ....*4,763*	11,585,763	.90	4.00	16.00	40.00	100	600	500
1910 ....*2,405*	30,166,948	.75	3.50	14.00	35.00	80.00	575	500
1911 ....*1,733*	39,557,639	.75	3.50	14.00	35.00	80.00	575	500
1912 ....*2,145*	26,234,569	.75	3.50	14.00	35.00	85.00	585	595
1912-D	8,474,000	1.25	4.50	37.50	75.00	170	600	
1912-S	238,000	37.50	60.00	350	475	590	3,750	
1913 (not an authorized Mint issue) ....*5 known*	—	—	—	—	—	—	—	1,840,000

"Buffalo" Portrait (1913–1938)

Bison Standing on Mound (1913)

	Mintage	Good-4	Fine-12	EF-40	AU-55	MS-63	MS-65	Proof-65
1913 .... *1,520*	30,992,000	$4.50	$6.00	$12.50	$20.00	$45.00	$85.00	$2,000
1913-D	5,337,000	7.50	10.00	20.00	32.50	55.00	190	
1913-S	2,105,000	12.50	17.50	35.00	45.00	65.00	700	

Bison Standing on Plain Line (1913–1938)

	Mintage	Good-4	Fine-12	EF-40	AU-55	MS-63	MS-65	Proof-65
1913 .... *1,514*	29,857,186	$4.50	$6.50	$13.00	$20.00	$40.00	$300	$1,000
1913-D	4,156,000	32.50	47.50	75.00	110	175	800	
1913-S	1,209,000	75.00	130	190	225	300	4,500	
1914 .... *1,275*	20,665,463	4.50	6.50	16.00	25.00	50.00	300	1,000
1914-D	3,912,000	27.50	47.50	90.00	125	205	1,750	
1914-S	3,470,000	5.50	12.50	37.50	52.50	200	2,500	
1915 .... *1,050*	20,986,220	2.25	4.50	12.00	20.00	50.00	210	1,000
1915-D	7,569,000	2.25	17.50	52.50	77.50	210	2,750	
1915-S	1,505,000	12.50	22.50	120	200	400	3,250	
1916 combined total	63,497,466							
1916 regular								
date *600*		.85	1.75	6.00	12.50	55.00	250	1,000
1916 with doubled obverse		1,500	6,000	17,500	30,000	110,000	180,000	
1916-D	13,333,000	5.25	9.50	47.50	75.00	190	2,100	
1916-S	11,860,000	3.25	7.00	42.50	70.00	225	1,950	
1917	51,424,019	.85	2.00	9.50	22.50	60.00	365	
1917-D	9,910,000	5.25	14.00	80.00	125	330	3,900	
1917-S	4,193,000	4.50	14.00	95.00	185	450	4,500	
1918	32,086,314	1.00	2.25	16.00	32.50	70.00	1,600	
1918-D combined total	8,362,000							
1918-D regular date		5.25	17.50	150	225	350	5,000	
1918/7-D overdate		400	850	3,750	7,500	26,000	275,000	
1918-S	4,882,000	4.50	12.50	140	200	840	34,000	
1919	60,868,000	.85	1.25	7.50	20.00	85.00	320	
1919-D	8,006,000	5.25	15.00	160	240	690	5,000	
1919-S	7,521,000	3.25	9.00	150	225	710	10,000	
1920	63,093,000	.75	1.25	8.50	22.50	45	500	

	Mintage	Good-4	Fine-12	EF-40	AU-55	MS-63	MS-65	Proof-65
1920-D	9,418,000	3.75	12.50	200	275	560	5,000	
1920-S	9,689,000	2.00	7.00	135	180	725	28,000	
1921	10,663,000	1.25	2.50	20.00	37.50	80.00	400	
1921-S	1,557,000	14.00	42.50	550	700	960	7,000	
1923	35,715,000	.75	1.25	7.50	15.00	48.00	350	
1923-S	6,142,000	2.25	5.25	160	225	440	11,000	
1924	21,620,000	.75	1.25	8.50	22.50	70.00	425	
1924-D	5,258,000	2.75	7.50	135	200	325	4,700	
1924-S	1,437,000	5.00	22.50	825	1,000	1,850	11,000	
1925	35,565,100	.75	1.50	7.50	20.00	48.00	180	
1925-D	4,450,000	4.50	16.00	120	180	395	5,000	
1925-S	6,256,000	2.00	7.50	135	200	750	45,000	
1926	44,693,000	.50	.85	4.50	13.50	33.00	125	
1926-D	5,638,000	2.50	12.50	125	170	285	5,000	
1926-S	970,000	6.00	15.00	750	1,000	2,000	52,500	
1927	37,981,000	.50	.75	4.50	15.00	37.00	180	
1927-D	5,730,000	1.50	4.00	37.50	70.00	142	4,000	
1927-S	3,430,000	.85	2.50	60.00	100	875	18,000	
1928	23,411,000	.50	.85	5.25	15.00	42.00	250	
1928-D	6,436,000	1.00	3.50	15.00	22.50	45.00	595	
1928-S	6,936,000	.80	1.75	12.50	25.00	325	5,000	
1929	36,446,000	.50	.75	5.00	12.50	40.00	165	
1929-D	8,370,000	1.00	1.75	14.00	22.50	55.00	2,000	
1929-S	7,754,000	.60	1.10	8.50	25.00	50.00	220	
1930	22,849,000	.50	.85	5.25	13.00	30.00	100	
1930-S	5,435,000	.60	.90	7.50	22.50	65.00	375	
1931-S	1,200,000	3.00	5.00	10.50	25.00	55.00	175	
1934	20,213,003	.40	.65	3.75	12.50	25.00	225	
1934-D	7,480,000	.45	.75	6.50	15.00	45.00	900	
1935	58,264,000	.30	.50	3.00	7.50	22.50	80.00	
1935-D	12,092,000	.35	.60	3.75	15.00	50.00	370	
1935-S	10,300,000	.35	.60	3.25	8.50	25.00	175	
1936 4,420	118,997,000	.30	.50	3.00	7.50	22.50	47.50	800
1936-D	24,814,000	.35	.60	3.25	9.00	25.00	60.00	
1936-S	14,930,000	.35	.60	3.25	11.00	25.00	75.00	
1937 5,769	79,480,000	.35	.50	3.00	6.50	20.00	30.00	800
1937-D combined total	17,826,000							
1937-D with normal reverse		.35	.60	3.25	8.00	22.50	30.00	
1937-D with 3-legged bison		125	300	350	650	3,750	22,500	
1937-S	5,635,000	.35	.60	3.25	8.00	20.00	40.00	
1938-D combined total	7,020,000							
1938-D with normal mint mark		.35	.50	2.50	7.50	17.50	30.00	
1938-D/D		.90	2.75	4.50	9.00	22.50	85.00	
1938-D/S		4.50	7.00	10.50	15.00	30.00	120	

Jefferson Portrait (1938–Present)

	Mintage	Good-4	Fine-12	EF-40	AU-55	MS-63	MS-65	Proof-65
1938 .... *19,365*	19,496,000	$.10	$.20	$.50	$.75	$1.50	$3.50	$35.00
1938-D	5,376,000	.50	.75	1.25	1.60	3.00	5.00	
1938-S	4,105,000	1.00	1.50	2.00	2.50	5.00	7.50	
1939 combined total	120,615,000							
1939 with regular reverse ... *12,535*			.10	.20	.25	.50	1.00	30.00
1939 with double image on MONTICELLO and FIVE CENTS		5.00	9.00	35.00	50.00			
1939-D	3,514,000	2.00	3.00	3.75	7.50	25.00	50.00	
1939-S	6,630,000	.25	.50	1.75	3.50	10.00	20.00	
1940 .... *14,158*	176,485,000	—	—	.10	.15	.75	1.25	30.00
1940-D	43,540,000	—	—	.20	.30	1.25	2.50	
1940-S	39,690,000	—	—	.15	.20	1.00	2.00	
1941 .... *18,720*	203,265,000	—	—	.10	.15	.60	1.20	25.00
1941-D	53,432,000	—	—	.10	.20	1.00	2.00	
1941-S	43,445,000	—	—	.10	.20	1.10	2.25	
1942 .... *29,600*	49,789,000	—	—	.10	.15	.60	1.20	20.00
1942-D	13,938,000	—	—	1.00	2.00	4.00	10.00	

Wartime Composition,
Mint Mark Above Monticello (1942–1945)

	Mintage	Good-4	Fine-12	EF-40	AU-55	MS-63	MS-65	Proof-65
1942-P *27,600*	57,873,000	—	—	$.50	$.60	$3.00	$7.50	$90
1942-S	32,900,000	—	—	.50	.60	2.50	5.00	
1943-P combined total	271,165,000							
1943-P regular date		—	—	.50	.60	2.00	4.00	
1943/2 overdate		—	—	90.00	150	350	750	
1943-D	15,294,000	—	—	.50	.60	2.50	4.50	
1943-S	104,060,000	—	—	.50	.60	2.00	4.00	
1944-P	119,150,000	—	—	.50	.60	2.00	4.00	
944-D	32,309,000	—	—	.50	.60	2.00	4.00	
1944-S	21,640,000	—	—	.50	.60	2.50	4.50	
1945-P	119,150,000	—	—	.50	.60	2.00	4.00	

	Mintage	Good-4	Fine-12	EF-40	AU-55	MS-63	MS-65	Proof-65
1945-D	37,158,000	—	—	.50	.60	2.00	4.00	
1945-S	58,939,000	—	—	.50	.60	2.00	4.00	

Regular Composition Returns (1946–Present)

	Mintage	Fine-12	EF-40	AU-55	MS-63	MS-65	Proof-65
1946	161,116,000	—	$.10	$.15	$.25	$.50	
1946-D	45,292,200	—	.15	.20	.35	.65	
1946-S	13,560,000	—	.20	.25	.40	.70	
1947	95,000,000	—	.10	.15	.25	.50	
1947-D	37,822,000	—	.15	.20	.35	.65	
1947-S	24,720,000	—	.15	.20	.35	.65	
1948	89,348,000	—	.10	.15	.25	.50	
1948-D	44,734,000	—	.15	.20	.35	1.00	
1948-S	11,300,000	—	.15	.20	.35	1.00	
1949	60,652,000	—	.10	.15	.25	.90	
1949-D combined total	36,498,000						
1949-D with regular mint mark		—	.15	.20	.30	.80	
1949-D/S		17.50	60.00	75.00	200	350	
1949-S	9,716,000	.10	.20	.25	.45	1.00	
1950 . . . . 51,386	9,796,000	.10	.20	.25	.45	1.00	$40.00
1950-D	2,630,030	5.00	5.50	6.00	7.50	9.00	
1951 . . . . 57,500	28,552,000	—	.10	.15	.25	.90	20.00
1951-D	20,460,000	—	.10	.15	.25	.90	
1951-S	7,776,000	.10	.15	.20	.35	1.25	
1952 . . . . 81,980	63,988,000	—	.10	.15	.25	.50	19.00
1952-D	30,638,000	—	.15	.20	.35	1.00	
1952-S	20,572,000	—	.10	.15	.25	.60	
1953 . . . . 128,800	46,644,000	—	.10	.15	.25	.50	18.00
1953-D	59,878,600	—	.10	.15	.25	.50	
1953-S	19,210,900	—	.10	.15	.25	.60	
1954 . . . . 233,300	47,684,050	—	.10	.15	.25	.50	10.00
1954-D	117,183,060	—	.10	.15	.25	.50	
1954-S combined total	29,384,000						
1954-S with regular mint mark		—	.10	.15	.25	.50	
1954-S/D		4.00	7.50	9.00	22.50	37.50	
1955 . . . . 378,200	7,888,000	.10	.15	.20	.35	1.00	10.00
1955-D combined total	74,464,100						
1955-D with regular mint mark		—	.10	.15	.25	.50	
1955-D/S		5.00	10.00	15.00	35.00	60.00	
1956 . . . . 669,384	35,216,000	—	—	.10	.20	.30	6.00
1956-D	67,222,940	—	—	.10	.20	.30	
1957 . . . . 1,247,952	38,408,000	—	—	.10	.20	.30	4.00

	Mintage	Fine-12	EF-40	AU-55	MS-63	MS-65	Proof-65
1957-D	136,828,900	—	—	.10	.20	.30	
1958 875,652	17,088,000	—	—	.15	.30	.40	5.00
1958-D	168,249,120	—	—	.10	.20	.30	
1959 1,149,291	27,248,000	—	—	.10	.25	.35	4.00
1959-D	160,738,240	—	—	.10	.20	.30	
1960 1,691,602	55,416,000	—	—	—	.10	.15	3.00
1960-D	192,582,180	—	—	—	.10	.15	
1961 3,028,144	73,640,100	—	—	—	.10	.15	2.50
1961-D	229,342,760	—	—	—	.10	.15	
1962 3,218,019	97,384,000	—	—	—	.10	.15	2.50
1962-D	280,195,720	—	—	—	.10	.15	
1963 3,075,645	175,776,000	—	—	—	.10	.15	2.50
1963-D	276,829,460	—	—	—	.10	.15	
1964 3,950,762	1,024,672,000	—	—	—	.10	.15	2.25
1964-D	1,787,297,160	—	—	—	.10	.15	
1965	136,131,380	—	—	—	.10	.15	
1966	156,208,283	—	—	—	.10	.15	
1967	107,325,800	—	—	—	.10	.15	
1968-D	91,227,880	—	—	—	.10	.15	
1968-S 3,041,506	100,396,004	—	—	—	.10	.15	1.00
1969-D	202,807,500	—	—	—	.10	.15	
1969-S 2,934,631	120,075,000	—	—	—	.10	.15	1.00
1970-D	515,485,380	—	—	—	.10	.15	
1970-S 2,632,810	238,832,004	—	—	—	.10	.15	1.60
1971	106,884,000	—	—	—	.25	.50	
1971-D	316,144,800	—	—	—	.10	.15	
1971-S combined total (proof only)	3,220,733						
1971-S with S		—	—	—	—	—	1.00
1971-S proof with no mint mark		—	—	—	—	—	700
1972	202,036,000	—	—	—	.10	.15	
1972-D	351,694,600	—	—	—	.10	.15	
1972-S (proof only)	3,260,996	—	—	—	—	—	1.10
1973	384,396,000	—	—	—	.10	.15	
1973-D	261,405,000	—	—	—	.10	.15	
1973-S (proof only)	2,760,339	—	—	—	—	—	1.20
1974	601,752,000	—	—	—	.10	.15	
1974-D	277,373,000	—	—	—	.15	.20	
1974-S (proof only)	2,612,568	—	—	—	—	—	1.35
1975	181,772,000	—	—	—	—	.10	
1975-D	401,875,300	—	—	—	—	.10	
1975-S (proof only)	2,845,450	—	—	—	—	—	1.60
1976	367,124,000	—	—	—	—	.10	
1976-D	563,964,147	—	—	—	—	.10	

	Mintage	Fine-12	EF-40	AU-55	MS-63	MS-65	Proof-65
1976-S (proof only)	4,149,730	—	—	—	—	—	1.40
1977	585,376,000	—	—	—	—	.10	
1977-D	297,313,422	—	—	—	—	.15	
1977-S (proof only)	3,251,152	—	—	—	—	—	1.50
1978	391,308,000	—	—	—	—	.10	
1978-D	313,092,780	—	—	—	—	.10	
1978-S (proof only)	3,127,781	—	—	—	—	—	1.60
1979	463,188,000	—	—	—	—	.10	
1979-D	325,867,672	—	—	—	—	.10	
1979-S combined total (proof only)	3,677,175						
1979-S with clear S		—	—	—	—	—	12.00
1979-S with clogged S		—	—	—	—	1.50	
1980-P	593,004,000	—	—	—	—	.10	
1980-D	502,323,448	—	—	—	—	.10	
1980-S (proof only)	3,554,806	—	—	—	—	—	1.60
1981-P	657,504,000	—	—	—	—	.10	
1981-D	364,801,843	—	—	—	—	.10	
1981-S (proof only)	4,063,083	—	—	—	—	—	1.40
1982-P	292,355,000	—	—	—	—	.10	
1982-D	373,726,544	—	—	—	—	.10	
1982-S (proof only)	3,857,479	—	—	—	—	—	1.50
1983-P	561,615,000	—	—	—	—	.10	
1983-D	536,726,276	—	—	—	—	.10	
1983-S (proof only)	3,279,126	—	—	—	—	—	1.60
1984-P	746,769,000	—	—	—	—	.10	
1984-D	517,675,146	—	—	—	—	.10	
1984-S (proof only)	3,065,110	—	—	—	—	—	2.50
1985-P	647,114,962	—	—	—	—	.10	
1985-D	459,747,446	—	—	—	—	.10	
1985-S (proof only)	3,362,821	—	—	—	—	—	1.60
1986-P	536,883,483	—	—	—	—	.10	
1986-D	361,819,140	—	—	—	—	.10	
1986-S (proof only)	3,010,497	—	—	—	—	—	4.50
1987-P	371,499,481	—	—	—	—	.10	
1987-D	410,590,604	—	—	—	—	.10	
1987-S (proof only)	3,792,233	—	—	—	—	—	1.50
1988-P	771,360,000	—	—	—	—	.10	
1988-D	663,771,652	—	—	—	—	.10	
1988-S (proof only)	3,262,948	—	—	—	—	—	2.50
1989-P	898,812,000	—	—	—	—	.10	
1989-D	570,842,474	—	—	—	—	.10	
1989-S (proof only)	3,215,728	—	—	—	—	—	2.00
1990-P	661,636,000	—	—	—	—	.10	
1990-D	663,938,503	—	—	—	—	.10	

NICKELS (1866–PRESENT)

	Mintage	Fine-12	EF-40	AU-55	MS-63	MS-65	Proof-65
1990-S (proof only)	3,299,559	—	—	—	—	—	3.50
1991-P	614,104,000	—	—	—	—	.10	
1991-D	436,496,678	—	—	—	—	.10	
1991-S (proof only)	2,867,787	—	—	—	—	—	2.50
1992-P	399,552,000	—	—	—	—	.10	
1992-D	450,565,113	—	—	—	—	.10	
1992-S (proof only)	4,176,544	—	—	—	—	—	2.00
1993-P	412,076,000	—	—	—	—	.10	
1993-D	406,084,135	—	—	—	—	.10	
1993-S (proof only)	3,360,876	—	—	—	—	—	2.00
1994-P	723,370,896	—	—	—	—	.10	
1994-D	716,973,006	—	—	—	—	.10	
1994-S (proof only)	3,212,792	—	—	—	—	—	2.00
1994-P matte finish	167,703	—	—	—	—	50.00	
1995-P	775,197,352	—	—	—	—	.10	
1995-D	889,153,352	—	—	—	—	.10	
1995-S (proof only)	2,796,345	—	—	—	—	—	2.00
1996-P	830,785,215	—	—	—	—	.10	
1996-D	819,190,215	—	—	—	—	.10	
1996-S (proof only)	2,925,305	—	—	—	—	—	2.00
1997-P	470,972,000	—	—	—	—	.10	
1997-D	468,840,000	—	—	—	—	.10	
1997-S (proof only)	2,788,020	—	—	—	—	—	2.00
1997-P matte finish	25,000	—	—	—	—	225	
1998-P	688,292,000	—	—	—	—	.10	
1998-D	635,380,000	—	—	—	—	.10	
1998-S (proof only)	2,965,503	—	—	—	—	—	2.00
1999-P	1,212,000,000	—	—	—	—	.10	
1999-D	1,066,720,000	—	—	—	—	.10	
1999-S (proof only)	(2,454,319)*	—	—	—	—	—	2.00
2000-P	846,240,000	—	—	—	—	.10	
2000-D	1,509,520,000	—	—	—	—	.10	
2000-S (proof only)	(3,934,000)*	—	—	—	—	—	2.00
2001-P	675,704,000	—	—	—	—	.10	
2001-D	627,680,000	—	—	—	—	.10	
2001-S (proof only)	(2,293,200)**	—	—	—	—	—	2.00
2002-P		—	—	—	—	.10	
2002-D		—	—	—	—	.10	
2002-S (proof only)		—	—	—	—	—	2.00
2003-P		—	—	—	—	.10	
2003-D		—	—	—	—	.10	
2003-S (proof only)		—	—	—	—	—	2.00

* Through March 31, 2001
** Through May 28, 2002

DIMES (1796–PRESENT)

Draped Bust Portrait with Small Eagle on Reverse (1796–1797)

	Mintage	Good-4	Fine-12	EF-40
1796	22,135	$825	$1,775	$4,000
1797 combined total	25,261			
1797 with 16 stars		850	1,800	4,500
1797 with 13 stars		850	1,800	4,400

Draped Bust Portrait with Heraldic Eagle on Reverse (1798–1807)

	Mintage	Good-4	Fine-12	EF-40
1798 combined total	27,550			
1798 regular date		$400	$700	$2,000
1798/7 overdate with 16 stars on reverse		440	800	2,400
1798/7 overdate with 13 stars on reverse		1,500	3,750	7,500
1798 with small 8	500	900	2,700	
1800	21,760	410	710	2,100
1801	34,640	410	800	2,800
1802	10,975	600	1,300	5,000
1803	33,040	385	750	2,300
1804	8,265	900	2,100	7,000
1805	120,780	370	675	1,900
1807	165,000	370	675	1,900

Capped Bust Portrait (1809–1837)

	Mintage	Good-4	Fine-12	EF-40	AU-55	MS-63
1809	51,065	$85.00	$325	$900	$2,100	$5,000
1811/09 overdate	65,180	41.00	120	725	1,750	5,000
1814 combined total	421,500					
1814 small date		30.00	90.00	475	1,100	3,500
1814 large date		16.00	40.00	300	675	2,250
1814 STATESOFAMERICA		16.00	40.00	330	725	2,300
1820 combined total	942,587					
1820 small 0		13.00	34.00	280	650	2,200
1820 large 0		13.00	32.00	270	650	2,200
1820 STATESOFAMERICA		16.00	40.00	350	875	2,500
1821 combined total	1,186,512					
1821 small date		18.00	46.00	300	700	2,600
1821 large date		13.00	32.00	275	675	2,200
1822	100,000	300	725	2,000	4,250	14,000
1823/2 overdate	440,000	13.00	30.00	260	700	2,400
1824/2 overdate	100,000	17.00	45.00	450	950	2,800
1825	410,000	12.00	30.00	260	625	2,000
1827	1,215,000	12.00	30.00	260	625	2,000
1828 combined total	125,000					
1828 large date		24.00	60.00	400	1,100	
1828 small date		24.00	70.00	300	800	2,100
1829 combined total	770,000					
1829 with curl-base 2		3,500	8,000			
1829 small 10c		14.00	28.00	180	500	1,800
1829 large 10c		30.00	80.00	350	750	2,400
1830 combined total	510,000					
1830 regular date		11.00	19.00	150	410	1,350
1830/29 overdate		35.00	90.00	350	750	3,000
1831	771,350	11.00	19.00	150	400	1,350
1832	522,500	11.00	19.00	150	400	1,350
1833	485,000	11.00	19.00	150	400	1,350
1834	635,000	11.00	19.00	150	400	1,350
1835	1,410,000	11.00	19.00	150	400	1,350
1836	1,190,000	11.00	19.00	150	400	1,350
1837	359,500	11.00	19.00	150	400	1,400

Seated Liberty Portrait (1837–1891)

Without Stars on Obverse (1837–1838)

	Mintage	Good-4	Fine-12	EF-40	AU-55	MS-63	MS-65
1837	682,500	$24.00	$52.50	$425	$675	$2,000	$5,500
1838-O	406,034	90.00	175	950	1,500	6,000	20,000

With Stars on Obverse (1838–1859)

	Mintage	Good-4	Fine-12	EF-40	AU-55	MS-63	MS-65
1838 combined total	1,992,500						
1838 with regular stars		$6.00	$10.00	$65.00	$130	$925	$3,250
1838 with small stars		18.00	42.50	150	225	2,500	6,000
1838 with partial drapery from elbow		27.50	65.00	190	385	3,850	4,000
1839	1,053,115	6.00	10.00	65.00	130	925	2,200
1839-O	1,323,000	7.50	15.00	75.00	300	1,500	4,500
1840	981,500	8.00	12.50	72.50	150	1,000	2,000
1840-O	1,175,000	12.50	25.00	100	350	3,750	5,500

Drapery Added from Liberty's Elbow (1840–1891)

	Mintage	Good-4	Fine-12	EF-40	AU-55	MS-63	MS-65
1840	377,500	$30.00	$75.00	$350	$1,100	—	—
1841	1,622,500	5.00	10.00	37.50	150	$675	$2,800
1841-O	2,007,500	9.00	17.50	42.50	175	975	4,000
1842	1,887,500	5.00	10.00	37.50	150	675	2,500
1842-O	2,020,000	9.00	17.50	42.50	250	—	—
1843	1,370,000	5.00	10.00	37.50	150	675	2,800
1843-O	150,000	50.00	150	750	1,250	—	—
1844	72,500	50.00	125	450	1,100	—	—
1845	1,755,000	5.00	10.00	37.50	150	675	2,800
1845-O	230,000	25.00	75.00	750	1,250	—	—
1846	31,300	80.00	175	900	1,500	—	—
1847	245,000	11.00	27.50	110	275	1,500	5,000

	Mintage	Good-4	Fine-12	EF-40	AU-55	MS-63	MS-65
1848	451,500	9.00	17.50	52.50	175	1,000	7,000
1849	839,000	9.00	14.00	37.50	95.00	900	3,000
1849-O	300,000	17.50	27.50	275	1,100	4,000	—
1850	1,931,500	5.00	10.00	42.50	150	675	2,800
1850-O	510,000	12.50	25.00	110	175	1,500	5,000
1851	1,026,500	6.00	11.00	32.50	100	700	2,850
1851-O	400,000	15.00	25.00	120	200	2,250	—
1852	1,535,500	5.00	10.00	32.50	90.00	675	2,850
1852-O	430,000	17.50	32.50	200	325	2,000	—
1853 without arrows	95,000	45.00	100	275	375	900	4,000

With Arrows Beside the Date (1853–1855)

	Mintage	Good-4	Fine-12	EF-40	AU-55	MS-63	MS-65	Proof-65
1853	12,078,010	$5.00	$7.50	$36.00	$110	$600	$2,500	
1853-O	1,100,000	8.00	12.00	92.50	350	1,650	7,500	
1854	4,470,000	5.00	7.50	36.00	110	600	2,500	$36,000
1854-O	1,770,000	6.00	9.00	38.00	120	800	3,000	
1855	2,075,000	5.00	7.50	36.00	110	775	3,500	35,000

Arrows Removed (1856)

	Mintage	Good-4	Fine-12	EF-40	AU-55	MS-63	MS-65	Proof-65
1856	5,780,000	$5.00	$10.00	$27.50	$75.00	$675	$2,000	$10,000
1856-O	1,100,000	7.50	12.50	30.00	85.00	700	2,000	
1856-S	70,000	65.00	200	350	600	5,000	—	
1857	5,580,000	4.00	8.00	24.00	70.00	475	2,850	5,600
1857-O	1,540,000	6.00	11.00	28.00	80.00	500	3,150	
1858	1,540,000	4.00	8.00	24.00	70.00	500	2,850	4,000
1858-O	290,000	15.00	35.00	75.00	250	800	4,500	
1858-S	60,000	80.00	200	300	500	—		
1859 800	429,200	6.00	11.00	28.00	80.00	500	2,000	4,000
1859-O	480,000	7.50	12.50	30.00	85.00	500	2,800	

With Motto on Obverse (1860–1873)

	Mintage	Good-4	Fine-12	EF-40	AU-55	MS-63	MS-65	Proof-65
1860 1,000	608,000	$4.00	$6.00	$25.00	$80.00	$200	$1,400	$1,200
1860-O	40,000	400	900	2,500	4,500	—	—	
1861 1,000	1,883,000	4.00	6.00	25.00	80.00	200	1,400	1,200
1861-S	172,500	25.00	40.00	200	400	5,000	14,000	
1862 550	847,000	4.00	6.00	25.00	80.00	200	1,400	1,200
1862-S	180,750	25.00	45.00	135	900	2,500	9,500	
1863 460	14,000	75.00	240	375	650	900	4,250	1,200

DIMES (1796–PRESENT)

	Mintage	Good-4	Fine-12	EF-40	AU-55	MS-63	MS-65	Proof-65
1863-S	157,500	25.00	75.00	185	900	2,500	9,000	
1864 .... *470*	11,000	75.00	240	375	650	900	3,000	1,200
1864-S	230,000	25.00	75.00	185	900	2,000	8,000	
1865 .... *500*	10,000	75.00	240	375	650	900	3,800	1,200
1865-S	175,000	22.50	65.00	160	800	2,500	7,800	
1866 .... *725*	8,000	140	425	675	1,000	3,200	9,000	1,200
1866-S	135,000	20.00	70.00	175	600	2,100	5,000	
1867 .... *625*	6,000	140	425	675	2,000	3,800	9,000	1,200
1867-S	140,000	15.00	65.00	150	600	1,500	4,000	
1868 .... *600*	464,000	12.00	24.00	40.00	90.00	500	2,500	1,200
1868-S	260,000	12.00	70.00	150	250	1,200	3,500	
1869 .... *600*	256,000	11.00	24.00	60.00	150	500	3,000	1,200
1869-S	450,000	9.00	42.50	95.00	210	610	3,800	
1870 .... *1,000*	470,500	5.00	8.00	38.00	110	300	1,800	1,200
1870-S	50,000	150	220	450	1,200	3,000	7,000	
1871 .... *960*	906,750	6.00	8.00	27.50	110	375	1,800	1,200
1871-CC	20,100	450	1,500	3,000	—	—	—	
1871-S	320,000	14.00	30.00	130	350	1,600	6,250	
1872 .... *950*	2,395,500	5.00	9.00	30.00	150	800	4,250	1,200
1872-CC	35,480	250	900	1,800	—	—	—	
1872-S	190,000	30.00	90.00	240	650	2,000	4,000	
1873 closed 3 .... *1,100*	1,506,900	4.00	6.00	45.00	90.00	300	1,400	1,200
1873 open 3	60,000	25.00	50.00	185	650	1,500	3,800	
1873-CC	(unique)	—	—	—	—	—	550,000	

With Arrows Beside the Date (1873–1874)

	Mintage	Good-4	Fine-12	EF-40	AU-55	MS-63	MS-65	Proof-65
1873 .... *800*	2,377,700	$6.00	$14.00	$110	$250	$1,000	$4,000	$5,000
1873-CC	18,791	500	1,450	3,000	9,000	—	—	
1873-S	455,000	20.00	75.00	150	350	1,300	5,000	
1874 .... *700*	2,940,000	6.00	14.00	110	250	1,000	4,000	5,000
1874-CC	10,817	850	1,400	2,450	11,000	—	—	
1874-S	240,000	20.00	95.00	250	450	1,500	6,850	

Arrows Removed (1875)

	Mintage	Good-4	Fine-12	EF-40	AU-55	MS-63	MS-65	Proof-65
1875 . . . . *700*	10,350,000	$4.00	$6.00	$15.00	$40.00	$175	$1,200	$1,500
1875-CC combined total	4,645,000							
1875-CC with CC below wreath		5.00	8.00	30.00	60.00	175	1,300	
1875-CC with CC inside wreath		4.00	6.00	20.00	110	175	1,300	
1875-S combined total	9,070,000							
1875-S with S below wreath		4.00	6.00	15.00	40.00	175	1,200	
1875-S with S inside wreath		4.00	6.00	17.50	100	175	1,200	
1876 . . . . *1,150*	11,460,000	4.00	6.00	15.00	40.00	175	1,200	1,500
1876-CC	8,270,000	5.00	6.50	20.00	42.50	175	1,200	
1876-S	10,420,000	4.00	6.00	15.00	40.00	175	1,200	
1877 . . . . *510*	7,310,000	4.00	6.00	15.00	40.00	175	1,200	1,500
1877-CC	7,700,000	5.00	6.50	20.00	42.50	175	1,200	
1877-S	2,340,000	4.00	6.00	15.00	40.00	175	1,200	
1878 . . . . *800*	1,678,000	6.00	8.00	18.00	55.00	250	2,000	1,500
1878-CC	200,000	40.00	130	250	400	1,100	2,500	
1879 . . . . . . *1,100*	14,000	140	325	475	800	1,250	2,000	
1880 . . . . . . *1,355*	36,000	75.00	140	340	650	1,100	1,800	1,500
1881 . . . . . . *975*	24,000	90.00	275	425	800	1,100	2,000	1,500
1882 . . . . . . *1,100*	3,910,000	4.00	6.00	15.00	40.00	300	1,200	1,500
1883 . . . . . . *1,039*	7,674,673	4.00	6.00	15.00	40.00	300	1,200	1,500
1884 . . . . . . *875*	3,365,505	4.00	6.00	15.00	40.00	300	1,200	1,500
1884-S	564,969	12.50	25.00	70.00	110	475	1,800	
1885, ... *930*	2,532,497	4.00	6.00	15.00	40.00	300	1,200	1,500
1885-S	43,690	150	350	600	1,250	2,250	2,800	
1886 . . . . . . *886*	6,376,684	4.00	6.00	15.00	40.00	300	1,200	1,500
1886-S	206,524	15.00	45.00	92.50	110	550	1,600	
1887 . . . . . . *710*	11,283,229	4.00	6.00	15.00	40.00	300	1,200	1,500
1887-S	4,454,450	4.00	6.00	15.00	40.00	300	1,200	
1888 . . . . . . *832*	5,495,655	4.00	6.00	15.00	40.00	300	1,200	1,500
1888-S	1,720,000	4.00	6.00	15.00	40.00	300	1,200	
1889 . . . . . . *711*	7,380,000	4.00	6.00	15.00	40.00	300	1,200	1,500
1889-S	972,678	9.00	20.00	92.50	110	475	1,300	
1890 . . . . . . *590*	9,910,951	4.00	6.00	15.00	40.00	300	1,200	1,500

	Mintage	Good-4	Fine-12	EF-40	AU-55	MS-63	MS-65	Proof-65
1890-S	1,423,076	7.50	15.00	50.00	100	475	1,500	
1891 600	15,310,000	4.00	6.00	15.00	40.00	300	1,200	1,500
1891-O	4,540,000	4.00	6.00	18.00	60.00	350	1,275	
1891-S	3,196,116	4.00	6.00	16.00	45.00	310	1,225	

Barber or Liberty Head Portrait (1892–1916)

	Mintage	Good-4	Fine-12	EF-40	AU-55	MS-63	MS-65	Proof-65
1892 1,245	12,120,000	$2.00	$6.00	$20.00	$50.00	$205	$800	$1,500
1892-O	3,841,700	4.00	10.00	25.00	65.00	300	1,500	
1892-S	990,710	30.00	65.00	95.00	180	700	3,500	
1893 combined total	3,340,000							
1893 regular date 792		5.00	10.00	25.00	55.00	210	900	1,500
1893/2 overdate	—	—	125	210	850	2,500		
1893-O	1,760,000	13.00	50.00	85.00	110	375	3,250	
1893-S	2,491,401	6.00	18.00	50.00	95.00	425	2,500	
1894 972	1,330,000	6.00	45.00	85.00	110	395	1,100	1,500
1894-S (proof only; not officially authorized)	24	50,000	—	—	—	—	—	451,000
1895 880	690,000	60.00	185	300	350	795	1,500	1,500
1895-O	440,000	150	400	750	1,850	2,850	8,000	
1895-S	1,120,000	20.00	45.00	80.00	175	990	4,000	
1896 762	2,000,000	5.00	15.00	45.00	95.00	250	1,500	1,500
1896-O	610,000	50.00	150	300	475	900	4,000	
1896-S	575,056	50.00	80.00	200	425	990	4,000	
1897 731	10,868,533	2.00	3.00	20.00	50.00	205	800	1,500
1897-O	666,000	35.00	110	250	495	900	5,000	
1897-S	1,342,844	8.00	30.00	75.00	175	675	5,000	
1898 735	16,320,000	2.00	4.00	20.00	50.00	205	800	1,500
1898-O	2,130,000	4.00	45.00	110	150	750	2,000	
1898-S	1,702,507	4.00	14.00	35.00	90.00	550	3,500	
1899 846	19,580,000	2.00	4.00	20.00	50.00	205	800	1,500
1899-O	2,650,000	4.00	35.00	100	195	750	2,500	
1899-S	1,867,493	4.00	11.00	30.00	80.00	495	2,850	
1900 912	17,600,000	2.00	4.00	20.00	50.00	205	800	1,500
1900-O	2,010,000	5.00	50.00	135	240	850	2,500	

DIMES (1796–PRESENT)

	Mintage	Good-4	Fine-12	EF-40	AU-55	MS-63	MS-65	Proof-65
1900-S	5,168,270	3.00	7.00	25.00	65.00	325	1,500	
1901 813	18,859,665	2.00	4.00	20.00	50.00	205	800	1,500
1901-O	5,620,000	3.00	8.00	40.00	110	495	2,000	
1901-S	593,022	35.00	175	350	525	900	3,000	
1902 777	21,380,000	2.00	4.00	20.00	50.00	205	800	1,500
1902-O	4,500,000	3.00	8.00	40.00	95.00	550	1,950	
1902-S	2,070,000	4.00	22.00	70.00	125	550	1,950	
1903 755	19,500,000	2.00	4.00	20.00	50.00	205	800	1,500
1903-O	8,180,000	3.00	6.00	25.00	85.00	475	4,000	
1903-S	613,300	25.00	165	650	750	875	3,700	
1904 670	14,600,357	2.00	4.00	20.00	50.00	205	800	1,500
1904-S	800,000	19.00	75.00	225	350	875	3,600	
1905 727	14,551,623	2.00	4.00	20.00	50.00	205	800	1,500
1905-O	3,400,000	3.00	12.00	35.00	95.00	390	3,800	
1905-S	6,855,199	3.00	7.00	25.00	70.00	365	1,000	
1906 675	19,957,731	2.00	4.00	20.00	50.00	205	800	1,500
1906-D	4,060,000	3.00	6.00	25.00	70.00	325	1,000	
1906-O	2,610,000	3.00	25.00	40.00	110	325	1,000	
1906-S	3,136,640	2.00	10.00	30.00	85.00	325	1,100	
1907 575	22,220,000	2.00	4.00	20.00	50.00	205	800	1,500
1907-D	4,080,000	2.00	7.00	30.00	80.00	225	2,000	
1907-O	5,058,000	2.00	13.00	25.00	70.00	375	1,500	
1907-S	3,178,470	3.00	9.00	40.00	95.00	425	2,900	
1908 545	10,600,000	2.00	4.00	20.00	50.00	205	800	1,500
1908-D	7,490,000	2.00	6.00	25.00	55.00	205	850	
1908-O	1,789,000	3.00	27.00	55.00	110	495	1,000	
1908-S	3,220,000	2.00	8.00	27.50	85.00	495	1,250	
1909 650	10,240,000	2.00	4.00	20.00	50.00	205	800	1,500
1909-D	954,000	3.00	25.00	80.00	140	550	2,000	
1909-O	2,287,000	2.00	8.00	27.50	85.00	325	1,000	
1909-S	1,000,000	3.00	39.00	125	250	475	2,500	
1910 551	11,520,000	2.00	4.00	20.00	50.00	205	800	1,500
1910-D	3,490,000	2.00	8.00	30.00	80.00	300	1,000	
1910-S	1,240,000	2.00	25.00	52.50	135	300	1,000	
1911 543	18,870,000	2.00	4.00	20.00	50.00	205	800	1,500
1911-D	11,209,000	2.00	4.00	20.00	50.00	205	800	
1911-S	3,520,000	2.00	8.00	25.00	80.00	325	900	
1912 700	19,350,000	2.00	4.00	20.00	50.00	205	850	1,500
1912-D	11,760,000	2.00	5.00	20.00	50.00	205	850	
1912-S	3,420,000	2.00	6.00	25.00	70.00	280	1,000	
1913 622	19,760,000	2.00	4.00	20.00	50.00	205	850	1,500
1913-S	510,000	8.00	50.00	155	275	375	1,000	
1914 425	17,360,230	2.00	4.00	20.00	50.00	205	800	1,800
1914-D	11,908,000	2.00	4.00	20.00	50.00	205	800	

DIMES (1796–PRESENT)

	Mintage	Good-4	Fine-12	EF-40	AU-55	MS-63	MS-65	Proof-65
1914-S	2,100,000	3.00	6.00	25.00	60.00	225	1,000	
1915........*450*	5,620,000	2.00	3.00	20.00	50.00	205	800	1,600
1915-S	960,000	2.00	8.00	40.00	110	400	1,100	
1916	18,490,000	2.00	3.00	20.00	55.00	205	850	
1916-S	5,820,000	2.00	3.00	20.00	55.00	205	850	

Winged Liberty Head or "Mercury" Portrait (1916–1945)

	Mintage	Good-4	Fine-12	EF-40	AU-55	MS-63	MS-65	Proof-65
1916	22,180,080	$3.00	$3.75	$10.00	$25.00	$50.00	$150	
1916-D	264,000	450	1,000	3,000	3,500	4,000	23,000	
1916-S	10,450,000	3.00	6.00	20.00	25.00	08.00	200	
1917	55,230,000	2.00	3.00	9.00	12.00	70.00	200	
1917-D	9,402,000	3.00	6.00	40.00	65.00	300	1,350	
1917-S	27,330,000	1.75	3.00	16.00	25.00	200	500	
1918	26,680,000	1.75	4.00	25.00	35.00	190	300	
1918-D	22,674,800	1.85	3.00	25.00	36.00	275	750	
1918-S	19,300,000	1.85	3.00	15.00	30.00	200	800	
1919	35,740,000	1.25	3.00	12.00	25.00	150	300	
1919 D	9,939,000	2.25	5.00	35.00	65.00	400	1,600	
1919-S	8,850,000	2.00	4.75	30.00	65.00	500	1,000	
1920	59,030,000	1.50	2.75	8.00	15.00	90.00	250	
1920-D	19,171,000	2.00	3.50	13.00	35.00	400	800	
1920-S	13,820,000	2.00	3.50	12.00	38.00	325	1,500	
1921	1,230,000	20.00	75.00	500	750	1,500	3,250	
1921-D	1,080,000	30.00	100	550	775	1,800	3,000	
1923	50,130,000	2.00	3.00	5.00	20.00	75.00	125	
1923-S	6,440,000	2.20	4.00	45.00	75.00	300	1,800	
1924	24,010,000	2.00	3.00	10.00	25.00	100	300	
1924-D	6,810,000	2.00	4.00	40.00	90.00	350	1,500	
1924-S	7,120,000	2.00	3.75	40.00	90.00	575	1,200	
1925	25,610,000	2.00	2.75	8.00	20.00	90.00	350	
1925-D	5,117,000	3.00	9.00	90.00	200	600	1,800	
1925-S	5,850,000	2.00	3.50	40.00	100	450	2,500	
1926	32,160,000	2.00	2.75	8.00	20.00	75.00	400	
1926-D	6,828,000	2.00	4.00	15.00	35.00	250	750	

	Mintage	Good-4	Fine-12	EF-40	AU-55	MS-63	MS-65	Proof-65
1926-S	1,520,000	4.00	15.00	200	400	1,500	3,500	
1927	28,080,000	2.00	3.00	6.00	12.00	75.00	200	
1927-D	4,812,000	2.00	4.00	40.00	80.00	450	1,200	
1927-S	4,770,000	2.00	3.00	20.00	35.00	350	1,750	
1928	19,480,000	2.00	2.00	6.00	15.00	75.00	150	
1928-D	4,161,000	3.00	5.00	40.00	80.00	250	900	
1928-S	7,400,000	2.00	4.00	9.00	30.00	150	400	
1929	25,970,000	2.00	3.00	5.00	10.00	35.00	75.00	
1929-D	5,034,000	2.50	4.00	12.00	20.00	40.00	70.00	
1929-S	4,730,000	2.00	2.50	5.00	15.00	42.00	100	
1930	6,770,000	2.00	2.25	6.00	12.00	45.00	140	
1930-S	1,843,000	2.50	4.00	10.00	40.00	100	135	
1931	3,150,000	2.25	3.00	8.00	20.00	75.00	175	
1931-D	1,260,000	5.00	10.00	30.00	42.00	100	200	
1931-S	1,800,000	2.50	4.00	10.00	35.00	75.00	200	
1934	24,080,000	1.00	1.10	1.20	2.50	20.00	45.00	
1934-D	6,772,000	1.25	1.50	3.50	7.50	35.00	65.00	
1935	58,830,000	.50	.60	.90	1.35	20.00	28.00	
1935-D	10,477,000	.50	.60	.90	1.35	35.00	65.00	
1935-S	15,840,000	.50	.60	.90	1.35	30.00	60.00	
1936 . . . . . . 4,130	87,500,000	.50	.60	.90	1.35	20.00	30.00	$800
1936-D	16,132,000	.50	.60	.90	1.35	28.00	40.00	
1936-S	9,210,000	.50	.60	.90	1.35	20.00	30.00	
1937 . . . . 5,756	56,860,000	.50	.60	.90	1.35	18.00	25.00	225
1937-D	14,146,000	.50	.60	.90	1.35	25.00	45.00	
1937-S	9,740,000	.50	.60	.90	1.35	26.00	35.00	
1938 . . . . . . 8,728	22,190,000	.50	.60	.90	1.35	20.00	28.00	180
1938-D	5,537,000	.50	.60	.90	1.35	22.00	30.00	
1938-S	8,090,000	.50	.60	.90	1.35	22.00	35.00	
1939 . . . . 9,321	67,740,000	.50	.60	.90	1.35	20.00	25.00	200
1939-D	24,394,000	.50	.60	.90	1.35	19.00	25.00	
1939-S	10,540,000	.50	.60	.90	1.35	28.00	40.00	
1940 . . . . 11,827	65,350,000	.40	.50	.75	1.25	15.00	25.00	125
1940-D	21,198,000	.40	.50	.75	1.25	15.00	25.00	
1940-S	21,560,000	.40	.50	.75	1.25	16.00	25.00	
1941 . . . . 16,557	175,090,000	.40	.50	.75	1.25	12.00	25.00	120
1941-D	45,634,000	.40	.50	.75	1.25	13.00	30.00	
1941-S	43,090,000	.40	.50	.75	1.25	15.00	25.00	
1942 combined total	205,410,000							
1942 regular date . . . 22,329		.40	.50	.75	1.25	12.00	25.00	120
1942/1 overdate		175	225	300	400	2,000	7,500	
1942-D combined total	60,740,000							
1942-D regular date		.40	.50	.75	1.25	15.00	25.00	
1942/1-D overdate		175	225	400	800	2,000	6,500	

	Mintage	Good-4	Fine-12	EF-40	AU-55	MS-63	MS-65	Proof-65
1942-S	49,300,000	.40	.50	.75	1.25	16.00	25.00	
1943	191,710,000	.40	.50	.75	1.25	15.00	24.00	
1943-D	71,949,000	.40	.50	.75	1.25	16.00	35.00	
1943-S	60,400,000	.40	.50	.75	1.25	15.00	25.00	
1944	231,410,000	.40	.50	.75	1.25	15.00	25.00	
1944-D	62,224,000	.40	.50	.75	1.25	15.00	25.00	
1944-S	49,490,000	.40	.50	.75	1.25	15.00	25.00	
1945	159,130,000	.40	.50	.75	1.25	12.00	28.00	
1945-D	40,245,000	.40	.50	.75	1.25	10.00	25.00	
1945-S combined total	41,920,000							
1945-S with regular S		.40	.50	.75	1.25	12.00	25.00	
1945-S with microscopic S		.40	.50	.75	1.25	20.00	58.00	

Roosevelt Portrait (1946–Present)

Silver Composition (1946–1964)

	Mintage	Fine-12	EF-40	AU-55	MS-60	MS-63	MS-65	Proof-65
1946	255,250,000	$.50	$.70	$1.10	$1.25	$1.75	$3.50	
1946-D	61,043,500	.60	.80	1.25	1.45	2.25	4.25	
1946-S	27,900,000	.75	.95	1.50	1.75	4.00	12.75	
1947	121,520,000	.60	.80	1.25	1.45	2.25	4.25	
1947-D	46,835,000	.85	1.05	2.00	2.75	5.75	16.50	
1947-S	34,840,000	.75	.95	1.50	1.75	4.00	12.00	
1948	74,950,000	.75	1.05	2.00	2.75	9.00	15.00	
1948-D	52,841,000	.60	1.05	2.50	2.75	8.00	16.50	
1948-S	35,520,000	.50	.70	1.25	2.75	8.00	18.00	
1949	30,940,000	.65	1.40	2.00	6.00	10.00	19.00	
1949-D	26,034,000	.65	1.00	1.25	3.00	5.00	12.00	
1949-S	13,510,000	1.00	1.50	5.00	12.00	15.00	23.00	
1950 ..... *51,386*	50,130,114	.50	.65	2.00	3.00	3.75	10.00	$20.00
1950-D	46,803,000	.50	.65	1.75	2.10	3.00	8.50	
1950-S	20,440,000	.65	1.40	2.00	6.00	10.00	19.00	
1951 ..... *57,500*	103,880,102	.50	.70	1.10	1.25	1.75	3.50	15.00
1951-D	56,529,000	.50	.70	1.10	1.25	1.75	3.50	
1951-S	31,630,000	.65	1.40	1.75	5.00	8.00	12.00	
1952 ..... *81,980*	99,040,093	.50	.70	1.10	1.25	1.75	3.50	16.00

	Mintage	Fine-12	EF-40	AU-55	MS-60	MS-63	MS-65	Proof-65
1952-D	122,100,000	.50	.70	1.10	1.25	1.75	3.50	
1952-S	44,419,500	.60	1.05	2.50	2.75	8.00	16.50	
1953 .... *128,800*	53,490,120	.50	.70	1.10	1.25	1.75	3.50	15.00
1953-D	136,433,000	.50	.70	1.00	1.10	1.25	2.00	
1953-S	39,180,000	.50	.65	.90	1.00	1.20	1.75	
1954 .... *233,300*	114,010,203	.50	.65	.90	1.00	1.40	1.90	12.00
1954-D	106,397,000	.50	.65	.90	1.00	1.30	1.85	
1054-S	22,860,000	.50	.65	.90	1.10	1.35	1.95	
1955 .... *378,200*	12,450,181	.65	.75	1.50	1.75	2.25	4.75	9.00
1955-D	13,959,000	.50	.65	.90	1.00	1.50	2.10	
1955-S	18,510,000	.50	.70	1.10	1.25	1.75	2.75	
1956 .... *669,384*	108,640,000	.50	.65	.90	1.00	1.20	1.50	4.00
1956-D	108,015,100	.05	.65	.90	1.00	1.20	1.50	
1957 .... *1,247,952*	160,160,000	.50	.70	1.00	1.10	1.35	1.60	3.00
1957-D	113,354,330	.50	.65	.90	1.00	1.50	2.00	
1958 .... *875,652*	31,910,000	.50	.65	.90	1.10	1.35	1.90	3.50
1958-D	136,564,600	.50	.65	.90	1.00	1.50	2.00	
1959 .... *1,149,291*	85,780,000	.50	.65	.90	1.10	1.35	1.90	2.25
1959-D	164,919,790	.50	.65	.90	1.00	1.50	2.00	
1960 .... *1,691,602*	70,390,000	.50	.65	.90	1.00	1.20	1.50	2.00
1960-D	200,160,400	.45	.60	.80	.90	1.00	1.35	
1961 .... *3,028,244*	93,730,000	.40	.50	.75	.85	.90	1.25	1.90
1961-d	209,146,550	.40	.50	.75	.85	.90	1.25	
1962 .... *3,218,019*	72,450,000	.40	.50	.75	.85	.90	1.25	1.90
1962-D	334,948,380	.40	.50	.75	.85	.90	1.35	
1963 .... *3,075,645*	123,650,000	.40	.50	.75	.85	.90	1.35	1.90
1963-D	421,476,530	.40	.50	.75	.85	.90	1.30	
1964 .... *3,950,762*	929,360,000	.40	.50	.75	.85	.90	1.30	1.75
1964-D	1,357,517,180	.40	.50	.75	.85	.90	1.30	

Copper-Nickel Clad Composition (1965–Present)

	Mintage	EF-40	MS-65	Proof-65
1965	1,652,140,570	—	$.25	
1966	1,382,734,540	—	.25	
1967	2,244,007,320	—	.25	
1968	424,470,400	—	.25	
1968-D	480,748,280	—	.25	
1968-S (proof only)	*3,041,506*	—	—	$.50
1969	145,790,000	—	.25	
1969-D	563,323,870	—	.25	
1969-S (proof only)	*2,934,631*	—	—	.50
1970	345,570,000	—	.20	
1970-D	754,942,100	—	.20	

	Mintage	EF-40	MS-65	Proof-65
1970-S combined total (proof only)	2,632,810			
1970-S proof with S		—	.50	
1970-S proof with no mint mark		—	400	
1971	162,690,000	—	.25	
1971-D	377,914,240	—	.25	
1971-S (proof only)	3,220,733	—	—	.50
1972	431,540,000	—	.25	
1972-D	330,390,000	—	.25	
1972-S (proof only)	3,260,996	—	—	.75
1973	315,670,000	—	.15	
1973-D	455,032,426	—	.15	
1973-S (proof only)	2,760,339	—	—	.75
1974	470,248,000	—	.15	
1974-D	571,083,000	—	.15	
1974-S (proof only)	2,612,568	—	—	.75
1975	585,673,900	—	.15	
1975-D	313,705,300	—	.15	
1975-S (proof only)	2,845,450	—	—	.75
1976	568,760,000	—	.15	
1976-D	695,222,774	—	.15	
1976-S (proof only)	4,149,730	—	—	.75
1977	796,930,000	—	.15	
1977-D	376,222,774	—	.15	
1977-S (proof only)	3,251,152	—	—	.75
1978	663,980,000	—	.15	
1978-D	282,847,540	—	.15	
1978 S (proof only)	3,127,781	—	—	.75
1979	315,440,000	—	.15	
1979-D	390,921,184	—	.15	
1979-S combined total (proof only)	3,677,175			
1979-S with clear S		—	1.00	
1979-S with clogged S		—	.75	
1980-P	735,170,000	—	.15	
1980-D	719,354,321	—	.15	
1980-S (proof only)	3,554,806	—	—	.65
1981-P	676,650,000	—	.15	
1981-D	712,284,143	—	.15	
1981-S (proof only)	4,063,083	—	—	.60
1982-P combined total	519,475,000			
1982-P with P		—	.15	
1982-P with no mint mark ...		—	100	

	Mintage	EF-40	MS-65	Proof-65
1982-D	542,713,584	—	.15	
1982-S (proof only)	3,857,479	—	—	.60
1983-P	647,025,000	—	.15	
1983-D	730,129,224	—	.15	
1983-S combined total (proof only)	3,279,126			
1983-S proof with S		—	—	.60
1983-S proof with no mint mark		—	—	310
1984-P	856,669,000	—	.15	
1984-D	704,803,976	—	.15	
1984-S (proof only)	3,065,110	—	—	1.00
1985-P	705,200,962	—	.15	
1985-D	587,979,970	—	.15	
1985-S (proof only)	3,362,821	—	—	.90
1986-P	682,649,693	—	.15	
1986-D	473,326,970	—	.15	
1986-S (proof only)	3,010,497	—	1.00	
1987-P	762,709,481	—	.15	
1987-D	653,203,402	—	.15	
1987-S (proof only)	3,792,233	—	—	1.00
1988-P	1,030,550,000	—	.15	
1988-D	962,385,489	—	.15	
1988-S (proof only)	3,262,948	—	—	1.00
1989-P	1,298,400,000	—	.15	
1989-D	896,535,597	—	.15	
1989-S (proof only)	3,215,728	—	—	1.00
1990-P	1,034,340,000	—	.15	
1990-D	839,995,824	—	.15	
1990-S (proof only)	3,299,559	—	—	1.00
1991-P	927,220,000	—	.15	
1991-D	601,241,114	—	.15	
1991-S (proof only)	· 2,867,787	—	—	1.00
1992-P	593,500,000	—	.15	
1992-D	616,273,932	—	.15	
1992-S (proof only)	4,176,544*	—	—	1.00
1993-P	766,180,000	—	.15	
1993-D	750,110,166	—	.15	
1993-S (proof only)	3,360,876*	—	—	1.00
1994-P	1,190,210,896	—	.15	
1994-D	1,304,479,006	—	.15	
1994-S (proof only)	3,212,792*	—	—	1.00
1995-P	1,126,541,352	—	.15	
1995-D	1,275,731,352	—	.15	
1995-S (proof only)	2,796,345*	—	.15	1.00

DIMES (1796–PRESENT)

	Mintage	EF-40	MS-65	Proof-65
1996-P	1,423,084,215	—	.15	
1996-D	1,401,754,215	—	.15	
1996-S (proof only)	2,925,305*	—	—	1.00
1996-W	1,258,334	—	15.00	
1997-P	991,640,000	—	.15	
1997-D	979,810,000	—	.15	
1997-S (proof only)	2,788,020*	—	—	1.00
1998-P	1,163,000,000	—	.15	
1998-D	1,172,300,000	—	.15	
1998-S (proof only)	2,086,507	—	—	1.00
1998-S (silver proof)	878,996	—	—	2.75
1999-P	2,164,000,000	—	.15	
1999-D	1,397,750,000	—	.15	
1999-S (proof only)	(2,454,319)**	—	—	1.00
1999-S (silver proof)	798,780	—	—	1.75
2000-P	1,842,500,000	—	.15	
2000-D	1,818,700,000	—	.15	
2000-S (proof only)	(3,030,000)**	—	—	1.00
2000-S (silver proof)	904,200**	—	—	1.75
2001-P	1,369,590,000	—	.15	
2001-D	1,412,800,000	—	.15	
2001-S (proof only)	(2,293,200)***	—	—	1.00
2001-S (silver proof)	891,400	—	—	1.75
2002-P		—	.15	
2002-D		—	.15	
2002-S (proof only)		—	—	1.00
2002-S (silver proof)		—	—	1.75
2003-P		—	.15	
2003-D		—	.15	
2003-S (proof only)		—	—	1.00
2003-S (silver proof)		—	—	1.75

* Includes 90% silver issue
** Through March 31, 2001
*** Through May 28, 2002

TWENTY-CENT PIECES (1875–1878)

	Mintage	Good-4	Fine-12	EF-40	AU-55	MS-63	MS-65	Proof-65
1875 . . . . *2,790*	36,910	$50.00	$65.00	$150	$400	$1,400	$6,800	$8,100
1875-CC	133,290	50.00	65.00	150	400	1,400	6,800	
1875-S	1,155,000	40.00	60.00	130	300	1,100	6,000	
1876 . . . . *1,150*	14,640	90.00	110	120	260	600	4,000	8,750
1876-CC (fewer than 20 known)	10,000	—	—	40,000	—	—	—	
1877 (proof only)	*510*	1,100	1,600	2,000	2,500	—	—	9,500
1878 (proof only)	*600*	800	1,000	1,275	1,500	—	—	8,500

QUARTER DOLLARS (1796–PRESENT)

Draped Bust Portrait with Small Eagle on Reverse (1796)

	Mintage	Good-4	Fine-12	EF-40
1796	6,146	$3,400	$7,250	$15,000

Draped Bust Portrait with Heraldic Eagle on Reverse (1804–1807)

	Mintage	Good-4	Fine-12	EF-40
1804	6,738	$800	$2,200	$7,500
1805	121,394	180	375	2,100
1806 combined total	206,124			
1806 regular date		170	330	2,000
1806/5 overdate		180	375	2,200
1807	220,643	170	330	2,000

Capped Bust Portrait (1815–1838)

Large Size (1815–1828)

	Mintage	Good-4	Fine-12	EF-40	AU-55	MS-63
1815	89,235	$38.00	$100	$610	$1,750	$4,100
1818 combined total	361,174					
1818 regular date		35.00	90.00	560	1,500	3,800
1818/5 overdate		40.00	120	700	1,850	3,900
1819 combined total	144,000					
1819 small 9		35.00	90.00	560	1,500	3,750
1819 large 9		35.00	90.00	560	1,500	3,750
1820 combined total	127,444					
1820 small 0		35.00	95.00	600	1,500	3,750
1820 large 0		35.00	90.00	560	1,500	3,750

	Mintage	Good-4	Fine-12	EF-40	AU-55	MS-63
1821	216,851	35.00	90.00	560	1,500	3,750
1822 combined total	64,080					
1822 regular 25c		46.00	130	850	2,200	4,200
1822 25/50c		800	1,600	8,000	16,000	—
1823/2 overdate	17,800	5,600	13,750	28,000	—	—
1824/2 overdate (mintage included with 1825)		65.00	180	1,100	3,000	—
1825 combined total	174,000					
1825/2 overdate		75.00	210	1,100	3,000	—
1825/3 overdate		35.00	90.00	560	1,500	3,750
1825/4 overdate		35.00	90.00	560	1,500	3,750
1827 original (curl-base 2 in 25c)	(only a few proofs known)				—	55,000
1827 restrike (square-base 2 in 25c)	(only a few proofs known)				—	27,500
1828 combined total	100,000					
1828 regular 25c		35.00	90.00	560	1,500	3,750
1828 25/50c		75.00	300	1,300	3,500	—

Reduced Size (1831–1838)

	Mintage	Good-4	Fine-12	EF-40	AU-55	MS-63
1831 combined total	398,000					
1831 with small letters		$32.00	$46.00	$200	$550	$1,600
1831 with large letters		32.00	46.00	200	550	1,600
1832	320,000	32.00	46.00	200	550	1,600
1833	156,000	35.00	50.00	210	600	1,700
1834	286,000	32.00	46.00	200	550	1,600
1835	1,952,000	32.00	46.00	200	550	1,600
1836	472,000	32.00	46.00	200	550	1,600
1837	252,400	32.00	46.00	200	550	1,600
1838	366,000	32.00	48.00	210	600	1,700

Seated Liberty Portrait (1838–1891)

	Mintage	Good-4	Fine-12	EF-40	AU-55	MS-63	MS-65
1838	466,000	$10.00	$23.00	$300	$600	$2,000	$35,000
1839	491,146	10.00	23.00	300	600	2,000	37,500
1840-O	382,200	10.00	30.00	350	705	4,000	—

With Drapery Hanging from Elbow (1840–1891)

	Mintage	Good-4	Fine-12	EF-40	AU-55	MS-63	MS-65
1840	188,127	$15.00	$40.00	$150	$300	$3,000	$9,750
1840-O	43,000	15.00	50.00	160	475	3,300	—

QUARTER DOLLARS (1796–PRESENT)

	Mintage	Good-4	Fine-12	EF-40	AU-55	MS-63	MS-65
1841	120,000	35.00	75.00	140	300	1,600	—
1841-O	452,000	15.00	35.00	135	310	1,800	7,500
1842 small date	(only a few proofs known)			—	—	—	
1842 large date	88,000	55.00	100	350	400	1,800	—
1842-O combined total	769,000						
1842-O small date		210	605	1,500	3,000	10,500	—
1842-O large date		15.00	28.00	70.00	300	2,800	—
1843	645,600	10.00	22.00	60.00	200	1,000	—
1843-O	968,000	15.00	40.00	150	350	2,000	—
1844	421,200	8.00	20.00	60.00	150	1,100	—
1844-O	740,000	8.00	22.00	90.00	175	1,800	—
1845	922,000	8.00	20.00	80.00	110	590	—
1846	510,300	8.00	23.50	85.00	130	1,000	—
1847	734,000	8.00	20.00	80.00	110	800	7,000
1847-O	368,000	20.00	60.00	152.50	260	4,000	—
1848	146,000	21.00	60.00	130	250	2,250	11,000
1849	340,000	15.00	40.00	110	200	1,600	8,750
1849-O	16,000	325	640	1,950	3,375	—	—
1850	190,800	22.50	46.00	100	205	1,385	—
1850-O	412,000	18.00	45.00	95.00	215	2,000	—
1851	160,000	30.00	54.00	110	205	1,800	8,000
1851-O	88,000	110	350	1,150	1,850	—	—
1852	177,060	38.00	55.00	150	200	905	—
1852-O	96,000	135	300	865	1,750	6,200	—
1853 without arrows or rays	44,200	140	345	440	825	3,775	—

With Arrows Beside the Date, Rays Around the Eagle (1853)

	Mintage	Good-4	Fine-12	EF-40	AU-55	MS-63	MS-65	Proof-65
1853 combined total	15,210,020							
1853 regular date		$10.00	$25.00	$175	$400	$3,500	$20,000	—
1853/4 overdate		50.00	110	300	900	4,500	—	
1853-O	1,332,000	12.50	30.00	200	1,000	5,500	—	

With Arrows Beside the Date, No Rays Around the Eagle (1854–1855)

	Mintage	Good-4	Fine-12	EF-40	AU-55	MS-63	MS-65	Proof-65
1854	12,380,000	$10.00	$25.00	$80.00	$200	$1,500	$10,000	
1854-O combined total	1,484,000							
1854-O regular date		10.00	20.00	80.00	200	1,900		
1854-O with huge O		110	180	400	1,000	4,500		

	Mintage	Good-4	Fine-12	EF-40	AU-55	MS-63	MS-65	Proof-65
1855	2,857,000	10.00	25.00	80.00	200	1,800	10,000	
1855-O	176,000	35.00	100	300	600		—	
1855-S	396,400	30.00	60.00	250	600	4,700	—	—

Arrows Removed, Without Motto (1856)

	Mintage	Good-4	Fine-12	EF-40	AU-55	MS-63	MS-65	Proof-65
1856	7,264,000	$10.00	$20.00	$65.00	$100	$900	$5,000	$12,500
1856-O	968,000	10.00	20.00	65.00	200	1,200	10,000	
1856-S combined total	286,000							
1856-S regular date		30.00	80.00	300	600	3,000	—	
1856-S/S		40.00	100	400	775		—	
1857	9,644,000	8.00	20.00	60.00	110	1,000	4,000	11,000
1857-O	1,180,000	8.00	20.00	60.00	225	2,000	—	
1857-S	82,000	35.00	125	485	750	6,000	—	
1858	7,368,000	10.00	20.00	50.00	110	900	4,000	9,500
1858-O	520,000	11.00	22.00	60.00	275	3,000	15,000	
1858-S	121,000	35.00	125	290	625	4,000	—	
1859 .... *800*	1,343,200	11.00	20.00	58.00	130	1,000	7,500	4,800
1859-O	260,000	12.00	35.00	65.00	250	2,500	15,000	
1859-S	80,000	68.00	125	390	675	4,500	—	
1860 .... *1,000*	804,400	9.00	20.00	60.00	100	1,000	4,500	5,250
1860-O	388,000	12.00	30.00	70.00	350	2,000	7,500	
1860-S	56,000	110	250	1,200	3,000	10,000	—	
1861 .... *1,000*	4,853,600	12.00	20.00	60.00	110	1,000	4,000	4,750
1861-S	96,000	50.00	275	1,500	4,000	—	—	4,800
1862 .... *550*	932,000	10.00	20.00	60.00	100	1,000	4,000	4,800
1862-S	67,000	50.00	80.00	280	550	—	—	
1863 .... *460*	191,600	35.00	40.00	100	225	1,000	4,500	4,600
1864 .... *470*	93,600	55.00	80.00	150	250	1,175	4,500	4,600
1864-S	20,000	135	250	900	1,500	—	—	
1865 .... *500*	58,800	38.00	80.00	150	250	1,000	8,000	5,000
1865-S	41,000	60.00	100	250	625	3,400	12,500	
1866	(unique)	—	—	—	250,000	—	—	

With Motto Above the Eagle (1866–1891)

	Mintage	Good-4	Fine-12	EF-40	AU-55	MS-63	MS-65	Proof-65
1866 . . . . 725	16,800	$150	$450	$550	$775	$2,500	$5,800	$3,000
1866-S	28,000	140	325	560	925	2,800	—	
1867 . . . . 625	20,000	100	300	400	475	1,800	—	2,400
1867-S	48,000	90.00	350	450	775	—		
1868 . . . . 600	29,400	90.00	230	273	425	2,000	4,500	2,500
1868-S	96,000	49.00	240	425	875	3,500	—	
1869 . . . . 600	16,000	150	425	450	675	2,200	—	2,550
1869-S	76,000	80.00	300	425	950	3,600	20,000	
1870 . . . . 1,000	86,400	50.00	200	225	375	1,000	7,000	2,400
1870-CC	8,340	1,100	3,500	3,900	7,000	—	—	
1871 . . . . 960	118,200	30.00	100	125	350	700	7,500	2,300
1871-CC	10,890	740	2,500	3,700	5,100	—	—	
1871-S	30,900	200	450	600	775	3,500	12,500	
1872 . . . . 950	182,000	25.00	80.00	100	225	1,500	7,500	2,300
1872-CC	22,850	250	1,800	2,300	5,000	—	—	
1872-S	83,000	200	500	600	975	3,600	35,000	
1873 closed 3 . . . . 600	40,000	69.00	300	400	475	2,200	—	2,500
1873 open 3	172,000	26.00	100	110	200	900	4,750	
1873-CC	(4 known)	—	—	—	—	—	—	

With Arrows Beside the Date (1873–1874)

	Mintage	Good-4	Fine-12	EF-40	AU-55	MS-63	MS-65	Proof-65
1873 . . . . 540	1,271,160	$12.00	$50.00	$200	$475	$1,600	$5,500	$5,000
1873-CC	12,462	1,200	3,000	5,000	9,000	—	—	
1873-S	156,000	18.00	50.00	200	475	2,000	—	
1874 . . . . 700	471,200	12.00	75.00	200	450	1,800	4,000	5,000
1874-S	392,000	15.00	80.00	200	460	1,800	4,000	

Arrows Removed, with Motto (1875)

	Mintage	Good-4	Fine-12	EF-40	AU-55	MS-63	MS-65	Proof-65
1875 . . . . 700	4,292,800	$9.00	$20.00	$50.00	$100	$600	$1,300	$1,350
1875-CC	140,000	50.00	200	300	500	2,000	—	
1875-S	680,000	35.00	150	200	400	1,800	2,800	
1876 . . . . 1,150	17,816,000	10.00	36.00	50.00	100	600	1,300	1,350
1876-CC	4,944,000	9.00	38.00	50.00	100	800	1,300	
1876-S	8,596,000	8.00	36.00	50.00	100	600	2,200	
1877 . . . . 510	10,911,200	8.00	36.00	50.00	100	600	1,300	1,350
1877-CC	4,192,000	9.00	38.00	50.00	100	775	1,400	
1877-S combined total	8,996,000							
1877-S with regular mint mark .		9.00	36.00	50.00	100	600	1,400	
1877-S with S struck over								
horizontal S		35.00	140	225	300	1,500	—	
1878 . . . . 800	2,260,000	9.00	30.00	50.00	100	675	2,000	1,350
1878-CC	996,000	18.00	80.00	100	135	775	3,500	
1878-S		60.00	190	300	450	2,000	—	
1879 . . . . 1,100	13,600	110	175	300	465	600	1,400	1,350
1880 . . . . 1,355	13,600	110	185	275	350	675	1,400	1,350
1881 . . . . 975	12,000	115	200	285	360	775	1,400	1,350
1882 . . . . 1,100	15,200	120	200	295	360	800	1,400	1,350
1883 . . . . 1,039	14,400	110	200	295	380	700	—	1,350
1884 . . . . 875	8,000	110	225	295	360	700	1,400	1,350
1885 . . . . 930	13,600	110	200	325	390	1,000	2,000	1,350
1886 . . . . 886	5,000	190	300	400	425	1,000	2,000	1,350
1887 . . . . 710	10,000	140	225	300	325	800	1,600	1,350
1888 . . . . 832	10,001	140	225	300	325	700	1,300	1,350
1888-S	1,216,000	10.00	30.00	50.00	100	600	3,000	
1889 . . . . 711	12,000	100	225	300	350	750	1,300	1,350
1890 . . . . 590	80,000	60.00	90.00	200	275	625	1,300	1,350
1891 . . . . 600	3,920,000	10.00	40.00	50.00	150	575	1,300	1,350
1891-O	68,000	100	265	475	650	4,500	—	
1891-S	2,216,000	10.00	50.00	75.00	125	575	2,000	

Barber or Liberty Head Portrait (1892–1916)

	Mintage	Good-4	Fine-12	EF-40	AU-55	MS-63	MS-65	Proof-65
1892 . . . . 1,245	8,236,000	$3.00	$15.00	$55.00	$110	$395	$1,250	$1,850
1892-O	2,640,000	4.00	16.00	60.00	130	395	2,500	
1892-S	964,079	12.00	35.00	100	250	750	4,000	
1893 792	5,444,023	3.00	15.00	55.00	110	395	1,350	1,850
1893-O	3,396,000	4.00	18.00	60.00	130	500	2,200	
1893-S	1,454,535	5.00	22.50	90.00	250	750	6,500	
1894 972	3,432,000	3.00	15.00	55.00	110	450	1,500	1,850
1894-O	2,852,000	4.00	18.00	60.00	170	1,700	3,800	
1894-S	2,648,821	4.00	17.50	60.00	150	650	5,600	
1895 880	4,440,000	4.00	15.00	55.00	125	525	1,250	1,850
1895-O	2,816,000	4.00	18.00	70.00	210	700	2,500	
1895-S	1,764,681	4.00	25.00	70.00	210	750	4,000	
1896 762	3,874,000	3.00	15.00	55.00	110	450	2,000	1,850
1896-O	1,484,000	5.00	40.00	300	600	1,400	6,000	
1896-S	188,039	200	550	1,250	2,700	5,000	10,000	
1897 731	8,140,000	3.00	15.00	55.00	110	395	1,250	1,850
1897-O	1,414,800	7.50	50.00	300	600	1,350	5,000	
1897-S	542,229	10.00	60.00	320	600	1,500	6,000	
1898 735	11,100,000	3.00	15.00	55.00	110	395	1,500	1,850
1898-O	1,868,000	5.00	30.00	140	350	950	7,000	
1898-S	1,020,592	5.00	20.00	60.00	160	750	4,500	
1899 846	12,624,000	3.00	15.00	55.00	110	395	1,500	1,850
1899-O	2,644,000	5.00	20.00	75.00	225	725	4,950	
1899-S	708,000	8.00	20.00	70.00	175	750	2,800	
1900 912	10,016,000	3.00	15.00	55.00	110	395	1,500	1,850
1900-O	3,416,000	5.00	25.00	85.00	215	700	3,200	
1900-S	1,858,585	5.00	18.00	60.00	110	625	4,500	
1901 813	8,892,000	3.00	15.00	55.00	110	395	1,500	1,850
1901-O	1,612,000	15.00	50.00	260	550	1,100	5,500	
1901-S	72,664	1,150	2,950	6,000	8,250	17,000	50,000	
1902 777	12,196,967	3.00	15.00	55.00	110	395	1,400	1,850
1902-O	4,748,000	5.00	20.00	90.00	175	795	5,000	
1902-S	1,524,612	8.00	20.00	75.00	175	750	3,500	
1903 755	9,669,309	3.00	15.00	55.00	110	395	1,500	1,850
1903-O	3,500,000	5.00	20.00	75.00	175	750	5,200	

	Mintage	Good-4	Fine-12	EF-40	AU-55	MS-63	MS-65	Proof-65
1903-S	1,036,000	8.00	25.00	85.00	225	700	2,750	
1904 670	9,588,143	3.00	15.00	55.00	110	395	1,500	1,850
1904-O	2,456,000	5.00	25.00	150	325	1,100	2,950	
1905 727	4,967,523	3.00	15.00	55.00	110	395	1,500	1,850
1905-O	1,230,000	5.00	23.00	110	250	700	5,250	
1905-S	1,884,000	7.50	15.00	75.00	175	725	3,500	
1906 675	3,655,760	3.00	15.00	55.00	110	395	1,250	1,850
1906-D	3,280,000	3.00	17.50	60.00	140	550	3,250	
1906-O	2,056,000	3.00	20.00	70.00	170	550	1,750	
1907 575	7,192,000	3.00	15.00	55.00	110	395	1,300	1,850
1907-D	2,484,000	4.00	17.50	60.00	160	750	3,250	
1907-O	4,560,000	4.00	17.50	55.00	130	650	2,200	
1907-S	1,360,000	4.00	20.00	90.00	195	750	3,950	
1908 545	4,232,000	3.00	15.00	55.00	110	395	1,300	1,850
1908-D	5,788,000	3.00	15.00	60.00	110	425	2,000	
1908-O	6,244,000	4.00	15.00	60.00	110	395	1,500	
1908-S	784,000	8.00	40.00	210	375	750	5,250	
1909 650	9,268,000	3.00	15.00	55.00	110	395	1,200	1,850
1909-D	5,114,000	4.00	15.00	60.00	150	450	1,950	
1909-O	712,000	10.00	32.50	150	325	1,100	7,500	
1909-S	1,348,000	4.00	17.50	65.00	165	650	2,100	
1910 551	2,244,000	3.00	15.00	55.00	110	395	1,400	1,850
1910-D	1,500,000	4.00	17.50	70.00	170	800	2,350	
1911 543	3,720,000	3.00	15.00	55.00	110	395	1,400	1,850
1911-D	933,600	4.00	65.00	275	395	875	4,500	
1911-S	988,000	4.00	15.00	80.00	185	475	1,650	
1912 700	4,400,000	3.00	15.00	55.00	110	395	1,400	1,850
1912-S	708,000	3.00	19.00	75.00	195	700	2,175	
1913 622	484,000	3.00	50.00	330	525	1,100	2,200	1,850
1913-D	1,450,800	3.00	17.50	60.00	150	475	1,500	
1913-S	40,000	275	1,350	2,950	3,750	5,500	8,000	
1914 425	6,244,230	3.00	15.00	55.00	110	395	1,400	1,950
1914-D	3,046,000	3.00	15.00	55.00	110	395	2,000	
1914-S	264,000	45.00	110	325	535	1,150	3,000	
1915 450	3,480,000	3.00	15.00	55.00	110	395	1,200	1,900
1915-D	3,694,000	3.00	15.00	55.00	110	395	2,000	
1915-S	704,000	5.00	17.50	70.00	175	395	2,050	
1916	1,788,000	3.00	15.00	55.00	110	395	2,000	
1916-D	6,540,800	3.00	15.00	55.00	110	395	2,000	

Standing Liberty Portrait (1916–1930)

Liberty with Bare Breast (1916–1917)

	Mintage	Good-4	Fine-12	EF-40	AU-55	MS-63	MS-65
1916	52,000	$1,000	$1,600	$2,800	$4,000	$6,350	$15,000
1917 (Type 1)	8,740,000	12.00	22.00	57.00	115	270	800
1917-D (Type 1)	1,509,200	16.00	26.00	85.00	120	325	1,000
1917-S (Type 1)	1,952,000	15.00	18.00	125	200	340	1,275

Liberty Wearing Coat of Mail (1917–1930)

	Mintage	Good-4	Fine-12	EF-40	AU-55	MS-63	MS-65
1917 (Type 2)	13,880,000	$12.00	$17.00	$40.00	$60.00	$200	$450
1917-D (Type 2)	6,224,400	20.00	45.00	85.00	100	300	1,200
1917-S (Type 2)	5,552,000	25.00	35.00	70.00	90.00	250	1,350
1918	14,240,000	15.00	20.00	40.00	75.00	175	500
1918-D	7,380,000	30.00	40.00	80.00	140	280	1,500
1918-S combined total	11,072,000						
1918-S regular date		15.00	25.00	50.00	80.00	300	1,500
1918/17-S overdate		1,200	1,600	4,500	8,600	22,000	90,000
1919	11,324,000	25.00	50.00	75.00	90.00	200	475
1919-D	1,944,000	60.00	90.00	300	325	900	2,500
1919-S	1,836,000	60.00	90.00	350	450	1,200	3,250
1920	27,860,000	15.00	20.00	30.00	60.00	200	425
1920-D	3,586,400	35.00	50.00	90.00	150	500	2,000
1920-S	6,380,000	18.00	20.00	50.00	80.00	600	2,500

	Mintage	Good-4	Fine-12	EF-40	AU-55	MS-63	MS-65
1921	1,916,000	90.00	125	240	350	725	2,100
1923	9,716,000	15.00	25.00	35.00	60.00	200	375
1923-S	1,360,000	100	150	325	425	690	1,850
1924	10,920,000	15.00	20.00	35.00	65.00	175	475
1924-D	3,112,000	30.00	40.00	80.00	95.00	160	475
1924-S	2,860,000	16.00	20.00	75.00	185	725	2,000

Date Recessed (1925–1930)

	Mintage	Good-4	Fine-12	EF-40	AU-55	MS-63	MS-65
1925	12,280,000	$3.00	$5.00	$30.00	$50.00	$185	$450
1926	11,316,000	3.00	5.00	30.00	50.00	185	450
1926-D	1,716,000	6.00	12.00	40.00	75.00	175	450
1926-S	2,700,000	4.00	10.00	100	200	600	2,000
1927	11,912,000	3.00	5.00	30.00	50.00	185	450
1927-D	976,000	6.00	12.00	75.00	125	200	465
1927-S	396,000	10.00	50.00	950	3,000	5,250	9,000
1928	6,336,000	3.00	5.00	30.00	60.00	175	450
1928-D	1,627,600	5.00	7.00	35.00	75.00	185	450
1928-S	2,644,000	5.00	7.00	35.00	75.00	185	450
1929	11,140,000	5.00	7.00	35.00	75.00	185	450
1929-D	1,358,000	5.00	7.00	35.00	75.00	185	450
1929-S	1,764,000	5.00	7.00	35.00	75.00	185	450
1930	5,632,000	5.00	7.00	35.00	75.00	185	450
1930-S	1,556,000	5.00	7.00	35.00	75.00	185	450

Washington Portrait (1932–Present)

Silver Composition (1932–1964)

	Mintage	Good-4	Fine-12	EF-40	AU-55	MS-63	MS-65	Proof-65
1932	5,404,080	$3.00	$4.00	$8.00	$15.00	$35.00	$450	
1932-D	436,800	40.00	45.00	140	250	800	20,000	
1932-S	408,000	30.00	37.50	50.00	125	500	6,007	
1934 combined total	31,912,052							

QUARTER DOLLARS (1796–PRESENT)

	Mintage	Good-4	Fine-12	EF-40	AU-55	MS-63	MS-65	Proof-65
1934 regular date	—	—	2.00	3.50	8.00	25.00	80.00	
1934 doubled die		20.00	50.00	100	200	600	4,000	
1934-D	3,527,200	4.00	5.00	9.00	40.00	100	1,600	
1935	32,484,000	—	1.75	3.00	9.00	25.00	50.00	
1935-D	5,780,000	2.00	3.00	10.00	50.00	85.00	650	
1935-S	5,660,000	2.00	3.00	5.75	20.00	50.00	300	
1936 ...... 3,837	41,300,000		1.50	3.00	7.50	25.00	75.00	$1,100
1936-D	5,374,000	3.00	3.25	25.00	105	350	675	
1936-S	3,828,000	2.00	2.50	9.75	25.00	70.00	140	
1937 ...... 5,542	19,696,000	—	1.50	2.25	12.00	25.00	70.00	450
1937-D	7,189,600	2.00	2.25	3.75	15.00	40.00	90.00	
1937-S	1,652,000	3.00	4.00	20.00	50.00	80.00	250	
1938 ...... 8,045	9,472,000	2.00	2.25	12.00	30.00	50.00	150	200
1938-S	2,832,000	2.00	2.25	12.00	30.00	50.00	160	
1939 ...... 8,795	33,540,000	—	1.25	3.00	6.00	18.00	50.00	200
1939-D	7,092,000	2.00	2.25	7.00	12.00	30.00	80.00	
1939-S	2,628,000	3.00	4.00	9.00	30.00	60.00	125	
1940 ...... 11,246	35,704,000	—	1.00	1.50	5.00	15.00	50.00	90.00
1940-D	2,797,600	3.00	4.00	9.00	30.00	60.00	125	
1940-S	8,244,000	1.50	1.75	2.00	9.00	20.00	50.00	
1941 .... 15,287	79,032,000	—	—	—	4.00	7.00	20.00	90.00
1941-D	16,714,800	—	—	—	6.00	15.00	35.00	
1941-S	16,080,000	—	—	—	6.00	17.00	75.00	
1942 .... 21,123	102,096,000	—	—	—	4.00	8.00	25.00	95.00
1942-D	17,487,200	—	—	—	5.00	12.00	26.00	
1942-S	19,384,000	—	—	—	14.00	75.00	150	
1943	99,700,000	—	—	—	3.00	8.00	26.00	
1943-D	16,095,000	—	—	—	6.00	15.00	30.00	
1943-S combined total	21,700,000							
1943-S regular strike		—	—	—	12.00	28.00	35.00	
1943-S with doubled obverse ..		—	—	800	890	1,375	—	
1944	104,956,000	—	—	—	2.75	6.00	14.00	
1944-D	14,600,800	—	—	—	4.00	12.00	24.00	
1944-S	12,560,000	—	—	—	4.75	11.50	28.00	
1945	74,372,000	—	—	—	2.00	5.00	15.00	
1945-D	12,341,600	—	—	—	4.00	8.00	20.00	
1945-S	17,004,001	—	—	—	3.00	5.00	20.00	
1946	53,436,000	—	—	—	2.00	5.00	15.00	
1946-D	9,072,800	—	—	—	3.00	5.00	12.00	
1946-S	4,204,000	—	—	—	2.00	6.00	16.00	
1947	22,556,000	—	—	—	3.00	7.00	12.00	
1947-D	15,338,400	—	—	—	3.50	7.80	12.75	
1947-S	5,532,000	—	—	—	2.00	6.00	15.00	
1948	35,196,000	—	—	—	2.00	6.00	10.00	

QUARTER DOLLARS (1796–PRESENT)

	Mintage	Good-4	Fine-12	EF-40	AU-55	MS-63	MS-65	Proof-65
1948-D	16,766,800	—	—	—	2.00	6.00	12.00	
1948-S	15,960,000	—	—	—	3.00	8.00	16.00	
1949	9,312,000	—	—	—	6.00	20.00	30.00	
1949-D	10,068,400	—	—	—	4.00	9.00	20.00	
1950 ...... 51,386	24,920,126	—	—	—	3.00	8.00	12.00	95.00
1950-D combined total	21,075,600							
1950-D with regular mint mark		—	—	—	2.50	6.00	9.00	
1950-D/S		30.00	140	200	200	300	500	
1950-S combined total	10,284,004							
1950-S with regular mint mark .		—	—	—	3.00	7.50	12.50	
1950-S/D		—	30.00	150	300	475	600	
1951 ...... 57,500	43,448,102	1.00	1.10	1.50	2.00	5.25	6.50	50.00
1951-D	35,354,800	1.00	1.10	1.50	2.00	5.25	6.00	
1951-S	9,048,000	1.00	1.10	1.50	2.50	12.50	16.00	
1952 ...... 81,980	38,780,093	1.00	1.10	1.50	2.00	3.50	4.50	45.00
1952-D	49,795,200	1.00	1.10	1.50	2.00	3.75	4.75	
1952-S	13,707,800	1.00	1.10	1.50	4.00	9.00	11.00	
1953 ...... 128,800	18,536,120	1.00	1.10	1.50	2.00	3.75	4.50	40.00
1953-D	56,112,400	1.00	1.10	1.50	1.70	2.50	4.00	
1953-S	14,016,000	1.00	1.10	1.50	2.25	4.50	6.00	
1954 ...... 233,300	54,412,203	1.00	1.10	1.50	1.75	2.50	3.75	18.00
1954-D	42,305,500	1.00	1.10	1.50	1.75	2.50	3.75	
1954-S	11,834,722	1.00	1.10	1.50	1.75	2.50	3.75	
1955 ...... 378,200	18,180,181	1.00	1.10	1.50	1.75	2.50	3.75	15.00
1955-D	3,182,400	1.00	1.10	1.50	2.00	2.75	7.00	
1956 ...... 669,384	44,144,000	1.00	1.10	1.50	1.65	2.25	3.50	8.00
1956-D	32,334,500	1.00	1.10	1.50	1.75	2.25	3.50	
1957 ...... 1,247,952	46,532,000	1.00	1.10	1.50	1.65	2.25	4.00	6.50
1957-D	77,924,160	1.00	1.10	1.50	1.65	2.25	3.50	
1958 ...... 875,652	6,360,000	1.00	1.10	1.50	2.00	3.00	5.00	6.00
1958-D	78,124,900	1.00	1.10	1.50	1.65	2.25	3.50	
1959 ...... 1,149,291	24,384,000	1.00	1.10	1.50	1.65	2.25	3.50	4.00
1959-D	62,054,232	1.00	1.10	1.50	1.65	2.25	3.50	
1960 ...... 1,691,602	29,164,000	1.00	1.10	1.50	1.65	2.50	3.75	3.90
1960-D	63,000,324	1.00	1.10	1.50	1.65	2.25	3.50	
1961 ...... 3,028,244	37,036,000	1.00	1.10	1.50	1.65	2.25	3.50	3.80
1961-D	88,656,928	1.00	1.10	1.50	1.65	2.25	3.50	
1962 ...... 3,218,019	36,156,000	1.00	1.10	1.50	1.65	2.25	3.50	3.80
1962-D	127,554,756	1.00	1.10	1.50	1.65	2.25	3.50	
1963 ...... 3,075,645	74,316,000	1.00	1.10	1.50	1.65	2.25	3.50	3.80
1963-D	135,288,184	1.00	1.10	1.50	1.65	2.25	3.50	
1964 ...... 3,950,762	560,390,585	1.00	1.10	1.50	1.65	2.25	3.50	3.80
1964-D	704,135,528	1.00	1.10	1.50	1.65	2.25	3.50	

Copper-Nickel Clad Composition (1965–Present)

	Mintage	EF-40	MS-65	Proof-65
1965	1,819,717,540	—	$.60	
1966	821,101,500	—	.60	
1967	1,524,031,848	—	.75	
1968	220,731,500	—	.60	
1968-D	101,534,000	—	.75	
1968-S (proof only)	3,041,506	—	—	$1.20
1969	176,212,000	—	.75	
1969-D	114,372,000	—	.75	
1969-S (proof only)	2,934,631	—	—	1.20
1970	136,420,000	—	.40	
1970-D	417,341,364	—	.35	
1970-S (proof only)	2,632,810	—	—	1.90
1971	109,284,000	—	.45	
1971-D	258,634,428	—	.35	
1971-S (proof only)	3,220,733	—	—	1.20
1972	215,048,000	—	.35	
1972-D	311,067,732	—	.35	
1972-S (proof only)	3,260,996	—	—	—
1973	346,924,000	—	.35	
1973-D	232,977,400	—	.35	
1973-S (proof only)	2,760,339	—	—	1.35
1974	801,456,000	—	.35	
1974-D	353,160,300	—	.35	
1974 S (proof only)	2,612,568	—	—	1.50

Bicentennial Portrait (1975–1976)

	Mintage	EF-40	MS-65	Proof-65
1776–1976 copper-nickel clad	809,784,016	—	$.40	
1776–1976-D copper-nickel clad	860,118,839	—	.40	
1776–1976-S copper-nickel clad (proof only; includes coins from both 1975 and 1976 proof sets)	6,968,506	—	—	1.60
1776–1976-S silver clad *3,998,621*	4,908,319	—	1.50	2.25

Regular Design Returns (1977)

	Mintage	EF-40	MS-65	Proof-65
1977	468,556,000	—	$.35	
1977-D	256,524,978	—	.35	
1977-S (proof only)	3,251,152	—	—	$1.75
1978	521,452,000	—	.35	
1978-D	287,373,152	—	.35	
1978-S (proof only)	3,127,781	—	—	1.80
1979	515,708,000	—	.40	
1979-D	489,789,780	—	.40	
1979-S combined total (proof only)	3,677,175			
1979-S with clear S		—	—	14.50
1979-S with clogged S		—	—	1.65
1980-P	635,832,000	—	.40	
1980-D	518,327,487	—	.40	
1980-S (proof only)	3,554,806	—	—	1.80
1981-P	601,716,000	—	.40	
1981-D	575,722,833	—	.40	
1981-S (proof only)	4,063,083	—	—	1.60
1982-P	500,931,000	—	3.50	
1982-D	480,042,788	—	2.25	
1982-S (proof only)	3,857,479	—	—	1.65
1983-P	673,535,000	—	4.50	
1983-D	617,806,446	—	6.00	
1983-S (proof only)	3,279,126	—	—	1.75
1984-P	676,545,000	—	.60	
1984-D	546,483,064	—	1.25	
1984-S (proof only)	3,065,110	—	—	3.00
1985-P	775,818,962	—	.90	
1985-D	519,962,888	—	2.00	
1985-S (proof only)	3,362,821	—	—	1.80
1986-P	551,199,333	—	2.50	
1986-D	504,298,660	—	2.50	
1986-S (proof only)	3,010,497	—	—	5.50
1987-P	582,499,481	—	.40	
1987-D	655,594,696	—	.40	
1987-S (proof only)	3,792,233	—	—	1.65
1988-P	562,052,000	—	.40	
1988-D	596,810,688	—	.40	
1988-S (proof only)	3,262,948	—	—	3.00
1989-P	512,868,000	—	.40	
1989-D	896,535,597	—	.40	
1989-S (proof only)	3,215,728	—	—	2.40
1990-P	613,792,000	—	.40	

	Mintage	EF-40	MS-65	Proof-65
1990-D	927,638,181	—	.40	
1990-S (proof only)	3,299,559	—	—	4.00
1991-P	570,968,000	—	.40	
1991-D	630,966,693	—	.40	
1991-S (proof only)	2,867,787	—	—	3.00
1992-P	384,764,000	—	.40	
1992-D	389,777,107	—	.40	
1992-S (proof only)	4,176,544*	—	—	3.00
1993-P	639,276,000	—	.40	
1993-D	645,476,128	—	.40	
1993-S (proof only)	3,360,876*	—	—	3.00
1994-P	827,010,896	—	.40	
1994-D	881,245,006	—	.40	
1994-S (proof only)	3,212,792*	—	—	3.00
1995-P	1,005,377,352	—	.40	
1995-D	1,104,257,352	—	.40	
1995-S (proof only)	2,796,345*	—	—	3.00
1996-P	926,494,215	—	.40	
1996-D	908,322,215	—	.40	
1996-S (proof only)	2,925,305*	—	—	3.00
1997-P	595,740,000	—	.40	
1997-D	599,680,000	—	.40	
1997-S (proof only)	2,788,030*	—	—	3.00
1998-P	960,400,000	—	.40	
1998-D	907,000,000	—	.40	
1998-S (proof only)	2,086,507	—	—	3.00
1998-S (silver proof)	878,996	—	—	6.00

Includes 90% silver issue

50 State Quarter Dollars (1999–)

Delaware

	Mintage	EF-40	MS-65	Proof-65
1999-P	373,400,000	—	$3.00	—
1999-D	401,424,000	—	3.00	—
1999-S (copper-nickel proof)	(3,624,009)*	—	—	$4.00
1999-S (silver proof)	(798,780)	—	—	7.00

Pennsylvania

1999-P	349,000,000	—	3.00	—
1999-D	358,332,000	—	3.00	—
1999-S (copper-nickel proof)	(3,624,009)*	—	—	4.00
1999-S (silver proof)	(798,780)	—	—	7.00

New Jersey

	Mintage	EF-40	MS-65	Proof-65
1999-P	363,200,000	—	2.00	—
1999-D	299,028,000	—	3.00	—
1999-S (copper-nickel proof)	(3,624,009)*	—	—	4.00
1999-S (silver proof)	798,780	—	—	7.00

Georgia

1999-P	451,188,000	—	2.00	—
1999-D	488,744,000	—	2.00	—
1999-S (copper-nickel proof)	(3,624,009)*	—	—	4.00
1999-S (silver proof)	798,780	—	—	7.00

Connecticut

1999-P	688,744,000	—	1.50	—
1999-D	657,880,000	—	1.50	—
1999-S (copper-nickel proof)	(3,624,009)	—	—	4.00
1999-S (silver proof)	798,780	—	—	7.00

Massachusetts

2000-P	628,600,000	—	1.00	—
2000-D	535,184,000	—	1.00	—
2000-S (copper-nickel proof)	(3,992,800)*	—	—	4.00
2000-S (silver proof)	904,200*	—	—	7.00

Maryland

2000-P	678,200,000	—	1.00	—
2000-D	556,532,000	—	1.00	—
2000-S (copper-nickel proof)	(3,992,800)*	—	—	4.00
2000-S (silver proof)	904,200*	—	—	7.00

South Carolina

2000-P	742,576,000	—	1.00	—
2000-D	566,208,000	—	1.00	—
2000-S (copper-nickel proof)	(3,992,800)	—	—	4.00
2000-S (silver proof)	904,200*	—	—	7.00

New Hampshire

2000-P	673,040,000	—	1.00	—
2000-D	495,576,000	—	1.00	—
2000-S (copper-nickel proof)	(3,992,800)*	—	—	4.00
2000-S (silver proof)	904,200*	—	—	7.00

Virginia

2000-P	943,000,000	—	1.00	—
2000-D	651,616,000	—	1.00	—
2000-S (copper-nickel proof)	(3,992,800)*	—	—	4.00
2000-S (silver proof)	904,200*	—	—	7.00

New York

	Mintage	EF-40	MS-65	Proof-65
2001-P	655,400,000	—	1.00	—
2001-D	619,640,000	—	1.00	—
2001-S (copper-nickel proof)	(3,093,200)**	—	—	4.00
2001-S (silver proof)	891,400	—	—	7.00

North Carolina

2001-P	627,600,000	—	1.00	—
2001-D	427,876,000	—	1.00	—
2001-S (copper-nickel proof)	(3,093,200)**	—	—	4.00
2001-S (silver proof)	891,400	—	—	7.00

Rhode Island

2001-P	423,000,000	—	1.00	—
2001-D	447,100,000	—	1.00	—
2001-S (copper-nickel proof)	(3,093,200)**	—	—	4.00
2001-S (silver proof)	891,400	—	—	7.00

Vermont

2001-P	423,400,000	—	1.00	—
2001-D	459,404,000	—	1.00	—
2001-S (copper-nickel proof)	(3,093,200)**	—	—	4.00
2001-S (silver proof)	891,400	—	—	7.00

Kentucky

2001-P	353,000,000	—	1.00	—
2001-D	370,564,000	—	1.00	—
2001-S (copper-nickel proof)	(3,093,200)**	—	—	4.00
2001-S (silver proof)	891,400	—	—	7.00

*Through March 31, 2001
**Through May 28, 2002

Tennessee

2002-P	—	—	1.00	—
2002-D	—	—	1.00	—
2002-S (copper-nickel proof)	—	—	—	4.00
2002-S (silver proof)	—	—	—	7.00

Ohio

2002-P	—	—	1.00	—
2002-D	—	—	1.00	—
2002-S (copper-nickel proof)	—	—	—	4.00
2002-S (silver proof)	—	—	—	7.00

Louisiana

	Mintage	EF-40	MS-65	Proof-65
2002-P	—	—	1.00	—
2002-D	—	—	1.00	—
2002-S (copper-nickel proof)	—	—	—	4.00
2002-S (silver proof)	—	—	—	7.00

Indiana

2002-P	—	—	1.00	—
2002-D	—	—	1.00	—
2002-S (copper-nickel proof)	—	—	—	4.00
2002-S (silver proof)	—	—	—	7.00

Mississippi

2002-P	—	—	1.00	—
2002-D	—	—	1.00	—
2002-S (copper-nickel proof)	—	—	—	4.00
2002-S (silver proof)	—	—	—	7.00

Illinois

2003-P	—	—	1.00	—
2003-D	—	—	1.00	—
2003-S (copper-nickel proof)	—	—	—	4.00
2003-S (silver proof)	—	—	—	7.00

Alabama

2003-P	—	—	1.00	—
2003-D	—	—	1.00	—
2003-S (copper-nickel proof)	—	—	—	4.00
2003-S (silver proof)	—	—	—	7.00

Maine

2003-P	—	—	1.00	—
2003-D	—	—	1.00	—
2003-S (copper-nickel proof)	—	—	—	4.00
2003-S (silver proof)	—	—	—	7.00

Missouri

2003-P	—	—	1.00	—
2003-D	—	—	1.00	—
2003-S (copper-nickel proof)	—	—	—	4.00
2003-S (silver proof)	—	—	—	7.00

Arkansas

2003-P	—	—	1.00	—
2003-D	—	—	1.00	—
2003-S (copper-nickel proof)	—	—	—	4.00
2003-S (silver proof)	—	—	—	7.00

HALF DOLLARS (1794–PRESENT)

Flowing Hair Portrait (1794–1795)

	Mintage	Good-4	Fine-12	EF-40
1794	23,464	$950	$2,750	$8,500
1795 combined total	299,680			
1795 with 2 leaves under each wing		375	750	3,300
1795 with 3 leaves under each wing		1,050	2,400	7,000

Draped Bust Portrait with Small Eagle on Reverse (1796–1797)

	Mintage	Good-4	Fine-12	EF-40
1796 combined total	934			
1796 with 15 stars		$9,250	$15,000	$45,000
1796 with 16 stars		10,500	17,000	55,000
1797	2,984	10,300	16,000	48,000

Draped Bust Portrait with Heraldic Eagle on Reverse (1801–1807)

	Mintage	Good-4	Fine-12	EF-40
1801	30,289	$180	$500	$2,000
1802	29,890	165	420	1,800
1803 combined total	188,234			
1803 with small 3		120	290	900
1803 with large 3		100	205	800
1805 combined total	211,722			
1805 with regular date		95	200	850
1805/4 overdate		175	425	1,600
1806 combined total	839,576			
1806/5 overdate		110	220	750
1806 with horizontal 0 in date		150	450	1,500
1806 with knob-top 6 and no stem through eagle's claw	(4 known)	16,000	40,000	80,000
1806, all others		95.00	185	550
1807	301,076	95.00	185	550

Capped Bust Portrait, Lettered Edge (1807–1836)

	Mintage	Good-4	Fine-12	EF-40	AU-55	MS-63
1807 combined total	750,500					
1807 with small stars		$60.00	$190	$750	$2,600	$7,000
1807 with large stars		50.00	170	750	2,600	5,000
1807 with 50c. over 20c.		36.00	105	550	2,100	5,500
1808 combined total	1,368,600					
1808 regular date		30.00	60.00	210	600	1,600
1808/7 overdate		34.00	80.00	285	900	3,250
1809	1,405,810	30.00	60.00	200	900	3,400
1810	1,276,276	28.00	45.00	175	550	2,000
1811 combined total	1,203,644					
1811 with small 8		27.00	46.00	150	375	1,900
1811 with large 8		27.00	46.00	175	425	2,000
1811/10 overdate		30.00	70.00	280	600	—
1812 combined total	1,628,059					
1812 regular date		26.00	44.00	150	450	1,900
1812/11 with small 8		35.00	80.00	300	1,000	3,000
1812/11 with large 8		1,500	3,000	7,500	—	—
1813 combined total	1,241,903					
1813 regular date		26.00	44.00	150	450	1,400
1813 with 50c. over UNI		30.00	70.00	250	1,100	—
1814 combined total	1,039,075					
1814 regular date		25.00	42.00	175	600	1,400
1814/3 overdate		42.00	70.00	340	850	—
1815/2 overdate	47,150	600	1,100	2,600	6,500	—
1817 combined total	1,215,567					
1817 regular date		25.00	42.00	150	450	1,400
1817/3 overdate		70.00	160	510	1,700	—
1817/4 overdate		25,000	50,000	—	—	—
1818 combined total	1,960,322					
1818 regular date		25.00	42.00	125	400	1,300
1818/7 overdate		28.00	44.00	180	550	—
1819 combined total	2,208,000					

	Mintage	Good-4	Fine-12	EF-40	AU-55	MS-63
1819 regular date		23.00	36.00	125	375	1,300
1819/8 overdate		28.00	55.00	140	450	1,300
1820	751,122	28.00	50.00	210	600	2,000
1821	1,305,797	25.00	42.00	125	375	1,300
1822 combined total	1,559,573					
1822 regular date		25.00	38.00	125	375	1,300
1822/1 overdate		45.00	70.00	275	900	2,850
1823 combined total	1,694,200					
1823 regular date		23.00	35.00	120	375	1,300
1823 with broken 3		40.00	70.00	300	800	2,500
1824 combined total	3,504,954					
1824 regular date		23.00	35.00	100	350	1,300
1824/1 overdate		26.00	42.00	160	450	1,800
1824/4 overdate		27.00	48.00	160	1,400	1,500
1825	2,943,166	23.00	30.00	85.00	300	1,200
1826	4,004,180	23.00	30.00	85.00	300	1,200
1827 combined total	5,493,400					
1827 with square-base 2		23.00	30.00	85.00	300	1,200
1827 with curl-base 2		26.00	38.00	115	325	1,300
1827/6 overdate		27.00	40.00	150	450	1,675
1828 combined total	3,075,200					
1828 with small 8's		23.00	30.00	75.00	300	1,200
1828 with large 8's		25.00	32.00	90.00	375	1,350
1828, all others		23.00	30.00	75.00	300	1,200
1829 combined total	3,712,156					
1829 regular date		23.00	30.00	75.00	300	1,200
1829/7 overdate		26.00	42.00	110	400	1,800
1830 combined total	4,764,800					
1830 with small O		23.00	30.00	75.00	300	1,200
1830 with large O		23.00	30.00	75.00	300	1,200
1831	5,873,660	23.00	30.00	75.00	300	1,200
1832 combined total	4,797,000					
1832 with regular letters on reverse		25.00	35.00	80.00	250	1,200
1832 with large letters		25.00	35.00	80.00	250	1,200
1833	5,206,000	25.00	35.00	80.00	200	1,200
1834	6,412,004	25.00	35.00	80.00	225	1,200
1835	5,352,006	25.00	35.00	80.00	200	1,200
1836 combined total	6,545,000					
1836 with regular 50c.		25.00	35.00	80.00	200	1,200
1836 with 50c. over 00 c.		30.00	50.00	150	625	2,175

Capped Bust Portrait, Reeded Edge (1836–1839)
"50 CENTS" on Reverse (1836–1837)

	Mintage	Good-4	Fine-12	EF-40	AU-55	MS-65
1836	1,200	$700	$975	$1,800	$3,800	$9,500
1837	3,629,820	30.00	50.00	150	350	1,750

"HALF DOL." on Reverse (1838–1839)

	Mintage	Good-4	Fine-12	EF-40	AU-55	MS-65
1838	3,546,000	$35.00	$45.00	$200	$300	$1,700
1838-O (proof only)	20	—	—	—	—	—
1839	1,392,976	35.00	45.00	200	300	1,700
1839-O	178,976	125	225	575	—	5,500

Seated Liberty Portrait (1839–1891)

	Mintage	Good-4	Fine-12	EF-40	AU-55	MS-63	MS-65
1839 combined total	1,972,400						
1839 with no drapery hanging from elbow		$40.00	$100	$675	$1,200	$5,200	$92,500
1839 with drapery from elbow		25.00	45.00	100	250	1,500	—
1840 with small letters	1,435,008	30.00	45.00	100	300	1,000	—
1840 with medium letters (struck at New Orleans without mint mark)		125	240	350	790	4,600	—
1840-O	855,100	25.00	45.00	125	250	1,400	—
1841	310,000	30.00	75.00	210	325	2,200	—
1841-O	401,000	20.00	35.00	110	200	1,175	—
1842 combined total	2,012,764						
1842 small date		25.00	75.00	120	190	1,100	—
1842 medium date		20.00	45.00	110	250	800	—
1842-O combined total	754,000						
1842-O small date		600	900	1,150	3,800	6,000	—
1842-O large date		25.00	35.00	110	240	—	—
1843	3,844,000	22.00	35.00	75.00	150	775	—
1843-O	2,268,000	22.00	35.00	80.00	175	1,150	—
1844	1,766,000	22.00	35.00	75.00	160	775	—
1844-O combined total	2,005,000						
1844-O regular date		22.00	32.00	75.00	140	—	—
1844-O with double date			800	2,400	4,000	—	—
1845	589,000	30.00	55.00	175	300	1,600	—
1845-O combined total	2,094,000						

	Mintage	Good-4	Fine-12	EF-40	AU-55	MS-63	MS-65
1845-O with drapery		20.00	35.00	75.00	180	775	—
1845-O with no drapery		30.00	65.00	175	350	—	—
1846 combined total	2,210,000						
1846 small date		20.00	35.00	85.00	150	1,400	—
1846 tall date		20.00	35.00	125	200	2,000	—
1846/horizontal 6 overdate		150	225	400	1,000	—	—
1846-O combined total	2,304,000						
1846-O medium date		25.00	35.00	100	300	—	—
1846-O tall date		150	300	750	1,500	—	—
1847 combined total	1,156,000						
1847 regular date		20.00	35.00	80.00	150	775	—
1847/6 overdate		1,200	3,000	4,500	9,000	—	—
1847-O	2,584,000	20.00	35.00	80.00	150	1,000	—
1848	580,000	30.00	65.00	200	450	1,600	—
1848-O	3,180,000	20.00	35.00	75.00	225	1,600	—
1849	1,252,000	25.00	50.00	150	300	12,00	—
1849-O	2,310,000	25.00	35.00	100	225	2,000	—
1850	227,000	175	300	550	800	—	—
1850-O	2,456,000	25.00	35.00	100	225	775	4,500
1851	200,750	190	300	450	525	2,100	—
1851-O	402,000	25.00	50.00	140	200	775	4,500
1852	77,130	250	400	625	700	1,600	—
1852-O	144,000	40.00	140	300	600	2,200	9,750
1853-O without arrows or rays	(3 known)	170,000	—	—	—	—	—

With Arrows Beside the Date, Rays Around the Eagle (1853)

	Mintage	Good-4	Fine-12	EF-40	AU-55	MS-63	MS-65	Proof-65
1853	3,532,708	$20.00	$40.00	$200	$600	$2,500	$18,500	—
1853-O	1,328,000	25.00	50.00	250	650	5,000	—	—

With Arrows Beside the Date, No Rays Around the Eagle (1854–1855)

	Mintage	Good-4	Fine-12	EF-40	AU-55	MS-63	MS-65	Proof-65
1854	2,982,000	$20.00	$40.00	$125	$250	$1,800	$7,500	—
1854-O	1,328,000	20.00	40.00	125	250	1,800	7,500	
1855 combined total	759,500							
1855 regular date		25.00	40.00	110	250	2,250	9,250	
1855/4 overdate		60.00	160	350	500	—	—	—
1855-O	3,688,000	20.00	35.00	120	240	1,600	7,500	
1855-S	129,950	390	600	2,500	3,500	—	—	

Arrows Removed (1856)

	Mintage	Good-4	Fine-12	EF-40	AU-55	MS-63	MS-65	Proof-65
1856	938,000	$20.00	$35.00	$80.00	$150	$975	$6,800	—
1856-O	2,658,000	20.00	35.00	80.00	150	975	—	
1856-S	211,000	45.00	85.00	325	600	—	—	
1857	1,988,000	20.00	40.00	80.00	140	950	5,800	$14,500
1857-O	818,000	20.00	40.00	75.00	160	1,650	—	
1857-S	158,000	45.00	110	350	450	—	—	
1858	4,226,000	20.00	40.00	80.00	150	1,200	6,000	12,500
1858-O	7,294,000	20.00	40.00	80.00	160	1,450	—	
1858-S	476,000	20.00	45.00	200	350	1,650	—	
1859 .... *800*	747,200	30.00	55.00	85.00	170	1,100	5,000	5,250
1859-O	2,834,000	20.00	40.00	80.00	150	1,100	5,000	
1859-S	566,000	20.00	50.00	150	275	1,400	—	
1860 .... *1,000*	302,700	20.00	40.00	75.00	300	900	5,000	5,250
1860-O	1,290,000	18.00	35.00	80.00	150	1,025	5,000	
1860-S	472,000	20.00	40.00	85.00	165	2,000	—	
1861 .... *1,000*	2,887,400	18.00	35.00	85.00	145	925	$5,000	5,250
1861-O	2,532,633	18.00	35.00	85.00	145	925	5,000	
1861-S	939,500	19.00	40.00	90.00	165	1,000	8,250	

	Mintage	Good-4	Fine-12	EF-40	AU-55	MS-63	MS-65	Proof-65
1862 . . . . 550	253,000	30.00	50.00	140	250	1,075	5,000	5,250
1862-S	1,352,000	18.00	35.00	80.00	150	1,000	—	
1863 . . . . 460	503,200	20.00	40.00	90.00	200	1,000	5,000	5,300
1863-S	916,000	18.00	35.00	80.00	150	1,000	—	
1864 . . . . 470	379,100	21.00	45.00	150	200	1,000	5,000	5,400
1864-S	658,000	20.00	30.00	80.00	150	1,175	—	
1865 . . . . 500	511,400	20.00	50.00	150	225	885	5,000	5,250
1865-S	675,000	15.00	35.00	80.00	175	1,175	—	
1866	(unique)	—	—	—	—	—	215,000	

With Motto Above the Eagle (1866–1891)

	Mintage	Good-4	Fine-12	EF-40	AU-55	MS-63	MS-65	Proof-65
1866 . . . . 725	744,900	$20.00	$45.00	$100	$190	$1,000	$4,000	$4,000
1866-S	994,000	20.00	35.00	75.00	150	1,250	—	
1867 . . . . 625	449,300	20.00	55.00	140	250	950	4,000	4,200
1867-S	1,196,000	20.00	35.00	75.00	135	1,500	—	
1868 . . . . 600	417,600	35.00	70.00	175	225	1,100	—	3,900
1868-S	1,160,000	20.00	40.00	125	200	1,100	—	
1869 . . . . 600	795,300	25.00	42.00	130	175	1,050	3,600	3,500
1869-S	656,000	18.00	35.00	150	190	1,200	—	
1870 . . . . 1,000	633,900	20.00	35.00	140	175	950	—	3,200
1870-CC	54,617	475	1,175	4,000	6,250	—	—	
1870-S	1,004,000	18.00	40.00	90.00	225	1,200	—	
1871 . . . . 960	1,203,600	20.00	35.00	80.00	140	975	3,800	3,200
1871-CC	153,950	140	210	750	1,250	—	—	
1871-S	2,178,000	16.00	35.00	80.00	190	950	4,600	
1872 . . . . 950	880,600	16.00	35.00	80.00	190	950	4,000	3,100
1872-CC	257,000	50.00	135	340	900	—	—	
1872-S	580,000	30.00	60.00	165	375	1,200	—	
1873 closed 3 . . . . 600	587,000	25.00	65.00	125	200	950	4,000	3,100
1873 open 3	214,200	2,250	3,500	6,000	7,800	—	—	
1873-CC	122,500	110	225	650	1,900	—	—	

With Arrows Beside the Date (1873–1874)

	Mintage	Good-4	Fine-12	EF-40	AU-55	MS-63	MS-65	Proof-65
1873 . . . . 540	1,815,150	$20.00	$35.00	$200	$475	$2,000	$21,000	$10,000
1873-CC	214,560	110	250	1,000	2,500	—	—	
1873-S	228,000	40.00	100	400	675	—	—	
1874 . . . . 700	2,359,600	20.00	30.00	175	450	2,000	21,000	10,500
1874-CC	59,000	210	525	1,650	3,000	—	—	
1874-S	394,000	32.00	60.00	375	500	3,250	—	

Arrows Removed (1875), with Motto

	Mintage	Good-4	Fine-12	EF-40	AU-55	MS-63	MS-65	Proof-65
1875 . . . . 700	6,026,800	$20.00	$35.00	$75.00	$150	$750	$3,500	$3,300
1875-CC	1,008,000	21.00	50.00	125	225	1,100		
1875-S	3,200,000	20.00	45.00	100	125	750	3,300	
1876 . . . . 1,150	8,418,000	20.00	35.00	75.00	150	750	2,800	3,300
1876-CC	1,956,000	20.00	38.00	90.00	190	900	3,000	
1876-S	4,528,000	20.00	35.00	75.00	175	750	3,600	
1877 . . . . 510	8,304,000	20.00	35.00	80.00	175	750	2,500	3,800
1877-CC	1,420,000	22.00	45.00	110	190	875	3,000	
1877-S	5,356,000	20.00	35.00	100	130	775	3,500	3,500
1878 . . . . 800	1,377,600	22.00	45.00	110	135	800	3,900	5,000

	Mintage	Good-4	Fine-12	EF-40	AU-55	MS-63	MS-65	Proof-65
1878-CC	62,000	275	360	1,250	2,900	7,800	—	
1878-S	12,000	6,500	7,000	12,000	15,000	50,000	—	
1879 1,100	4,800	200	300	400	480	900	2,500	3,300
1880 1,355	8,400	200	250	300	380	900	3,000	3,300
1881 975	10,000	190	240	300	380	900	3,000	3,300
1882 1,100	4,400	200	340	375	410	900	3,000	3,300
1883 1,039	8,000	190	300	350	400	900	3,000	3,300
1884 875	4,400	210	360	425	485	900	3,000	3,300
1885 930	5,200	200	240	325	410	900	3,000	3,300
1886 . . . . ;. . . 886	5,000	210	310	360	490	900	3,000	3,300
1887 710	5,000	225	400	500	575	900	3,000	3,300
1888 832	12,001	190	250	300	400	900	3,000	3,300
1889 711	12,000	190	250	325	360	900	3,000	3,300
1890 590	12,000	200	225	335	400	900	3,000	3,300
1891 600	200,000	60.00	100	135	245	900	3,000	3,300

Barber or Liberty Head Portrait (1892–1915)

	Mintage	Good-4	Fine-12	EF-40	AU-55	MS-63	MS-65	Proof-65
1892 1,245	934,000	$12.50	$35.00	$170	$275	$895	$2,500	$3,300
1892-O	390,000	70.00	150	390	475	1,150	5,500	
1892-S	1,029,028	95.00	165	375	550	1,550	5,000	
1893 792	1,826,000	10.00	35.00	150	300	850	3,250	3,300
1893-O	1,389,000	15.00	45.00	250	325	1,150	7,600	
1893-S	740,000	50.00	110	325	450	1,800	7,250	
1894 972	1,148,000	10.00	45.00	170	295	925	3,750	3,200
1894-O	2,138,000	9.00	43.00	240	325	1,100	5,000	
1894-S	4,048,690	9.00	40.00	185	300	925	11,000	
1895 880	1,834,338	8.00	35.00	170	285	950	2,800	3,200
1895-O	1,766,000	8.00	40.00	210	325	1,100	5,000	
1895-S	1,108,086	15.00	50.00	235	325	950	6,800	
1896 762	950,000	10.00	35.00	175	275	895	4,500	3,200
1896-O	924,000	15.00	70.00	325	600	2,100	9,500	
1896-S	1,140,948	50.00	90.00	340	525	1,950	8,500	

	Mintage	Good-4	Fine-12	EF-40	AU-55	MS-63	MS-65	Proof-65
1897 . . . . 731	2,480,000	5.00	25.00	110	275	850	3,250	3,200
1897-O	632,000	40.00	225	725	950	2,100	4,000	
1897-S	933,900	70.00	225	600	900	2,050	7,500	
1898 . . . . 735	2,956,000	5.00	25.00	110	275	850	3,500	3,200
1898-O	874,000	15.00	55.00	285	425	1,900	5,500	
1898-S	2,358,550	10.00	30.00	190	325	1,450	7,500	
1899 . . . . 846	5,538,000	5.00	25.00	110	275	850	3,250	3,200
1899-O	1,724,000	10.00	40.00	210	310	1,250	5,500	
1899-S	1,686,411	10.00	35.00	175	300	1,250	5,750	
1900 . . . . 912	4,762,000	5.00	25.00	110	275	850	3,250	3,200
1900-O	2,744,000	10.00	35.00	225	325	1,425	9,000	
1900-S	2,560,322	10.00	30.00	175	300	1,250	7,000	
1901 . . . . 813	4,268,000	5.00	25.00	110	275	850	3,250	3,200
1901-O	1,124,000	10.00	40.00	250	425	1,750	10,000	
1901-S	847,044	15.00	80.00	500	825	2,500	10,000	
1902 . . . . 777	4,922,000	5.00	25.00	110	275	850	3,250	3,200
1902-O	2,526,000	8.00	35.00	170	325	1,250	7,500	
1902-S	1,460,670	8.00	40.00	180	350	1,400	4,900	
1903 . . . . 755	2,278,000	8.00	28.00	135	275	1,050	4,500	3,200
1903-O	2,100,000	8.00	35.00	170	325	950	5,500	
1903-S	1,920,772	7.50	35.00	200	330	1,250	6,500	
1904 . . . . 670	2,992,000	5.00	25.00	110	275	850	3,250	3,200
1904-O	1,117,000	10.00	45.00	275	450	1,350	7,500	
1904-S	553,038	12.50	75.00	450	750	2,500	9,500	
1905 . . . . 727	662,000	10.00	40.00	175	350	1,150	4,950	3,200
1905-O	505,000	10.00	25.00	200	350	1,150	5,000	
1905-S	2,494,000	7.50	35.00	175	325	1,450	6,500	
1906 . . . . 675	2,638,000	5.00	25.00	110	275	850	3,250	3,200
1906-D	4,028,000	6.00	25.00	135	275	900	3,950	
1906-O	2,446,000	6.00	30.00	150	280	950	5,500	
1906-S	1,740,154	6.00	35.00	175	325	1,000	4,500	
1907 . . . . 575	2,598,000	5.00	25.00	110	275	850	2,500	3,200
1907-D	3,856,000	5.00	25.00	110	275	850	2,500	
1907-O	3,946,600	5.00	25.00	110	275	850	4,000	
1907-S	1,250,000	6.00	35.00	250	350	2,000	10,000	
1908 . . . . 545	1,354,000	5.00	25.00	110	275	850	3,750	3,200
1908-D	3,280,000	5.00	25.00	110	275	850	2,500	
1908-O	5,360,000	5.00	25.00	110	275	850	2,500	
1908-S	1,644,828	6.00	35.00	175	300	1,300	6,000	
1909 . . . . 650	2,368,000	5.00	25.00	110	275	850	2,500	3,200
1909-O	925,400	10.00	35.00	250	425	1,600	6,000	
1909-S	1,764,000	6.00	25.00	165	300	1,000	3,950	
1910 . . . . 551	418,000	10.00	50.00	250	350	950	4,250	3,200
1910-S	1,948,000	6.00	26.00	160	290	1,200	4,500	
1911 . . . . 543	1,406,000	5.00	25.00	110	275	850	2,500	3,200
1911-D	695,080	6.00	30.00	150	300	850	2,500	

	Mintage	Good-4	Fine-12	EF-40	AU-55	MS-63	MS-65	Proof-65
1911-S	1,272,000	6.00	30.00	150	300	1,000	6,000	
1912 .... *700*	1,550,000	5.00	25.00	130	300	850	3,800	3,200
1912-D	2,300,800	6.00	25.00	120	275	850	3,000	
1912-S	1,370,000	6.00	27.50	150	290	1,000	5,000	
1913 .... *627*	188,000	14.00	75.00	300	625	1,250	3,500	3,500
1913-D	534,800	6.00	35.00	170	300	900	4,500	
1913-S	604,000	6.00	35.00	170	350	1,100	4,700	
1914 .... *380*	124,230	18.00	150	425	700	1,500	8,000	3,600
1914-S	992,000	6.00	30.00	170	350	1,100	4,000	
1915 .... *450*	138,000	15.00	80.00	325	650	1,700	5,500	3,500
1915-D	1,170,400	5.00	25.00	110	275	850	2,500	
1915-S	1,604,000	5.00	25.00	110	275	850	2,500	

Walking Liberty Portrait (1916–1947)

	Mintage	Good-4	Fine-12	EF-40	AU-55	MS-63	MS-65	Proof-65
1916	608,080	$23.00	$52.50	$105	$190	$300	$1,700	
1916-D	1,014,400	17.50	29.00	80.00	150	330	2,000	
1916-S	508,000	44.00	95.00	400	580	1,050	5,600	
1917	12,292,000	6.50	8.00	30.00	60.00	140	800	
1917-D with D on obverse	765,400	8.00	28.00	110	270	750	6,000	
1917-D with D on reverse	1,940,000	6.00	17.50	115	350	1,400	14,500	
1917-S with S on obverse	952,000	9.00	30.00	430	600	3,000	17,000	
1917-S with S on reverse	5,554,000	4.00	11.00	40.00	140	800	11,000	
1918	6,634,000	4.00	15.00	100	420	650	3,500	
1918-D	3,853,040	5.00	18.00	120	350	1,250	22,000	
1918-S	10,282,000	4.00	12.50	50.00	140	1,050	18,000	
1919	962,000	9.00	28.00	300	625	1,825	5,000	
1919-D	1,165,000	7.00	29.00	370	1,100	5,000	95,000	
1919-S	1,552,000	8.00	24.00	500	1,000	4,200	15,000	
1920	6,372,000	5.00	11.00	50.00	115	475	6,000	
1920-D	1,551,000	6.00	24.00	275	625	2,200	10,000	
1920-S	4,624,000	7.00	15.00	140	400	1,250	10,000	
1921	246,000	40.00	170	1,200	1,200	2,800	11,000	
1921-D	208,000	60.00	200	1,700	1,700	3,500	11,000	

	Mintage	Good-4	Fine-12	EF-40	AU-55	MS-63	MS-65	Proof-65
1921-S	548,000	15.00	65.00	3,400	4,600	12,500	58,500	
1923-S	2,178,000	6.00	17.50	170	625	2,250	10,500	
1927-S	2,392,000	3.00	9.00	65.00	375	1,200	8,000	
1928-S	1,940,000	4.00	10.50	85.00	325	1,500	7,250	
1929-D	1,001,200	4.00	8.50	55.00	165	400	1,700	
1929-S	1,902,000	3.00	8.50	50.00	135	400	1,925	
1933-S	1,786,000	4.00	8.00	45.00	225	750	2,850	
1934	6,964,000	2.25	2.75	10.00	26.00	165	400	
1934-D	2,361,400	3.50	4.75	23.00	58.00	450	850	
1934-S	3,652,000	2.75	3.50	22.50	125	450	2,600	
1935	9,162,000	2.25	2.75	6.50	23.00	50.00	300	
1935-D	3,003,800	3.50	3.75	23.00	55.00	225	1,200	
1935-S	3,854,000	3.00	3.25	22.50	75.00	210	1,600	
1936 3,901	12,614,000	2.25	3.50	6.50	24.00	50.00	150	$2,950
1936-D	4,252,400	2.75	5.00	15.00	46.00	90.00	300	
1936-S	3,884,000	2.75	5.50	15.50	52.00	130	450	
1937 5,728	9,522,000	2.25	3.75	6.75	22.50	45.00	175	800
1937-D	1,676,000	4.75	7.00	29.00	72.50	150	500	
1937-S	2,090,000	4.75	5.00	16.00	58.00	130	360	
1938 8,152	4,110,000	2.75	5.50	12.00	33.00	70.00	300	700
1938-D	491,600	16.50	17.00	35.00	90.00	375	900	
1939 8,808	6,812,000	2.25	4.75	9.00	40.00	40.00	120	690
1939-D	4,267,800	2.75	4.75	9.25	23.00	40.00	120	
1939-S	2,552,000	5.50	4.00	7.00	25.00	95.00	170	
1940 11,279	9,156,000	2.25	3.75	6.00	15.00	30.00	100	600
1940-S	4,550,000	2.50	3.00	10.00	24.00	32.50	350	
1941 15,412	24,192,000	2.25	3.75	5.50	15.00	30.00	90.00	600
1941-D	11,248,400	2.50	3.75	5.75	25.00	35.00	100	
1941-S	8,098,000	2.75	5.00	8.00	43.00	85.00	1,150	
1942 21,120	47,818,000	2.25	2.75	6.00	15.00	35.00	80.00	500
1942-D combined total	10,973,800							
1942-D regular mint mark		2.50	4.10	7.50	20.00	50.00	200	
1942-D/S		25.00	45.00	325	800	1,600	3,000	
1942-S	12,708,000	2.50	4.10	6.75	25.00	40.00	500	
1943	53,190,000	2.25	2.75	6.25	15.00	35.00	85.00	
1943-D	11,346,000	2.50	4.10	6.25	24.00	45.00	120	
1943-S	13,450,000	2.50	4.45	6.50	25.00	40.00	400	
1944	28,206,000	2.25	2.75	6.00	15.00	30.00	85.00	
1944-D	9,769,000	2.50	4.10	6.25	20.00	35.00	100	
1944-S	8,904,000	2.50	4.10	6.25	24.00	35.00	400	
1945	31,502,000	2.25	2.75	6.00	15.00	35.00	85.00	
1945-D	9,966,800	2.75	4.00	6.25	22.50	35.00	95.00	
1945-S	10,156,000	2.75	4.10	6.25	24.00	35.00	145	
1946	12,118,000	2.25	2.75	6.25	18.00	35.00	150	
1946-D	2,151,000	2.75	6.25	12.50	29.00	35.00	85.00	

	Mintage	Good-4	Fine-12	EF-40	AU-55	MS-63	MS-65	Proof-65
1946-S	3,724,000	2.75	3.00	6.25	23.00	35.00	125	
1947	4,094,000	2.75	3.20	7.50	24.00	35.00	90.00	
1947-D	3,900,600	2.75	3.20	7.50	23.00	35.00	90.00	

Franklin Portrait (1948–1963)

	Mintage	Fine-12	EF-40	AU-55	MS-60	MS-63	MS-65	Proof-65
1948	3,006,814	$3.00	$5.00	$4.00	$15.00	$18.00	$55.00	
1948-D	4,028,600	2.00	3.50	4.00	7.50	12.50	100	
1949	5,614,000	2.00	4.00	9.00	32.50	35.00	60.00	
1949-D	4,120,600	2.00	6.00	11.00	32.50	33.00	600	
1949-S	3,744,000	2.00	9.00	18.00	41.00	50.00	125	
1950 51,386	7,742,123	2.00	4.00	17.00	34.00	40.00	70.00	215
1950-D	8,031,600	2.00	4.00	12.50	21.00	24.00	320	
1951 7,500	16,802,102	1.85	3.25	8.00	10.00	16.00	55.00	150
1951-D	9,475,200	1.85	5.25	15.00	31.00	35.00	110	
1951-S	13,696,000	1.85	4.00	8.00	20.00	30.00	45.00	
1952 81,980	21,192,093	1.85	4.00	5.00	6.50	12.50	40.00	75.00
1952-D	25,395,600	1.85	3.50	4.00	6.50	12.50	95.00	
1952-S	5,526,000	1.85	3.25	12.50	28.00	36.00	35.00	
1953 128,800	2,668,120	4.00	6.00	9.00	18.00	23.00	110	50.00
1953-D	20,900,400	1.85	4.00	5.00	6.25	12.50	110	
1953-S	4,148,000	1.85	3.25	8.00	12.00	16.00	50.00	
1954 233,300	13,188,203	1.85	3.25	3.50	4.50	10.00	70	35.00
1954-D	25,445,580	1.85	3.25	3.50	4.50	10.00	110	
1954-S	4,993,400	1.85	3.25	3.50	5.00	11.00	32.00	
1955 378,200	2,498,181	4.00	4.50	5.00	6.00	11.00	28.00	30.00
1956 669,384	4,032,000	1.85	3.50	4.00	5.25	9.00	28.00	11.00
1957 1,247,952	5,114,000	1.85	3.50	4.50	5.75	11.00	28.00	10.00
1957-D	19,966,850	1.65	1.70	1.80	4.50	10.00	28.00	
1958 875,652	4,042,000	1.65	1.70	1.75	4.00	10.00	28.00	10.00
1958-D	23,962,412	1.65	1.70	1.75	3.00	8.00	28.00	
1959 1,149,291	6,200,000	1.65	1.70	1.75	3.75	9.00	50.00	10.00
1959-D	13,053,750	1.65	1.70	1.75	3.75	7.50	50.00	

	Mintage	Fine-12	EF-40	AU-55	MS-60	MS-63	MS-65	Proof-65
1960 . . . . *1,691,602*	6,024,000	2.00	3.00	3.25	4.00	6.25	100	10.00
1960-D	18,215,812	2.00	3.00	3.25	4.00	6.00	530	
1961 . . . . *3,028,244*	8,290,000	2.00	3.00	3.25	4.00	6.00	150	11.00
1961-D	20,276,442	2.00	3.00	3.25	4.00	6.00	370	
1962 . . . . *3,218,019*	9,714,000	2.00	3.00	3.25	4.00	6.00	145	10.00
1962-D	35,473,281	2.00	3.00	3.25	4.00	5.00	280	
1963 . . . . *3,075,645*	22,164,000	2.00	3.00	3.25	3.50	5.00	70.00	10.00
1963-D	67,069,292	2.00	3.00	3.25	3.50	5.00	70.00	

Kennedy Portrait (1964–Present)

Silver Composition (1964)

	Mintage	EF-40	MS-65	Proof-65
1964 . . . . *3,950,762*	273,304,004	$2.50	$8.00	$7.00
1964-D	156,205,446	2.50	8.00	

Silver Clad Composition (1965–1970)

	Mintage	EF-40	MS-65	Proof-65
1965	65,879,366	$1.25	$5.00	
1966	108,984,932	1.25	5.00	
1967	295,046,978	1.25	7.00	
1968-D	246,951,930	1.25	5.00	
1968-S (proof only)	*3,041,506*	—	—	$3.00
1969-D	129,881,800	1.25	4.00	
1969-S (proof only)	*2,934,631*	—	—	3.00
1970-D	2,150,000	10.00	36.00	
1970-S (proof only)	*2,632,810*	—	—	3.00

Copper-Nickel Clad Composition (1971–Present)

	Mintage	EF-40	MS-65	Proof-65
1971	155,164,000	—	$3.50	
1971-D	302,097,424	—	2.00	
1971-S (proof only)	3,220,733	—	—	$3.00
1972	153,180,000	—	3.00	
1972-D	141,890,000	—	3.00	
1972-S (proof only)	3,260,996	—	—	3.00
1973	64,964,000	—	3.00	
1973-D	83,171,400	—	3.00	
1973-S (proof only)	2,760,339	—	—	3.00
1974	201,596,000	—	1.75	
1974-D	79,066,300	—	.75	
1974-S (proof only)	2,612,568	—	—	2.00

Bicentennial Portrait (1975–1976)

	Mintage	EF-40	MS-65	Proof-65
1776–1976 copper-nickel clad	234,308,000		$.75	
1776–1976-D copper-nickel clad	287,565,248		.75	
1776–1976-S copper-nickel clad (proof only; includes coins from both 1975 and 1976 proof sets)	6,995,180	—	—	$2.00
1776–1976-S silver clad .... 3,998,621 ...	4,908,319	—	2.50	3.50

Regular Design Returns (1977–Present)

	Mintage	EF-40	MS-65	Proof-65
1977	43,598,000	—	$.75	
1977-D	31,449,106	—	1.00	
1977-S (proof only)	3,251,152	—	—	$2.00
1978	14,350,000	—	1.00	
1978-D	13,765,799	—	1.25	
1978-S (proof only)	3,127,781	—	—	2.25
1979	68,312,000	—	.75	
1979-D	15,815,422	—	1.00	
1979-S combined total (proof only)	3,677,175			
1979-S with clear S		—	—	18.00
1979-S with clogged S		—	—	2.00
1980-P	44,134,000	—	.75	
1980-D	33,456,449	—	.75	

HALF DOLLARS (1794–PRESENT)

	Mintage	EF-40	MS-65	Proof-65
1980-S (proof only)	3,554,806	—	—	2.00
1981-P	29,544,000	—	.75	
1981-D	27,839,533	—	.75	
1981-S (proof only)	4,063,083	—	—	2.00
1982-P	10,819,000	—	.75	
1982-D	13,140,102	—	.75	
1982-S (proof only)	3,857,479	—	—	2.25
1983-P	34,139,000	—	.75	
1983-D	32,472,244	—	1.00	
1983-S (proof only)	3,279,126	—	—	2.50
1984-P	26,029,000	—	1.25	
1984-D	26,262,158	—	.75	
1984-S (proof only)	3,065,110	—	—	4.00
1985-P	18,706,962	—	1.25	
1985-D	19,814,034	—	1.25	
1985-S (proof only)	3,362,821	—	—	2.50
1986-P	13,107,633	—	.75	
1986-D	15,336,145	—	1.00	
1986-S (proof only)	3,010,497	—	—	6.50
1987-P	2,890,758	—	1.50	
1987-D	2,890,758	—	1.50	
1987-S (proof only)	3,792,233	—	—	2.50
1988-P	13,626,000	—	.75	
1988-D	12,000,096	—	.75	
1988-S (proof only)	3,262,948	—	—	3.75
1989-P	24,542,000	—	.75	
1989-D	23,000,216	—	.75	
1989-S (proof only)	3,215,728	—	—	3.25
1990-P	22,278,000	—	.75	
1990-D	20,096,242	—	.75	
1990-S (proof only)	3,299,559	—	—	5.25
1991-P	14,874,000	—	.75	
1991-D	15,054,678	—	.75	
1991-S (proof only)	2,867,787	—	—	8.00
1992-P	17,628,000	—	.75	
1992-D	17,000,106	—	.75	
1992-S (proof only)	4,176,544*	—	—	10.00
1993-P	15,510,000	—	.75	
1993-D	15,000,006	—	.75	
1993-S (proof only)	3,360,876*	—		12.00
1994-P	24,928,896	—	.75	
1994-D	25,039,006	—	.75	
1994-S (proof only)	3,212,792*	—		10.00
1995-P	27,537,352	—	.75	
1995-D	27,329,352	—	.75	

	Mintage	EF-40	MS-65	Proof-65
1995-S (proof only)	2,799,213*			20.00
1996-P	25,896,215		.75	
1996-D	26,198,215		.75	
1996-S (proof only)	2,925,305*			6.00
1997-P	20,882,000		.75	
1997-D	40,758,000		.75	
1997-S (proof only)	2,788,020			12.00
1998-P	15,646,000		.75	
1998-D	15,064,000		.75	
1998-S (proof only)	2,086,507			8.00
1998-P matte finish silver . .	64,141		100	
1998-S (silver proof)	878,996			20.00
1999-P	8,900,000		.75	
1999-D	10,682,000		.75	
1999-S (proof only)	(2,454,319)**			8.00
1999-S (silver proof)	798,780			20.00
2000-P	22,600,000		.75	
2000-D	19,466,000		.75	
2000-S (proof only)	(3,030,000)**			8.00
2000-S (silver proof)	904,200**			20.00
2001-P	21,200,000		.75	
2001-D	19,504,000		.75	
2001-S (proof only)	(2,293,200)***			8.00
2001-S (silver proof)	891,400			20.00
2002-P			.75	
2002-D			.75	
2002-S (proof only)				8.00
2002-S (silver proof)				20.00
2003-P			.75	
2003-D			.75	
2003-S (proof only)				8.00
2003-S (silver proof)				20.00

*Includes 90% silver issue
**Through March 31, 2001
***Through May 28, 2002

SILVER DOLLARS (1794–1935)

Flowing Hair Portrait (1794–1795)

	Mintage	Good-4	Fine-12	EF-40
1794	1,758	$15,000	$30,000	$100,000
1795 combined total	160,295			
1795 with 2 leaves under each wing		750	1,300	4,500
1795 with 3 leaves under each wing		750	1,300	4,500

Draped Bust Portrait with Small Eagle on Reverse (1795–1798)

	Mintage	Good-4	Fine-12	EF-40
1795	42,738	$600	$1,100	$3,750
1796 combined total	72,920			
1796 with small date and small letters		600	1,100	3,250
1796 with small date and large letters		600	1,100	3,250

	Mintage	Good-4	Fine-12	EF-40
1796 with large date and small letters		600	1,000	3,250
1797 combined total	7,776			
1797 with 9 stars left, 7 right and small letters ...		1,100	2,100	8,500
1797 with 9 stars left, 7 right and large letters ...		550	1,000	3,250
1797 with 10 stars left, 6 right		550	1,000	3,250
1798 combined total	327,536			
1798 with 13 stars		950	1,750	4,250
1798 with 15 stars		950	1,800	4,250

Draped Bust Portrait with Heraldic Eagle on Reverse (1798–1804)

	Mintage	Good-4	Fine-12	EF-40	Proof
1798 (mintage included above)		$350	$600	$1,850	
1799 combined total	423,515				
1799 regular date		325	500	1,400	
1799 with 8 stars left, 5 right		350	600	1,500	
1799/8 overdate		400	700	1,500	
1800	220,920	325	530	1,400	
1801	54,454	325	550	1,700	
1802 combined total	41,650				
1802 regular date		325	550	1,500	
1802/1 overdate		325	550	1,600	
1803 combined total	85,634				
1803 with small 3		350	575	1,650	
1803 with large 3	325	550	1,600		
1804 original .... (8 proofs)		—	—	—	$4,140,000
1804 restrike .... (7 proofs)		—	—	—	300,000

(NOTE: All silver dollars dated 1804 were actually minted decades later, and all are extremely rare. The so-called "original" specimens were struck in the 1830s as presentation pieces intended as gifts for monarchs in the Far and Middle East. The restrikes were produced in 1859 to fill demand from collectors who wanted examples of this great rarity. All 15 known examples are accounted for, and all bring enormous premiums whenever they're offered for sale. In 1999, one of the eight known original examples changed hands for $4,140,000 at a major auction.)

Gobrecht Dollars (1836–1839)

	Mintage	Fine-12	EF-40	AU-55	MS 65	Proof 65
1836 pattern*	(unknown)					$50,000
1836 circulation strike with 416 grains of silver	*1,000*	$3,000	$4,250	$9,000	$35,000	45,000
1836 circulation strike with 412½ grains of silver	*600*	3,000	4,750	9,500	48,000	47,500
1838 pattern	(unknown)	3,250	5,250	17,000	60,000	95,000
1839 circulation strike	*300*	3,500	5,000	12,000	45,000	95,000

* The 1836 pattern has C. Gobrecht F. just above the date and below the figure of Liberty.

Seated Liberty Portrait (1840–1873)

	Mintage	Good-4	Fine-12	EF-40	AU-55	MS-63	MS-65	Proof-65
1840	61,005	$140	$200	$400	$850	$3,000	$40,000	—
1841	173,000	110	190	350	750	3,000	20,000	—
1842	184,618	100	180	350	750	3,000	20,000	—
1843	165,100	100	180	350	750	3,500	20,000	—
1844	20,000	175	250	550	1,000	4,500	25,000	—
1845	24,500	175	250	500	900	8,500	45,000	—
1846	110,600	100	175	350	750	3,500	20,000	—
1846-O	59,000	175	250	600	900	5,500	25,000	—
1847	140,750	100	190	400	750	3,500	20,000	—
1848	15,000	250	500	800	1,250	3,750	25,000	—
1849	62,600	125	225	350	750	3,500	20,000	—
1850	7,500	300	600	900	1,350	7,500	35,000	—
1850-O	40,000	250	350	1,200	2,250	11,500	25,000	—
1851 original	1,300	3,000	8,000	10,000	12,500	20,000	50,000	—
1851 restrike	(unknown)	—	—	—	—	—	—	—
1852 original	1,100	1,500	7,500	9,500	12,000	15,000	35,000	—
1852 restrike	(unknown)	—	—	—	—	—	—	—
1853	46,118	135	300	600	850	3,500	20,000	—
1854	33,140	650	1,250	2,750	4,000	7,500	35,000	—
1855	26,000	600	1,250	2,750	3,500	11,000	25,000	—
1856	63,500	180	340	765	1,150	3,750	20,000	—
1857	94,000	190	350	600	1,100	3,500	20,000	—
1858 (proof only)	(about 300)	—	—	—	—	—	—	$35,000
1859 800	255,700	—	—	—	—	3,250	25,000	20,000
1859-O	360,000	200	400	650	800	2,250	20,000	—
1859-S	20,000	300	400	650	1,500	3,250	20,000	—
1860 1,330	217,600	275	375	675	800	3,000	20,000	20,000
1860-O	515,000	95.00	175	375	475	2,250	50,000	—
1861 1,000	77,500	325	550	1,100	2,200	3,500	20,000	17,500
1862 550	11,540	350	550	1,100	2,000	2,500	20,000	20,000
1863 460	27,200	200	300	650	1,000	2,500	16,000	15,000
1864 470	30,700	180	250	600	1,100	2,500	8,000	12,500

	Mintage	Good-4	Fine-12	EF-40	AU-55	MS-63	MS-65	Proof-65
1865 . . . . *500*	46,500	180	250	550	1,000	2,500	20,000	15,000
1866 with no motto above the eagle	*(2 known)*	—	—	—	—	—	—	—1,500,000*

* Proof 63

With Motto Above the Eagle (1866–1873)

	Mintage	Good-4	Fine-12	EF-40	AU-55	MS-63	MS-65	Proof-65
1866 . . . . *725*	48,900	$110	$250	$550	$600	$2,250	$27,500	$9,000
1867 . . . . *625*	46,900	110	260	600	700	2,500	27,500	9,000
1868 . . . . *600*	162,100	110	250	550	700	2,500	30,000	9,000
1869 . . . . *600*	423,700	100	225	500	600	2,250	27,500	9,000
1870 . . . . *1,000*	415,000	100	200	400	500	2,250	27,500	9,000
1870-CC	12,462	250	475	1,100	2,350	15,000	50,000	
1870-S	*(about 10)*	—	—	85,000	90,000	—	—	
1871 . . . . *960*	1,073,800	100	175	375	500	2,250	27,500	9,000
1871-CC	1,376	2,000	3,300	8,500	15,000	25,000	65,000	
1872 . . . . *950*	1,105,500	100	175	375	500	2,250	27,500	9,000
1872-CC	3,150	650	1,400	3,800	6,000	20,000	45,000	
1872-S	9,000	180	410	900	1,500	12,500	35,000	
1873 . . . . *600*	293,000	110	225	400	500	2,250	27,500	11,500
1873-CC	2,300	2,250	4,750	12,500	17,500	50,000	100,000	
1873-S	700				(no examples known to exist)			

Morgan or Liberty Head Portrait (1878–1921)

(NOTE: Values shown for MS-65 examples apply only to coins which have been certified in that grade by the Professional Coin Grading Service or the Numismatic Guaranty Corporation of America.)

	Mintage	Fine-12	EF-40	AU-55	MS-63	MS-65	Proof-65
1878 with 8 tail feathers *500*	749,500	$14.00	$22.00	$30.00	$75.00	$1,200	$6,500
1878 with 7 tail feathers, combined total *50*	9,759,300						
1878 with 7 tail feathers, reverse of 1878		11.00	14.00	20.00	75.00	1,000	
1878 with 7 tail feathers, reverse of 1879		11.00	25.00	28.00	225	2,200	8,500
1878 with 7 tail feathers over 8		14.00	36.00	45.00	125	2,600	
1878-CC	2,212,000	35.00	40.00	50.00	150	1,050	
1878-S	9,774,000	14.00	15.00	18.00	40.00	200	
1879 . . . . *1,100*	14,806,000	10.00	13.00	16.00	50.00	800	4,500
1879-CC combined total	756,000						
1879-CC with regular mint mark		30.00	185	550	2,750	13,000	
1879-CC with muddled mint mark		28.00	210	450	2,500	16,500	
1879-O	2,887,000	9.00	12.00	22.00	215	3,000	
1879-S combined total	9,110,000						
1879-S with reverse of 1878		18.00	23.00	38.00	350	4,800	
1879-S with reverse of 1879		9.00	14.00	16.00	35.00	90.00	
1880 . . . . *1,355*	12,600,000	9.00	12.00	16.00	45.00	675	3,500
1880-C	591,000	50.00	90.00	130	180	800	
1880-O	5,305,000	9.00	14.00	22.00	400	12,000	

	Mintage	Fine-12	EF-40	AU-55	MS-63	MS-65	Proof-65
1880-S	8,900,000	9.00	13.00	16.00	30.00	75.00	
1881 975	9,163,000	9.00	12.00	16.00	45.00	675	3,500
1881-CC	296,000	85.00	120	140	200	575	
1881-O	5,708,000	9.00	12.00	16.00	45.00	1,200	
1881-S	12,760,000	9.00	12.00	16.00	30.00	75.00	
1882 1,100	11,100,000	9.00	12.00	17.00	35.00	400	3,500
1882-CC	1,133,000	30.00	45.00	55.00	85.00	350	
1882-O	6,090,000	9.00	12.00	15.00	38.00	600	
1882-S	9,250,000	10.00	17.00	18.00	30.00	90.00	
1883 1,039	12,290,000	9.00	12.00	14.00	32.00	95.00	3,500
1883-CC	1,204,000	30.00	45.00	55.00	80.00	300	
1883-O	8,725,000	9.00	12.00	14.00	30.00	90.00	
1883-S	6,250,000	15.00	22.00	100	1,300	20,000	
1884 875	14,070,000	9.00	12.00	17.00	38.00	200	3,500
1884-CC	1,136,000	45.00	55.00	70.00	75.00	300	
1884-O	9,730,000	9.00	12.00	14.00	30.00	90.00	
1884-S	3,200,000	15.00	30.00	225	17,000	150,000	
1885 930	17,786,837	9.00	12.00	16.00	30.00	95.00	3,500
1885-CC	228,000	175	195	210	235	700	
1885-O	9,185,000	9.00	12.00	14.00	30.00	90.00	
1885-S	1,497,000	15.00	22.00	45.00	225	1,650	
1886 886	19,963,000	9.00	12.00	14.00	29.00	90.00	3,500
1886-O	10,710,000	12.00	18.00	50.00	1,600	175,000	
1886-S	750,000	15.00	35.00	55.00	285	3,600	
1887 combined total 710	20,290,000						
1887 with regular date		9.00	12.00	14.00	30.00	90.00	3,500
1887/6 overdate		15.00	28.00	43.00	2,100	3,250	3,500
1887-O combined total	11,550,000						
1887-O with regular date		9.00	14.00	25.00	160	3,350	
1887/6-O overdate		15.00	25.00	43.00	2,750	15,000	
1887-S	1,771,000	15.00	20.00	32.00	210	3,000	
1888 832	19,183,000	9.00	12.00	15.00	30.00	150	3,500
1888-O	12,150,000	9.00	13.00	17.00	36.00	350	
1888-S	657,000	20.00	27.00	50.00	280	3,500	
1889 811	21,726,000	9.00	12.00	14.00	30.00	300	3,500
1889-CC	350,000	175	750	2,700	15,000	150,000	
1889-O	11,875,000	11.00	17.00	35.00	210	4,000	
1889-S	700,000	15.00	30.00	50.00	200	1,800	
1890 590	16,802,000	9.00	12.00	17.00	50.00	2,000	4,000
1890-CC	2,309,041	30.00	40.00	85.00	375	5,500	
1890-O	10,701,000	10.00	13.00	30.00	80.00	1,800	
1890-S	8,230,373	10.00	13.00	30.00	80.00	900	
1891 650	8,693,556	9.00	12.00	28.00	130	6,000	4,000
1891-CC	1,618,000	25.00	45.00	75.00	300	2,500	

SILVER DOLLARS (1794–1935)

	Mintage	Fine-12	EF-40	AU-55	MS-63	MS-65	Proof-65
1891-O	7,954,529	12.00	20.00	32.00	190	5,500	
1891-S	5,296,000	12.00	15.00	25.00	85.00	1,000	
1892 .... 1,245	1,036,000	15.00	20.00	50.00	290	3,000	4,000
1892-CC	1,352,000	35.00	85.00	190	750	5,000	
1892-O	2,744,000	15.00	20.00	50.00	210	5,000	
1892-S	1,200,000	20.00	140	1,600	30,000	70,000	
1893 .... 792	389,000	45.00	75.00	150	500	6,000	4,000
1893-CC	677,000	60.00	425	700	2,500	40,000	
1893-O	300,000	60.00	160	400	4,500	150,000	
1893-S	100,000	1,000	2,750	12,500	50,000	200,000	
1894 .... 972	110,000	225	300	500	2,250	13,000	3,500
1894-O	1,723,000	20.00	30.00	140	2,500	40,000	
1894-S	1,260,000	30.00	85.00	180	650	5,000	
1895 .... 880	12,000*	8,500	10,000	11,000	24,000		35,000
1895-O	450,000	65.00	180	800	20,000	200,000	
1895-S	400,000	100	400	650	2,250	15,000	
1896 .... 762	9,976,000	9.00	12.00	14.00	35.00	150	4,000
1896-O	4,900,000	12.00	18.00	110	5,000	125,000	
1896-S	5,000,000	17.00	95.00	295	1,100	8,000	
1897 .... 731	2,822,000	9.00	12.00	16.00	33.00	225	4,500
1897-O	4,004,000	12.00	16.00	65.00	3,250	42,000	
1897-S	5,825,000	12.00	14.00	22.00	75.00	600	
1898 .... 725	5,884,000	9.00	12.00	16.00	33.00	190	4,000
1898-O	4,440,000	13.00	14.00	25.00	33.00	90.00	
1898-S	4,102,000	14.00	24.00	55.00	285	1,700	
1899 .... 846	330,846	35.00	45.00	70.00	115	500	4,300
1899-O	12,290,000	9.00	14.00	16.00	33.00	90.00	
1899-S	2,562,000	15.00	26.00	70.00	260	1,800	
1900 .... 912	8,830,000	9.00	12.00	16.00	30.00	150	4,300
1900-O combined total	12,590,000						
1900-O with regular mint mark		9.00	12.00	16.00	30.00	120	
1900-O/CC		20.00	30.00	90.00	350	1,500	
1900-S	3,540,000	15.00	25.00	55.00	265	1,400	
1901 .... 813	6,962,000	20.00	40.00	175	7,500	105,000	6,000
1901-O	13,320,000	9.00	12.00	16.00	33.00	150	
1901-S	2,284,000	20.00	45.00	100	390	3,000	
1902 .... 777	7,994,000	10.00	14.00	28.00	65.00	400	4,000
1902-O	8,636,000	10.00	12.00	17.00	32.00	150	
1902-S	1,530,000	30.00	65.00	90.00	310	3,000	
1903 .... 755	4,652,000	12.00	17.00	22.00	50.00	180	3,750
1903-O	4,450,000	125	140	165	180	400	
1903-S	1,241,000	25.00	165	675	3,000	7,000	
1904 .... 650	2,788,000	9.00	17.00	35.00	170	2,500	3,750
1904-O	3,720,000	10.00	12.00	15.00	30.00	90.00	

	Mintage	Fine-12	EF-40	AU-55	MS-63	MS-65	Proof-65
1904-S	2,304,000	30.00	115	425	1,450	5,250	
1921	44,690,000	7.00	8.00	9.00	22.00	95.00	
1921-D	20,345,000	7.00	8.00	11.00	33.00	275	
1921-S	21,695,000	7.00	8.00	11.00	36.00	1,250	

* Only proofs are known to exist for 1895 silver dollars from the Philadelphia Mint.

Peace Portrait (1921–1935)

	Mintage	Fine-12	EF-40	AU-55	MS-63	MS-65	Proof-65
1921	1,006,473	$30.00	$45.00	$80.00	$260	$2,300	
1922	51,737,000	7.00	8.00	9.00	20.00	90.00	
1922-D	15,063,000	7.00	8.00	11.00	50.00	325	
1922-S	17,475,000	7.00	8.00	11.00	70.00	1,850	
1923	30,800,000	7.00	8.00	9.00	20.00	90.00	
1923-D	6,811,000	7.00	9.00	13.00	80.00	875	
1923-S	19,020,000	7.00	9.00	13.00	80.00	4,600	
1924	11,811,000	7.00	10.00	14.00	28.00	95.00	
1924-S	1,728,000	12.00	20.00	55.00	400	8,000	
1925	10,198,000	7.00	10.00	14.00	25.00	90.00	
1925-S	1,610,000	11.00	17.00	30.00	170	12,500	
1926	1,939,000	8.00	14.00	20.00	43.00	350	
1926-D	2,348,700	10.00	15.00	30.00	125	600	
1926-S	6,980,000	9.00	13.00	20.00	80.00	750	
1927	848,000	17.00	25.00	35.00	130	1,250	
1927-D	1,268,900	17.00	22.00	75.00	375	3,800	
1927-S	866,000	15.00	20.00	60.00	185	7,500	
1928	360,649	95.00	125	155	300	2,800	
1928-S	1,632,000	15.00	19.00	50.00	375	15,500	
1934	954,057	18.00	22.00	35.00	150	875	
1934-D	1,569,500	16.00	19.00	38.00	190	1,500	
1934-S	1,011,000	20.00	150	450	2,500	5,250	
1935	1,576,000	15.00	19.00	25.00	90.00	575	
1935-S	1,964,000	15.00	18.00	65.00	275	825	

TRADE DOLLARS (1873–1885)

	Mintage	Fine-12	EF-40	AU-55	MS-63	MS-65	Proof-65
1873 . . . . *865*	396,635	$110	$225	$400	$1,300	$10,000	$9,000
1873-CC	124,500	175	450	750	3,500	20,000	
1873-S	703,000	110	250	425	1,750	10,000	
1874 . . . . *700*	987,100	110	225	400	1,300	10,000	9,000
1874-CC	1,373,200	120	225	450	1,750	20,000	
1874-S	2,549,000	90.00	185	350	2,250	10,250	
1875 . . . . *700*	218,200	275	550	850	2,000	12,500	8,500
1875-CC	1,573,700	85.00	225	400	2,000	16,000	
1875-S combined total	4,487,000						
1875-S with regular mint							
mark		75.00	140	325	1,300	8,000	
1875-S/CC		600	1,700	2,200	3,000	30,000	
1876 . . . . *1,150*	455,000	75.00	150	350	1,300	8,000	8,500
1876-CC	509,000	110	290	425	3,000	20,000	
1876-S	5,227,000	90.00	150	325	1,300	8,000	
1877 . . . . *510*	3,039,200	90.00	150	350	1,500	8,000	8,500
1877-CC	534,000	185	350	600	1,550	20,000	
1877-S	9,519,000	80.00	150	325	1,300	8,000	
1878 (proof only)	*900*	—	—	—	—	—	10,000
1878-CC	97,000	500	1,400	2,750	17,500	35,000	
1878-S	4,162,000	90.00	150	325	1,300	8,000	
1879 (proof only)	*1,541*	—	—	—	—	—	7,500
1880 (proof only)	*1,987*	—	—	—	—	—	7,500
1881 (proof only)	*960*	—	—	—	—	—	7,500
1882 (proof only)	*1,097*	—	—	—	—	—	7,500
1883 (proof only)	*979*	—	—	—	—	—	7,500
1884 (proof only)	*10*	—	—	—	—	—	300,000
1885 (proof only)	*5*	—	—	—	—	—	1,100,000

CLAD DOLLARS (1971–1981)

Eisenhower Portrait (1971–1978)

	Mintage	MS-65	Proof-65
1971 copper-nickel clad	47,799,000	$275	
1971-D copper-nickel clad	68,587,424	35.00	
1971-S silver clad *4,265,234*	6,868,530	18.00	$12.00
1972 copper-nickel clad	75,890,000	450	
1972-D copper-nickel clad	92,548,511	50.00	
1972-S silver clad *1,811,631*	2,193,056	14.00	13.00
1973 copper-nickel clad	2,000,056	65.00	
1973-D copper-nickel clad	2,000,000	45.00	
1973-S copper-nickel clad (proof only)	*2,760,339*	—	13.00
1973-S silver clad *1,013,646*	1,883,140	16.00	20.00
1974 copper-nickel clad	27,366,000	60.00	
1974-D copper-nickel clad	45,517,000	40.00	
1974-S copper-nickel clad (proof only)	*2,612,568*	—	13.00
1974-S silver clad *1,306,579*	1,900,156	17.00	10.50

Bicentennial Portrait (1975–1976)

	Mintage	MS-65	Proof-65
1776–1976 copper-nickel clad with thick lettering on reverse	4,019,000	$150	
1776–1976 copper-nickel clad with thin lettering	113,318,000	45.00	
1776–1976-D copper-nickel clad with thick lettering	21,048,710	55.00	
1776–1976-D copper-nickel clad with thin lettering	82,179,564	35.00	
1776–1976-S copper-nickel clad (proof only; includes coins from both 1975 and 1976 proof sets)	*6,995,180*		$15.00
1776–1976-S silver clad *3,998,621*	4,908,319	17.00	15.00

Regular Design Returns (1977–1978)

	Mintage	MS-65	Proof-65
1977 copper-nickel clad	12,596,000	$50.00	
1977-D copper-nickel clad	32,983,006	40.00	
1977-S copper-nickel clad (proof only)	3,251,152	—	$12.00
1978 copper-nickel clad	25,702,000	50.00	
1978-D copper-nickel clad	33,012,890	45.00	
1978-S copper-nickel clad (proof only)	3,127,781	—	4.50

Susan B. Anthony Portrait (1979–1981)

	Mintage	MS-65	Proof-65
1979-P	360,222,000	$2.00	
1979-D	288,015,744	2.00	
1979-S combined total 3,677,175	109,576,000		
1979-S with clear S		2.00	$70.00
1979-S with clogged S		2.00	5.00
1980-P	27,610,000	2.00	
1980-D	41,628,708	2.00	
1980-S 3,554,806	20,422,000	2.00	5.00
1981-P	3,000,000	3.00	
1981-D	3,250,000	3.00	
1981-S combined total 4,063,083	3,492,000		
1981-S with clear S		3.00	65.00
1981-S with clogged S		3.00	7.00
1999-P	25,592,000	1.50	
1999-D	11,776,000	1.50	
1999-S (proof only)	(555,276)	—	15.00

Sacagawea Dollars (2000–)

	Mintage	EF-40	MS-65	Proof-65
2000-P	767,140,000		$1.50	
2000-D	518,916,000		1.50	
2000-S (proof only)	(3,030,000)*		—	
2001-P	62,468,000		1.50	

	Mintage	EF-40	MS-65	Proof-65
2001-D	70,939,500	—	1.50	
2001-S (proof only)	*(2,293,200)***	—	—	
2002-P		—	1.50	
2002-D		—	1.50	
2002-S (proof only)		—	—	

* Through March 31, 2001
** Through May 28, 2002

GOLD DOLLARS (1849–1889)

Liberty Head Portrait (1849–1854)

	Mintage	Fine-12	EF-40	AU-50	MS-65	Proof-65
1849 combined total	688,567					
1849 with open wreath		$110	$150	$200	$5,500	
1849 with closed wreath		110	150	200	5,000	
1849-C combined total	11,634					
1849-C with open wreath		150,000	300,000	—	—	
1849-C with closed wreath		275	925	2,000	—	
1849-D	21,588	250	610	1,000	—	
1849-O	215,000	125	210	400	—	
1850	481,953	100	150	200	5,850	
1850-C	6,966	325	805	2,000	—	
1850-D	8,382	300	950	2,000	—	
1850-O	14,000	200	300	775	32,500	
1851	3,317,671	100	150	200	5,850	
1851-C	41,267	250	600	900	30,000	
1851-D	9,882	225	700	1,500	—	
1851-O	290,000	110	175	200	—	
1852	2,045,351	100	150	200	5,850	
1852-C	9,434	240	785	1,475	40,000	
1852-D	6,360	300	1,200	1,500	—	
1852-O	140,000	125	185	260	—	
1853	4,076,051	100	200	225	5,750	
1853-C	11,515	200	850	1,500	—	
1853-D	6,583	300	875	2,150	—	
1853-O	290,000	140	175	195	5,600	

	Mintage	Fine-12	EF-40	AU-50	MS-65	Proof-65
1854	855,502	110	175	200	6,500	—
1854-D	2,935	515	1,740	6,000	—	
1854-S	14,632	240	385	650	21,500	

Indian Head Portrait with Small Head (1854–1856)

	Mintage	Fine-12	EF-40	AU-50	MS-65	Proof-65
1854	783,943	$200	$450	$550	$50,000	—
1855	758,269	200	450	550	50,000	$225,000
1855-C	9,803	600	2,000	4,000	—	
1855-D	1,811	1,600	4,000	9,000	—	
1855-O	55,000	300	710	1,000	—	
1856-S	24,600	400	910	1,600	—	

Indian Head Portrait with Large Head (1856–1889)

	Mintage	Fine-12	EF-40	AU-50	MS-65	Proof-65
1856 combined total	1,762,936					
1856 with upright 5		$125	$200	$300	$3,000	
1856 with slanted 5		100	110	160	2,875	—
1856-D	1,460	2,500	6,000	8,000	—	
1857	774,789	90.00	135	150	2,875	—
1857-C	13,280	290	950	2,750	—	
1857-D	3,533	275	1,600	3,000	—	
1857-S	10,000	250	775	1,000	—	
1858	117,995	105	140	160	3,000	$22,500
1858-D	3,477	400	1,100	2,400	—	
1858-S	10,000	250	525	1,575	—	
1859 _80_	168,164	100	140	160	2,800	—
1859-C	5,235	250	1,175	3,200	—	
1859-D	4,952	400	1,310	2,450	—	
1859-S	15,000	240	500	1,700	—	
1860 _154_	36,514	100	140	170	4,000	8,775
1860-D	1,566	2,000	3,800	6,500	—	
1860-S	13,000	300	400	700	50,000	

	Mintage	Fine-12	EF-40	AU-50	MS-65	Proof-65
1861 ....349	527,150	100	140	200	3,000	13,000
1861-D ....(unknown)		4,000	9,000	12,500	140,000	
1862 ....35 1,361,355		100	140	160	2,650	14,500
1863 ....50	6,200	325	750	1,600	21,000	—
1864 ....50	5,900	250	400	600	5,000	22,500
1865 ....25	3,700	250	400	600	7,700	10,000
1866 ....30	7,100	275	400	675	5,200	9,750
1867 ....50	5,200	300	500	600	5,000	—
1868 ....25	10,500	250	400	500	5,000	—
1869 ....25	5,900	300	500	700	4,000	—
1870 ....35	6,300	250	400	500	5,000	—
1870-S	3,000	300	700	1,400	30,000	
1871 ....30	3,900	275	400	500	4,250	—
1872 ....30	3,500	250	400	500	4,250	16,500
1873 closed 3 ....25	1,800	300	700	1,000	16,500	—
1873 open 3	123,300	100	150	200		
1874 ....20	198,800	100	150	200	1,800	—
1875 ....20	400	1,600	3,500	5,000	25,000	36,500
1876 ....45	3,200	200	300	400	3,500	15,000
1877 ....20	3,900	150	300	425	3,500	20,000
1878 ....20	3,000	175	310	395	3,000	—
1879 ....30	3,000	140	250	375	1,800	—
1880 ....36	1,600	140	175	190	1,800	—
1881 ....87	7,620	140	175	190	1,800	—
1882 ....125	5,000	135	190	190	1,875	8,600
1883 ....207	10,800	115	175	190	1,775	8,600
1884 ....1,006	5,230	115	175	190	1,875	8,600
1885 ....1,105	11,156	115	175	190	1,800	8,600
1886 1,016	5,000	115	175	190	1,700	8,600
1887 ....1,043	7,500	115	175	190	1,700	8,600
1888 ....1,079	15,501	115	175	190	1,700	8,600
1889 ....1,779	28,950	115	175	190	1,700	8,600

QUARTER EAGLES, OR $2.50 GOLD PIECES (1796–1929)

Capped Bust Portrait Facing Right (1796–1807)

	Mintage	Fine-12	EF-40	MS-60
1796 with no stars	963	$9,500	$26,000	$130,000
1796 with stars	432	8,000	18,000	100,000
1797	427	7,750	15,000	125,000
1798	1,094	3,000	4,000	30,000
1802/1 overdate	3,035	3,000	4,000	20,000
1804 combined total	3,327			
1804 with 13 stars		13,000	28,000	
1804 with 14 stars		3,250	4,800	26,000
1805	1,781	2,800	4,000	26,000
1806/4 overdate	1,136	3,000	5,000	27,000
1806/5 overdate	480	5,000	9,000	
1807	6,812	3,000	4,000	22,000

Capped Bust Portrait Facing Left (1808)

	Mintage	Fine-12	EF-40	MS-60
1808	2,710	$8,000	$16,000	$60,000

Capped Head Portrait (1821–1834)

	Mintage	Fine-12	EF-40	AU-50	MS-60	MS-63
1821	6,448	$3,000	$4,800	$6,000	$12,000	$40,000
1824/1 overdate	2,600	3,200	4,000	5,000	10,000	30,000
1825	4,434	3,000	4,000	5,000	9,000	30,000
1826	760	3,000	5,000	7,000	20,000	50,000
1827	2,800	4,000	6,000	7,000	13,000	38,000

Size Reduced (1829–1834)

	Mintage	Fine-12	EF-40	AU-50	MS-60	MS-63
1829	3,403	$3,000	$4,000	$4,850	$7,250	$12,500
1830	4,540	3,000	4,000	4,850	7,250	12,500
1831	4,520	3,000	4,000	4,850	7,250	12,500
1832	4,400	3,000	4,000	4,850	7,250	15,000
1833	4,160	3,000	4,000	4,850	7,750	—
1834 (E PLURIBUS UNUM on reverse)	4,000	6,000	15,000	22,000	28,000	—

Classic Head Portrait (1834–1839)

	Mintage	Fine-12	EF-40	AU-50	MS-60	MS-63
1834 (no motto on reverse)	112,234	$200	$425	$700	$2,000	$5,000
1835	131,402	200	425	700	2,800	6,000
1836	547,986	200	425	700	2,000	5,000
1837	45,080	200	425	800	3,000	6,000
1838	47,030	200	425	800	2,900	5,000
1838-C	7,880	500	1,425	4,000	20,000	—

	Mintage	Fine-12	EF-40	AU-50	MS-60	MS-63
1839	27,021	200	600	2,000	6,000	12,850
1839-C	18,140	400	1,600	4,000	14,000	25,000
1839-D	13,674	475	2,600	5,000	18,000	—
1839-O	17,781	400	1,000	2,200	5,800	14,750

Coronet Portrait (1840–1907)

	Mintage	Fine-12	EF-40	AU-50	MS-60	MS-63	Proof-65
1840	18,859	$100	$500	$3,500	$9,000	$20,000	
1840-C	12,822	300	1,200	4,000	14,000	30,000	
1840-D	3,532	1,000	3,500	7,000	25,000		
1840-O	33,580	300	800	1,800	7,500	20,000	
1841 (proof only)	(very rare)	20,000	50,000	100,000	—	—	
1841-C	10,281	300	1,000	3,000	16,000	32,000	
1841-D	4,164	1,400	3,000	9,000	16,000	35,000	
1842	2,823	600	2,500	5,500	14,000	32,000	
1842-C	6,729	1,100	2,500	7,500	20,000	60,000	
1842-D	4,643	1,000	3,000	14,000	15,500	42,500	
1842-O	19,800	275	1,200	2,800	14,000	35,000	
1843	100,546	120	400	800	300	6,000	
1843-C small date	2,988	2,500	5,000	11,000	30,000	50,000	
1843-C large date	23,076	500	900	2,650	7,000	24,000	
1843-D	36,209	600	1,000	2,000	7,000	24,350	
1843-O small date	288,002	225	300	400	1,200	4,000	
1843-O large date	76,000	200	325	1,800	7,000	—	
1844	6,784	375	900	2,500	7,600	20,000	
1844-C	11,622	600	1,300	7,000	20,000	40,000	
1844-D	17,332	600	1,200	2,000	6,000	20,000	
1845	91,051	300	400	500	900	5,000	
1845-D	19,460	600	900	3,000	10,000	22,500	
1845-O	4,000	1,000	3,000	5,000	14,000	42,000	
1846	21,598	375	785	2,250	18,000	40,000	
1846-C	4,808	1,000	1,600	8,000	20,000	42,500	
1846-D	19,303	750	1,100	2,800	10,000	22,500	
1846-O	62,000	300	450	1,400	6,000	16,000	
1847	29,814	200	400	900	4,000	9,000	
1847-C	23,226	500	900	2,000	7,000	20,000	

	Mintage	Fine-12	EF-40	AU-50	MS-60	MS-63	Proof-65
1847-D	15,784	500	1,000	2,000	7,000	21,500	
1847-O	124,000	250	400	1,000	3,000	8,000	
1848	7,497	300	800	3,000	7,500	20,000	
1848 with CAL. above eagle	1,389	6,850	14,000	20,000	35,000	62,500	
1848-C	16,788	500	1,200	3,000	12,000	30,000	
1848-D	13,771	500	1,200	2,000	8,250	30,000	
1849	23,294	300	600	1,200	3,600	7,000	
1849-C	10,220	500	1,300	4,250	16,000	42,500	
1849-D	10,945	750	1,200	2,750	14,000	35,000	
1850	252,923	100	200	300	800	4,000	
1850-C	9,148	500	1,500	3,000	14,000	38,500	
1850-D	12,148	600	1,000	2,500	15,000	34,000	
1850-O	84,000	200	575	1,500	5,000	14,250	
1851	1,372,748	200	300	400	500	1,200	
1851-C	14,923	500	1,450	3,850	12,750	32,500	
1851-D	11,264	625	1,200	2,600	12,500	30,000	
1851-O	148,000	200	300	900	4,000	8,000	
1852	1,159,681	200	275	375	410	1,000	
1852-C	9,772	550	1,400	3,200	15,500	38,500	
1852-D	4,078	850	2,600	5,000	18,000	40,000	
1852-O	140,000	200	300	700	5,000	11,000	
1853	1,404,668	200	400	450	600	1,050	
1853 D	3,178	1,500	2,500	5,000	17,500	35,000	
1854	596,258	100	200	250	450	1,000	
1854-C	7,295	600	2,000	4,000	15,000	32,500	
1854 D	1,760	2,500	4,500	13,000	25,000	50,000	
1854-O	153,000	100	300	600	1,500	5,850	
1854-S	246	25,000	70,000	100,000	—	—	
1855	235,480	200	225	250	425	1,600	
1855-C	3,677	1,200	3,000	6,000	25,000	50,000	
1855-D	1,123	4,000	8,000	15,000	30,000	50,000	
1856	384,240	100	200	300	400	1,400	$74,850
1856-C	7,913	800	1,600	4,600	20,000	40,000	
1856-D	874	6,000	10,000	18,000	37,000	85,000	
1856-O	21,100	225	775	1,800	6,250	24,000	
1856-S	72,120	100	400	900	6,000	22,000	
1857	214,130	200	300	340	350	1,500	
1857-D	2,364	800	1,700	3,400	12,000	30,000	
1857-O	34,000	150	325	1,500	6,000	14,000	
1857-S	69,200	200	400	1,500	6,000	15,000	
1858	47,377	150	300	400	1,400	4,250	18,500
1858-C	9,056	600	1,300	2,500	12,000	30,000	
1859 _80_	39,364	200	300	900	1,500	4,000	18,500
1859-D	2,244	1,200	2,200	6,000	22,000	41,850	
1859-S	15,200	200	1,500	2,500	6,000	14,000	

	Mintage	Fine-12	EF-40	AU-50	MS-60	MS-63	Proof-65
1860 ...... 112	22,563	200	300	500	1,200	3,300	18,500
1860-C	7,469	775	1,600	4,000	20,000	32,500	
1860-S	35,600	250	700	1,500	4,600	9,000	
1861 ...... 90	1,283,788	200	300	375	410	1,050	18,500
1861-S	24,000	300	1,800	3,000	6,000	15,000	
1862 combined total	98,543						
1862 regular date 35		200	300	500	1,500	3,000	18,500
1862/1 overdate		675	2,000	3,500	13,750	32,000	
1862-S	8,000	800	3,000	4,500	15,000	34,000	
1863 (proof only)	30	—	—	—	—	—	75,000
1863-S	10,800	400	1,500	5,000	19,000	30,000	
1864 ...... 50	2,824	5,000	14,000	25,000	40,000	65,000	18,500
1865 ...... 25	1,520	3,000	9,000	20,000	32,500	68,000	28,000
1865-S	23,376	225	740	1,200	3,800	9,000	
1866 ...... 30	3,080	1,200	2,200	6,900	16,000	40,000	24,000
1866-S	38,960	300	900	2,500	8,000	20,000	
1867 ...... 50	3,200	300	900	1,400	5,000	11,000	18,500
1867-S	28,000	300	900	1,900	5,000	10,000	
1868 ...... 25	3,600	300	600	900	3,000	7,000	18,500
1868-S	34,000	200	600	1,500	4,000	9,000	
1869 ...... 25	4,320	225	450	900	5,000	9,500	18,500
1869-S	29,500	200	600	925	4,000	10,000	
1870 ...... 35	4,520	250	500	900	4,000	9,000	18,500
1870-S	16,000	225	400	1,000	5,000	12,000	
1871 ...... 30	5,320	250	475	925	2,600	6,000	18,500
1871-S	22,000	200	400	900	3,000	6,000	
1872 ...... 30	3,000	350	750	1,800	4,000	12,000	18,500
1872-S	18,000	200	500	1,200	4,000	11,000	
1873 closed 3 .... 25	55,200	300	375	600	1,100	3,000	18,500
1873 open 3	122,800	200	300	325	375	1,050	
1873-S	27,000	200	500	1,000	3,000	8,000	
1874 ...... 20	3,920	300	500	1,000	3,000	8,000	18,500
1875 ...... 20	400	3,000	6,000	7,000	14,000	—	42,500
1875-S	11,600	100	300	800	4,000	10,000	
1876 ...... 45	4,176	150	700	1,100	5,000	11,000	18,500
1876-S	5,000	200	600	1,100	4,000	11,000	
1877 ...... 20	1,632	400	800	1,000	3,000	7,000	35,000
1877-S	35,400	200	300	375	900	3,000	
1878 ...... 20	286,240	200	300	375	350	1,075	18,500
1878-S	178,000	200	275	300	1,100	2,500	
1879 ...... 30	88,960	200	300	375	425	1,500	18,500
1879-S	43,500	150	300	500	2,200	5,500	
1880 ...... 36	2,960	200	325	750	1,400	3,500	22,000
1881 ...... 51	640	1,400	3,000	5,000	11,000	30,000	22,000
1882 ...... 67	4,000	200	300	400	1,100	3,100	13,750

	Mintage	Fine-12	EF-40	AU-50	MS-60	MS-63	Proof-65
1883 82	1,920	150	400	700	2,000	5,000	17,500
1884 73	1,950	150	400	700	1,600	3,000	18,500
1885 87	800	600	1,500	2,600	6,000	8,000	—
1886 88	4,000	200	300	400	1,200	3,000	17,000
1887 122	6,160	200	300	400	1,200	3,000	—
1888 97	16,001	200	300	400	500	500	—
1889 48	17,600	205	240	260	280	500	—
1890 93	8,720	140	190	240	410	500	17,750
1891 80	10,960	200	250	260	410	500	14,850
1892 105	2,440	130	200	300	800	2,575	14,700
1893 106	30,000	200	225	240	260	500	13,000
1894 122	4,000	225	250	275	800	2,000	12,000
1895 119	6,000	140	160	190	400	600	12,000
1896 132	19,070	120	150	180	250	500	11,750
1897 136	29,768	120	150	180	250	500	11,750
1898 165	24,000	120	150	180	250	500	11,750
1899 150	27,200	120	150	180	250	500	11,750
1900 205	67,000	120	150	180	250	500	11,750
1901 223	91,100	120	150	180	250	500	11,750
1902 193	133,540	120	150	180	250	500	11,750
1903 197	201,060	120	150	180	250	500	11,750
1904 170	160,790	120	150	180	250	500	11,750
1905 144	217,800	120	150	180	250	500	11,750
1906 160	176,330	120	150	180	250	500	11,750
1907 154	336,294	120	150	180	250	500	11,750

Indian Head Portrait (1908–1929)

	Mintage	AU-50	MS-60	MS-63	MS-65	Proof-65
1908 236	564,821	$170	$250	$650	$2,800	$14,500
1909 139	441,760	170	250	650	2,800	15,500
1910 682	492,000	170	300	650	4,000	14,000
1911 191	704,000	170	275	650	4,000	14,500
1911-D	55,680	900	3,000	5,800	35,000	
1912 197	616,000	170	300	900	6,000	14,500
1913 165	722,000	170	250	600	4,000	14,500
1914 117	240,000	190	300	2,500	10,000	15,500
1914-D	448,000	190	300	1,700	14,000	

	Mintage	AU-50	MS-60	MS-63	MS-65	Proof-65
1915 ....*100*	606,000	170	275	500	4,000	15,500
1925-D	578,000	170	250	500	3,000	
1926	446,000	170	250	500	3,000	
1927	388,000	170	250	500	3,000	
1928	416,000	170	250	500	3,000	
1929	532,000	170	250	500	9,000	

$3 GOLD PIECES (1854–1889)

	Mintage	Fine-12	EF-40	AU-50	MS-60	MS-63	Proof-65
1854	138,618	$400	$600	$1,000	$2,000	$4,500	$150,000
1854-D	1,120	5,000	13,000	25,000	75,000	—	
1854-O	24,000	380	800	2,500	20,000	—	
1855	50,555	400	750	1,000	2,000	4,350	—
1855-S	6,600	850	2,000	5,000	19,000	—	
1856	26,010	550	750	1,000	2,000	—	—
1856-S	34,500	500	900	2,000	7,500	—	
1857	20,891	500	875	1,000	3,500	8,000	65,000
1857-S	14,250	750	1,200	4,000	9,600	—	
1858	2,133	750	1,000	2,500	4,500	—	58,000
1859 ....*80*	15,558	500	775	1,000	2,500	4,500	40,000
1860 ....*119*	7,036	600	775	1,000	2,500	4,500	33,000
1860-S	4,408	700	1,600	4,000	10,000	20,000	
1861 ....*113*	5,959	650	850	1,200	3,500	4,600	33,000
1862 ....*35*	5,750	650	900	1,200	3,500	5,500	34,000
1863 ....*39*	5,000	650	900	1,200	3,500	4,900	34,000
1864 ....*50*	2,630	650	925	1,200	3,200	5,800	34,000
1865 ....*25*	1,140	900	2,000	3,500	6,800	10,500	35,000
1866 ....*30*	4,000	650	925	1,200	3,500	5,000	34,000
1867 ....*50*	2,600	650	925	1,200	3,500	4,500	35,000
1868 ....*25*	4,850	600	875	1,200	3,300	4,500	35,000
1869 ....*25*	2,500	675	900	1,500	3,700	5,900	35,000
1870 ....*35*	3,500	600	925	1,500	4,000	10,000	35,000
1870-S	(1 known)	—	750,000	—	—		
1871 ....*30*	1,300	500	800	1,500	3,600	5,250	35,000
1872 ....*30*	2,000	500	775	1,300	3,300	5,250	35,000
1873 closed 3	(unknown)	2,000	4,000	8,000	16,750	—	

	Mintage	Fine-12	EF-40	AU-50	MS-60	MS-63	Proof-65
1873 open 3 (proof only)	25	—	—	—	—	—	70,000
1874 ....20	41,800	400	650	800	2,000	4,500	38,000
1875 (proof only)	20	—	—	—	—	—	200,000
1876 (proof only)	45	—	—	18,000	—	—	85,000
1877 ....20	1,468	600	2,550	5,000	6,000	15,000	42,500
1878 ....20	82,304	400	725	900	2,000	4,500	32,500
1879 ....30	3,000	400	800	900	2,100	4,500	32,500
1880 ....36	1,000	300	1,400	1,600	2,100	4,500	32,500
1881 ....54	500	400	1,750	3,000	4,000	4,800	30,000
1882 ....76	1,500	400	725	900	2,000	4,800	30,000
1883 ....89	900	400	925	1,500	2,000	4,800	30,000
1884 ......106	1,000	650	1,250	1,600	1,900	4,600	28,000
1885 ......109	801	700	1,300	1,800	2,000	4,500	28,000
1886 ......142	1,000	700	1,275	1,900	3,250	5,300	28,000
1887 ......160	6,000	450	750	850	2,000	4,600	28,000
1888 ......291	5,000	475	790	850	2,000	4,600	28,000
1889 ......129	2,300	475	750	850	2,000	4,500	28,000

$4 GOLD PIECES, OR "STELLAS" (1879–1880)

	Mintage	Proof-60	Proof-63	Proof-65
1879 with flowing hair (proof only)	425	$28,000	$40,000	$125,000
1879 with coiled hair (proof only)	10	100,000	175,000	360,000
1880 with flowing hair (proof only)	15	45,000	75,000	190,000
1880 with coiled hair (proof only)	10	110,000	225,000	600,000

HALF EAGLES, OR $5 GOLD PIECES (1795–1929)

Capped Bust Portrait Facing Right with Small Eagle on Reverse (1795–1798)

	Mintage	Fine-12	EF-40	MS-60
1795	8,707	$5,000	$8,000	$40,000
1796/5 overdate	6,196	6,000	13,000	50,000
1797 combined total	3,609			
1797 with 15 stars		8,000	20,000	60,000
1797 with 16 stars		7,000	20,000	60,000
1798	(7 known)	100,000	200,000	450,000

Capped Bust Portrait Facing Right with Heraldic Eagle on Reverse (1795–1807)

	Mintage	Fine-12	EF-40	MS-60
1795 (mintage included in 1798)		$6,000	$14,000	$85,000
1797/5 overdate (mintage included in 1798)		8,000	15,000	160,000
1797 with 16 stars (mintage included in 1798)	(1 known)	—	—	—
1798 combined total	24,867			
1798 with small 8		1,500	3,000	8,000

	Mintage	Fine-12	EF-40	MS-60
1798 with large 8 and 13 stars .		1,500	3,000	8,000
1798 with large 8 and 14 stars .		2,000	2,600	—
1799	7,451	1,800	3,500	12,000
1800	37,628	1,600	2,000	6,000
1802/1 overdate	53,176	1,600	2,000	6,000
1803/2 overdate	33,506	1,600	2,000	6,000
1804 combined total	30,475			
1804 with small 8		1,600	2,000	6,000
1804 with small 8 over large 8 .		1,600	2,000	6,000
1805	33,183	1,600	2,000	6,000
1806 with pointed 6	9,676	1,400	2,500	5,800
1806 with round-top 6	54,417	1,400	2,500	5,600
1807	32,488	1,400	2,500	5,600

Capped Draped Bust Portrait Facing Left
(1807–1812)

	Mintage	Fine-12	EF-40	MS-60
1807	51,605	$1,300	$2,400	$5,500
1808 combined total	55,578			
1808 regular date		1,300	2,400	5,500
1808/7 overdate		1,500	3,000	10,000
1809/8 overdate		1,500	2,250	5,250
1810 combined total	100,287			
1810 small date with small 5 ..		8,000	35,000	87,500
1810 small date with tall 5		1,600	2,700	5,800
1810 large date with small 5 ...		7,600	33,000	95,000
1810 large date with large 5 ...		1,600	2,450	5,800
1811	99,581	1,600	2,450	5,800
1812	58,087	1,600	2,450	5,800

Capped Head Portrait (1813–1829)

	Mintage	Fine-12	EF-40	AU-55	MS-60	MS-63
1813	95,428	$1,500	$2,200	$3,000	$5,000	$12,000
1814/3 overdate	15,454	1,800	2,700	4,200	8,500	22,750
1815	635	38,250	55,000	100,000		—
1818 combined total	48,588					
1818 regular strike		2,000	3,000	4,000	6,000	12,000
1818 with 5D over 50		—	—	—	—	70,000
1819 combined total	51,723					
1819 regular strike		—	—	—	—	—
1819 with 5D over 50		—	—	—	—	—
1820	263,806	2,000	3,000	4,000	8,000	16,500
1821	34,641	2,500	6,500	9,500	—	—
1822 (3 known)	17,796	—	—	—	—	—
1823	14,485	2,500	3,500	6,000	12,500	18,000
1824	17,340	5,000	16,000	18,000	28,000	40,000
1825 combined total	29,060					
1825/1		4,000	6,000	8,000		
1825/4 (2 known)		—	—	—	—	—
1826	18,069	3,000	7,000	12,000	19,000	32,750
1827	24,913	7,200	8,500	14,850	24,000	47,000
1828 combined total	28,029					
1828 regular date		—	—	—	—	—
1828/7 overdate		—	—	—	—	—
1829 large date	57,442	—	—	—	—	—

Size Reduced (1829–1834)

	Mintage	Fine-12	EF-40	AU-50	MS-60	MS-63
1829 small date (mintage included with large date)		—	—	—	—	—
1830	126,351	$4,000	$5,000	$6,000	$12,000	$30,000
1831	140,594	4,000	5,000	6,000	12,000	30,000
1832 combined total	157,487					
1832 with 12 stars (6 known) ...		30,000	48,000	—	—	—
1832 with 13 stars		4,000	8,000	11,000	14,000	26,000
1833 with large date	193,630	3,000	5,000	6,000	10,000	22,500
1834 combined total	50,141					
1834 with plain 4		3,000	5,000	5,200	12,000	24,000
1834 with crosslet 4		3,000	5,000	5,200	12,000	24,000

Classic Head Portrait (1834–1838)

	Mintage	Fine-12	EF-40	AU-50	MS-60	MS-63
1834 combined total	657,460					
1834 with plain 4		$300	$400	$800	$3,000	$6,500
1834 with crosslet 4		900	3,000	5,000	15,000	
1835	371,534	300	500	800	2,500	7,500
1836	553,147	300	500	800	2,500	7,500
1837	207,121	300	500	800	2,500	9,000
1838	286,588	300	500	800	2,500	9,000
1838-C	17,179	875	4,500	14,000	22,000	—
1838-D	20,583	725	3,000	6,500	16,750	—

Coronet Portrait (1839–1907)
No Motto over Eagle (1839–1866)

	Mintage	Fine-12	EF-40	AU-50	MS-60	MS-63	Proof-65
1839	118,143	$200	$350	$1,400	$3,000	—	
1839-C	17,205	1,000	2,500	7,000	20,000	—	
1839-D	18,939	1,000	2,000	6,000	12,000	—	
1840	137,382	100	1,000	1,500	8,000	—	
1840-C	18,992	1,500	3,000	9,000	25,000	—	
1840-D	22,896	1,000	2,000	4,000	15,000	—	
1840-O	40,120	400	900	2,000	9,250	—	
1841	15,833	500	1,000	1,800	6,000	—	
1841-C	21,467	1,000	1,675	3,000	22,000	—	
1841-D	29,392	1,000	1,200	3,000	11,000	—	
1841-O	50	(unknown in any collection)					
1842 combined total	27,578						
1842 with small letters		250	975	4,000	12,500	—	
1842 with large letters		500	1,800	4,000	16,500	—	
1842-C combined total	27,432						
1842-C small date		2,500	20,000	72,000	125,000	—	
1842-C large date		725	1,600	3,500	26,000	—	
1842-D combined total	59,608						
1842-D small date		600	1,200	3,850	15,000	—	
1842-D large date		1,800	6,000	14,000	45,000	—	
1842-O	16,400	600	2,650	10,000	30,000	—	
1843	611,205	300	210	305	2,000	—	
1843-C	44,277	400	1,150	3,000	10,000	—	
1843-D	98,452	525	850	2,600	8,000	—	
1843-O with small letters	19,075	300	900	3,000	9,600	—	
1843-O with large letters	82,000	200	900	3,000	13,250	—	
1844	340,330	100	150	475	2,000	$5,000	
1844-C	23,631	600	1,600	4,800	30,000	—	
1844-D	88,982	400	1,000	2,600	12,000	—	
1844-O	364,600	150	325	600	4,000	11,000	
1845	417,099	100	200	350	2,000	6,500	
1845-D	90,629	400	900	2,000	14,000	—	
1845-O	41,000	300	600	3,000	13,000	—	

HALF EAGLES, OR $5 GOLD PIECES (1795–1929)

	Mintage	Fine-12	EF-40	AU-50	MS-60	MS-63	Proof-65
1846	395,942	100	160	400	2,500	9,000	
1846-C	12,995	700	3,000	7,000	25,000	80,000	
1846-D	80,294	500	600	3,000	10,000	—	
1846-O	58,000	100	600	4,000	15,000	—	
1847	915,981	100	150	400	2,000	8,000	
1847-C	84,151	300	1,000	3,000	18,000	—	
1847-D	64,405	300	1,000	2,000	7,000	—	
1847-O	12,000	510	6,000	12,000	25,000	50,000	
1848	260,775	100	300	400	3,000	8,000	
1848-C	64,472	400	1,000	2,500	19,000	—	
1848-D	47,465	300	800	2,600	14,000	—	
1849	133,070	100	200	750	3,000	—	
1849-C	64,823	300	950	3,000	15,000	—	
1849-D	39,036	500	1,000	3,000	10,000	—	
1850	64,491	200	750	1,000	4,000	10,000	
1850-C	63,591	300	1,000	2,000	15,000	—	
1850-D	43,984	300	1,650	4,000	15,000	—	
1851	377,505	100	200	300	2,000	9,000	
1851-C	49,176	490	1,200	3,400	19,000	—	
1851-D	62,710	475	1,400	3,000	15,000	—	
1851-O	41,000	400	910	5,000	13,000	—	
1852	573,901	100	175	200	1,200	8,000	
1852-C	72,574	400	800	2,000	8,000	25,000	
1852-D	91,584	400	800	2,000	10,000	—	
1853	305,770	100	200	200	1,600	9,000	
1853-C	65,571	300	800	2,000	11,000	—	
1853-D	89,678	300	800	2,000	6,000	22,500	
1854	160,675	100	300	600	3,000	—	
1854-C	39,283	400	1,200	4,000	22,000	—	
1854-D	56,413	300	900	2,000	9,000	—	
1854-O	46,000	200	400	900	6,000	—	
1854-S	268	—	—	300,000	—	—	
1855	117,098	100	200	300	3,000	7,000	—
1855-C	39,788	400	1,400	3,000	17,000	60,000	
1855-D	22,432	500	1,100	3,000	16,000	—	
1855-O	11,100	400	2,000	4,000	20,000	—	
1855-S	61,000	200	800	3,000	9,000	—	
1856	197,990	100	200	300	2,000	9,000	—
1856-C	28,457	400	1,000	4,000	21,000	—	
1856-D	19,786	400	1,000	3,000	14,000	—	
1856-O	10,000	400	1,650	5,000	15,500	—	
1856-S	105,100	225	700	1,500	5,000	—	
1857	98,188	100	150	300	2,000	9,000	—
1857-C	31,360	400	1,000	2,600	12,000	—	
1857-D	17,046	400	850	2,500	15,000	—	

	Mintage	Fine-12	EF-40	AU-50	MS-60	MS-63	Proof-65
1857-O	13,000	400	1,500	4,600	12,000	—	
1857-S	87,000	300	710	1,250	6,000	—	
1858	15,136	300	575	1,600	3,000	15,000	—
1858-C	38,856	300	1,000	3,000	18,000	—	
1858-D	15,362	300	1,000	1,600	13,000	—	
1858-S	18,600	300	1,675	7,000	15,000	—	
1859 80	16,734	200	500	1,000	4,000	—	—
1859-C	31,847	300	1,000	3,500	18,000	50,000	—
1859-D	10,366	400	1,700	2,800	13,000	—	
1859-S	13,220	900	2,950	8,000			
1860 62	19,763	150	300	900	6,000	—	—
1860-C	14,813	500	1,000	3,500	15,000	—	
1860-D	14,635	500	1,000	2,000	14,000	32,500	—
1860-S	21,200	600	1,100	9,000	25,000	—	
1861 66	688,084	100	150	200	2,000	6,000	$65,500
1861-C	6,879	900	2,000	8,000	32,000	—	
1861-D	1,597	2,000	3,000	16,000	41,000	—	
1861-S	18,000	800	2,000	10,000	32,500	—	
1862 35	4,430	300	1,500	4,000	20,000	—	—
1862-S	9,500	900	8,000	18,000	60,000	—	
1863 30	2,442	500	2,000	8,000	22,500	—	
1863-S	17,000	400	3,000	13,000	30,000	—	
1864 50	4,170	200	1,200	4,000	12,500	—	65,000
1864-S	3,888	3,000	20,000	45,000	90,000	—	
1865 25	1,270	600	2,000	9,000	28,000	—	—
1865-S	27,612	500	2,000	8,000	25,000	—	
1866-S	9,000	900	2,800	12,500	25,000	—	

Motto over Eagle (1866–1908)

	Mintage	Fine-12	EF-40	AU-50	MS-60	MS-63	Proof-65
1866 30	6,700	$400	$1,000	$4,600	$10,000	—	—
1866-S	34,920	600	2,000	9,000	18,000	—	
1867 50	6,870	200	1,000	4,650	8,650	—	—
1867-S	29,000	900	2,500	14,000	26,500	—	
1868 25	5,700	400	1,000	3,600	6,000	—	—
1868-S	52,000	300	1,100	5,000	10,000	—	
1869 25	1,760	500	2,000	5,000	10,000	—	—
1869-S	31,000	525	2,300	9,000	23,500	—	
1870 35	4,000	650	1,950	4,300	12,000	—	—
1870-CC	7,675	2,400	15,000	40,000	65,000	—	
1870-S	17,000	1,075	2,800	13,000	25,000	—	
1871 30	3,200	775	2,050	6,000	21,000	—	—
1871-CC	20,770	825	3,500	15,000	60,000	—	
1871-S	25,000	500	1,250	4,000	18,500	—	—

HALF EAGLES, OR $5 GOLD PIECES (1795–1929)

	Mintage	Fine-12	EF-40	AU-50	MS-60	MS-63	Proof-65
1872 ....30	1,660	725	1,900	3,750	15,000	$42,000	—
1872-CC	16,980	775	5,000	17,000	60,000	—	—
1872-S	36,400	500	1,350	5,000	20,500	—	
1873 combined total	112,480						
1873 closed 3 ....25 ..		150	175	550	2,400	11,500	—
1873 open 3	122,800	150	175	500	2,300	11,000	
1873-CC	7,416	1,400	12,000	25,000	40,000	—	
1873-S	31,000	615	2,700	5,000	20,000	—	
1874 ....20	3,488	580	2,050	4,600	16,000	—	—
1874-CC	21,198	625	2,500	11,000	28,000	—	
1874-S	16,000	700	2,500	6,600	19,500	—	
1875 ....20	200	42,000	57,000	96,000	—	—	—
1875-CC	11,828	1,250	3,700	10,500	30,000	—	
1875-S	9,000	725	2,750	8,650	22,000	—	
1876 ....45	1,432	925	2,500	4,750	18,000	42,000	—
1876-CC	6,887	1,000	3,500	11,000	20,000	45,000	
1876-S	4,000	1,450	3,100	13,000	27,000	—	
1877 ,........20	1,132	750	2,400	4,200	11,400	—	—
1877-CC	8,680	850	3,600	9,000	28,000	—	
1877-S	26,700	330	700	3,000	15,000	—	
1878 ....20	131,720	125	150	190	600	3,100	—
1878-CC	9,054	1,900	6,800	18,000	32,500	—	
1878-S	144,700	135	185	350	1,300	4,350	
1879 ....30	301,920	125	145	210	450	1,500	—
1879-CC	17,281	400	900	3,000	15,000	—	
1879-S	426,200	160	240	285	600	3,950	
1880 ....36	3,166,400	115	125	155	195	1,400	—
1880-CC	51,017	315	650	1,300	10,000	—	
1880-S	1,348,900	150	200	250	400	1,400	
1881 combined total	5,708,760						
1881 regular date ....42 ..		105	150	175	250	1,400	$35,000
1881/0 overdate		300	600	1,500	5,000	—	
1881-CC	13,886	400	1,200	6,000	16,000	22,000	
1881-S	969,000	150	200	225	275	600	
1882 ....48	2,514,520	150	200	225	275	600	35,000
1882-CC	82,817	285	425	1,600	7,000	20,000	
1882-S	969,000	150	200	225	275	550	
1883 ....61	233,400	150	200	225	600	2,000	—
1883-CC	12,958	400	600	6,000	16,000	35,000	
1883-S	83,200	150	200	275	995	2,000	
1884 ....48	191,030	150	175	200	900	1,600	—
1884-CC	16,402	400	700	3,500	13,000	20,000	
1884-S	177,000	200	275	300	600	1,600	
1885 ....66	601,440	105	120	125	200	550	—
1885-S	1,211,500	110	115	135	175	550	

HALF EAGLES, OR $5 GOLD PIECES (1795–1929)

	Mintage	Fine-12	EF-40	AU-50	MS-60	MS-63	Proof-65
1886 ....72	388,360	150	175	195	450	1,000	—
1886-S	3,268,000	110	120	150	175	600	
1887 (proof only)	87	—	—	—	—	—	—
1887-S	1,912,000	105	120	140	175	550	
1888 ....95	18,201	130	200	275	995	2,000	—
1888-S	293,900	135	240	650	2,100	2,800	
1889 ....45	7,520	220	450	795	1,400	2,000	35,000
1890 ....88	4,240	375	600	1,200	4,000	5,800	29,000
1890-CC	53,800	250	300	450	1,600	3,000	
1891 ....53	61,360	120	160	210	700	2,000	27,000
1891-CC	208,000	175	250	350	700	2,600	
1892 ....92	753,480	110	120	130	195	650	—
1892-CC	82,968	250	350	500	1,900	5,200	
1892-O	10,000	400	900	1,900	5,900	8,000	
1892-S	298,400	150	200	275	1,200	4,300	
1893 ....77	1,528,120	100	115	140	195	550	27,000
1893-CC	60,000	200	500	600	1,900	5,000	
1893-O	110,000	195	225	350	1,200	5,000	
1893-S	224,000	150	175	225	550	1,000	
1894 ....75	957,880	110	120	140	200	800	29,500
1894-O	16,600	160	250	375	1,500	4,850	
1894-S	55,900	250	300	550	3,300	8,900	
1895 ....81	1,345,855	105	115	140	200	550	29,000
1895-S	112,000	175	275	900	3,800	6,000	
1896 ....103	58,960	130	150	175	255	1,000	24,000
1896-S	155,400	185	250	600	2,000	6,700	
1897 ....83	867,800	110	115	145	195	550	—
1897-S	354,000	135	195	395	1,300	4,250	
1898 ....75	633,420	110	115	135	225	550	25,000
1898-S	1,397,400	120	130	140	190	1,000	
1899 ....99	1,710,630	110	120	130	175	575	25,000
1899-S	1,545,000	120	130	140	225	575	
1900 ....230	1,405,500	115	120	130	200	525	26,000
1900-S	329,000	130	150	250	850	750	
1901 ....140	615,900	115	120	130	175	525	26,000
1901-S combined total	3,648,000						
1901-S regular date		110	115	135	175	525	
1901/0-S overdate		140	195	350	900	3,000	
1902 ....162	172,400	110	115	135	175	525	25,000
1902-S	939,000	110	115	135	175	525	
1903 ....154	226,870	110	115	135	175	525	25,000
1903-S	1,855,000	110	115	135	175	525	
1904 ....136	392,000	110	115	135	175	575	25,000
1904-S	97,000	130	175	295	750	3,850	
1905 ....108	302,200	115	125	145	195	575	27,000

	Mintage	Fine-12	EF-40	AU-50	MS-60	MS-63	Proof-65
1905-S	880,700	130	175	295	750	2,500	
1906 85	348,735	115	125	145	195	575	27,000
1906-D	320,000	115	125	145	195	575	
1906-S	598,000	115	125	145	195	575	
1907 92	626,100	115	125	145	195	575	27,000
1907-D	888,000	115	125	145	195	575	
1908	421,874	115	125	145	195	575	

Indian Head Portrait (1908–1929)

	Mintage	Fine-12	EF-40	AU-50	MS-60	MS-63	Proof-65
1908 167	577,845	$100	$200	$225	$300	$1,200	$24,000
1908-D	148,000	110	200	225	300	1,200	
1908-S	82,000	195	200	295	3,000	3,700	
1909 78	627,060	110	200	225	300	1,200	30,000
1909-D	3,423,560	110	200	225	300	1,200	
1909-O	34,200	700	900	1,450	7,000	39,000	
1909-S	297,200	195	200	300	995	6,500	
1910 250	604,000	110	200	225	300	2,000	26,000
1910-D	193,600	125	200	300	450	2,000	
1910-S	770,200	200	300	350	1,000	6,000	
1911 139	915,000	110	200	225	300	1,000	24,500
1911-D	72,500	110	200	275	4,000	19,000	
1911-S	1,416,000	110	200	225	600	2,500	
1912 144	790,000	110	300	500	400	1,200	24,500
1912-S	392,000	110	300	500	995	9,950	
1913 99	915,901	110	200	225	300	1,500	25,000
1913-S	408,000	200	300	500	1,700	12,000	
1914 125	247,000	110	200	225	300	1,500	25,500
1914-D	247,000	200	300	500	400	2,500	
1914-S	263,000	200	300	900	995	9,500	
1915 75	588,000	110	200	225	300	1,500	30,000
1915-S	164,000	300	375	400	2,500	8,000	
1916-S	240,000	200	300	375	600	2,200	
1929	662,000	2,900	3,750	6,000	7,500	8,000	

EAGLES, OR $10 GOLD PIECES (1795–1933)

Capped Bust Portrait Facing Right with Small Eagle on Reverse (1795–1797)

	Mintage	VF-20	EF-40	MS-60
1795 combined total	5,583			
1795 with 9 leaves below eagle		$37,000	$50,000	$200,000
1795 with 13 leaves below eagle		9,000	11,000	55,000
1796	4,146	10,000	13,000	50,000
1797	3,615	12,000	19,000	80,000

Capped Bust Portrait Facing Right with Heraldic Eagle on Reverse (1797–1804)

	Mintage	VF-20	EF-40	MS-60
1797	10,940	$2,500	$3,900	$12,950
1798/7 overdate with 9 stars left, 4 right	900	6,000	15,000	55,000

	Mintage	VF-20	EF-40	MS-60
1798/7 overdate with 7 stars left, 6 right	842	12,000	50,000	—
1799	37,449	2,300	4,000	8,500
1800	5,999	2,800	4,700	10,000
1801	44,344	2,300	4,700	9,000
1803	15,017	2,300	4,700	9,000
1804	3,757	3,000	6,000	19,000

Coronet Portrait (1838–1907)

No Motto over Eagle (1838–1866)

	Mintage	VF-20	EF-40	AU-50	MS-60	MS-63	Proof-65
1838	7,200	$785	$2,500	$4,500	$19,500	$75,000	
1839 with large letters	25,801	750	1,400	3,500	12,500	70,000	

Modified Portrait of Liberty, Smaller Letters (1839–1907)

	Mintage	VF-20	EF-40	AU-50	MS-60	MS-65	Proof-65
1839 with small letters	12,447	$1,500	$3,200	$8,000	$24,000	—	
1840	47,338	330	700	2,500	14,000	—	
1841	63,131	400	650	2,200	11,000	$38,000	
1841-O	2,500	2,000	6,000	17,000	37,000	—	
1842 small date	18,623	350	500	2,000	8,000	29,000	
1842 large date	62,884	400	600	2,500	10,000	—	
1842-O	27,400	350	750	4,000	20,000	—	
1843	75,462	350	650	2,500	12,000	—	
1843-O	175,162	350	600	1,500	17,000	—	
1844	6,361	995	2,995	8,000	29,500	—	
1844-O	118,700	350	500	1,200	9,950	—	
1845	26,153	500	1,200	5,500	19,000	—	
1845-O	47,500	400	900	2,500	20,000	—	
1846	20,095	800	2,200	7,300	24,000	—	
1846-O	81,780	500	1,000	6,700	14,000	—	
1847	862,258	350	380	700	5,000	22,000	

EAGLES, OR $10 GOLD PIECES (1795–1933)

	Mintage	VF-20	EF-40	AU-50	MS-60	MS-65	Proof-65
1847-O	571,500	350	400	800	5,000	17,500	
1848	145,484	350	450	750	5,500	35,000	
1848-O	35,850	500	1,350	5,500	17,000	—	
1849	653,618	350	450	750	4,800	12,000	
1849-O	23,900	800	2,400	5,000	21,000	—	
1850 combined total	291,451						
1850 small date		600	900	2,000	18,000	—	
1850 large date		350	600	995	5,500	18,000	
1850-O	57,500	350	600	6,000	13,000	75,000	
1851	176,328	350	400	1,100	9,000	30,000	
1851-O	263,000	350	500	1,700	11,000	—	
1852	263,106	350	500	700	5,500	19,000	
1852-O	18,000	700	1,400	4,900	25,000	—	
1853 combined total	201,253						
1853 regular date		350	400	700	5,200	32,000	
1853/2 overdate		550	1,100	2,400	11,000	—	
1853-O	51,000	350	450	1,500	9,000	—	
1854	54,250	350	500	1,500	10,000	—	
1854-O combined total	52,500						
1854-O small date		350	1,000	2,700	11,000	—	
1854-O large date		450	1,600	3,600	13,000	—	
1854-S	123,826	350	500	1,500	13,000	—	
1855	121,701	350	400	700	5,500	—	
1855-O	18,000	600	1,900	5,000	15,000	—	
1855-S	9,000	1,400	3,500	7,500	29,000	—	
1856	60,490	350	400	800	5,000	14,000	—
1856-O	14,500	950	2,100	5,000	16,000	—	
1856-S	68,000	350	450	1,300	10,000	—	
1857	16,666	350	900	3,600	13,000	—	—
1857-O	5,500	1,100	2,400	5,500	25,000	—	
1857-S	26,000	400	950	2,500	11,000	—	
1858	2,521	5,500	12,000	25,000	65,000	—	—
1858-O	20,000	350	700	1,800	14,000	—	
1858-S		11,800	2,000	4,500	12,000	32,000	—
1859 ...... *80*	16,013	350	575	2,500	13,000	—	—
1859-O	2,300	3,500	9,500	25,000	47,500	—	
1859-S	7,000	3,000	7,000	17,500	45,000	—	
1860 ...... *50*	15,055	400	950	3,000	12,000	—	—
1860-O	11,100	500	1,400	3,300	14,000	—	
1860-S	5,000	2,500	6,500	19,000	42,000	—	
1861 ...... *69*	113,164	350	400	800	5,400	17,000	—
1861-S	15,500	1,400	4,000	12,000	32,000	—	
1862 ...... *35*	10,960	400	1,200	3,900	12,000	—	—
1862-S	12,500	1,700	4,200	12,000	40,000	—	
1863 ...... *30*	1,218	4,000	10,000	24,000	57,500	—	—

EAGLES, OR $10 GOLD PIECES (1795–1933)

	Mintage	VF-20	EF-40	AU-50	MS-60	MS-65	Proof-65
1863-S	10,000	1,500	4,000	10,000	52,000	—	
1864 .... 50	3,530	1,800	3,950	9,000	27,000	—	—
1864-S	2,500	4,200	11,000	21,000	50,000	—	
1865 .... 25	3,980	1,500	5,000	11,000	35,000	—	—
1865-S combined total	16,700						
1865-S regular date		5,000	10,000	21,000	45,000	—	
1865-S with 865 over inverted							
186		3,600	8,000	15,000	50,000	—	
1866-S	8,500	3,600	6,000	20,000	45,000	—	

Motto over Eagle (1866–1907)

	Mintage	VF-20	EF-40	AU-50	MS-60	MS-63	Proof-65
1866 .... 30	3,750	$800	$2,000	$5,000	$17,000	—	$60,000
1866-S	11,500	1,700	4,000	8,500	25,000	—	
1867 .... 50	3,090	1,500	2,500	6,000	28,000	—	60,000
1867-S	9,000	2,300	7,000	12,000	42,500	—	
1868 .... 5	10,630	570	1,000	2,500	15,000	—	60,000
1868-S	13,500	1,700	3,000	5,000	33,000	—	
1869 .... 25	1,830	1,500	3,000	8,000	29,500	$65,000	60,000
1869-S	6,430	1,500	3,000	8,000	30,000	—	
1870 .... 35	3,990	700	1,200	2,500	18,000	—	60,000
1870-CC	5,908	10,000	25,000	70,000	—	—	
1870-S	8,000	1,500	3,000	7,500	37,000	—	
1871 .... 30	1,790	1,100	4,000	7,000	20,000	—	60,000
1871-CC	8,085	2,000	5,000	20,000	60,000	—	
1871-S	16,500	1,200	2,000	8,000	30,000	—	
1872 .... 30	1,620	2,000	4,000	15,000	30,000	—	60,000
1872-CC	4,680	3,200	11,000	35,000	60,000	—	
1872-S	17,300	600	1,000	2,500	15,000	—	
1873 .... 25	800	4,000	10,000	29,000	55,000	—	60,000
1873-CC	4,543	2,000	13,000	30,000	—	—	
1873-S	12,000	1,150	2,500	5,000	20,000	—	
1874 .... 20	53,140	250	300	350	2,300	10,000	58,000
1874-CC	16,767	700	3,900	11,000	25,000	—	
1874-S	10,000	1,100	3,600	9,500	45,000	—	

	Mintage	VF-20	EF-40	AU-50	MS-60	MS-63	Proof-65
1875 ....20.............	100	40,000	70,000	120,000	—	—	170,000
1875-CC	7,715	3,800	10,000	35,000	50,000	—	
1876 ....45..............	687	3,500	7,000	19,000	49,000	—	50,000
1876-CC	4,696	3,500	7,000	24,000	50,000	—	
1876-S	5,000	1,300	2,000	7,000	40,000	—	
1877 ....20.............	797	2,500	4,000	10,000	45,000	60,000	60,000
1877-CC	3,332	3,000	6,000	14,000	40,000	—	
1877-S	17,000	500	1,000	3,000	20,000	—	
1878 ....20.............	73,780	240	280	350	1,500	6,000	58,000
1878-CC	3,244	3,900	7,900	17,000	40,000	—	
1878-S	26,100	400	600	3,000	21,000	—	
1879 ....30............ ...	384,740	240	260	290	800	3,500	50,000
1879-CC	1,762	4,500	13,000	25,000	49,000	—	
1879-O	1,500	1,800	4,500	11,000	40,000	—	
1879-S	224,000	240	260	290	1,600	8,000	
1880 ....36..............	1,644,840	240	260	290	330	3,000	50,000
1880-CC	11,190	400	800	2,000	12,000	—	
1880-O	9,200	300	600	1,500	9,000	—	
1880-S	506,250	240	260	290	500	4,000	
1881 ....40..............	3,877,220	240	260	280	300	700	50,000
1881-CC	24,015	400	600	1,100	7,500	20,000	
1881-O	8,350	330	700	2,000	7,300	—	
1881-S	970,000	240	260	290	400	6,000	
1882 ....40..............	2,324,440	240	260	290	300	700	50,000
1882-CC	6,764	500	1,200	3,500	12,000	30,000	
1882-O	10,820	300	700	1,300	9,000	19,500	
1882-S	132,000	240	280	350	500	5,000	
1883 ....40..............	208,700	240	280	290	370	2,500	50,000
1883-CC	12,000	400	700	2,200	12,000	27,000	
1883-O	800	3,000	8,000	12,000	50,000	—	
1883-S	38,000	300	350	375	1,300	7,000	
1884 ....45..............	76,860	300	350	375	1,000	2,500	
1884-CC	9,925	500	900	3,000	11,000	25,000	
1884-S	124,250	240	260	300	700	6,700	
1885 ....65..............	253,462	240	260	300	500	4,000	48,000
1885-S	228,000	240	260	300	325	5,000	
1886 ....60..............	236,100	240	250	300	400	3,000	48,000
1886-S	826,000	240	260	300	400	800	
1887 ....80..............	53,600	240	260	400	1,000	5,000	48,000
1887-S	817,000	240	260	285	300	3,000	
1888 ....75..............	132,921	240	260	325	1,000	7,000	47,000
1888-O	21,335	240	260	285	650	7,000	
1888-S	648,700	240	260	300	350	3,600	
1889 ....45..............	4,440	250	475	900	3,600	8,500	47,000
1889-S	425,400	240	260	285	375	2,400	

	Mintage	VF-20	EF-40	AU-50	MS-60	MS-63	Proof-65
1890 . . . . 63	57,980	240	260	300	1,000	5,000	46,000
1890-CC	17,500	360	475	700	2,000	15,000	
1891 . . . . 48	91,820	240	260	285	325	2,500	47,000
1891-CC	103,732	240	375	425	800	4,300	
1892 . . . . 72	797,480	240	260	300	310	1,200	46,000
1892-CC	40,000	300	475	550	3,500	11,000	
1892-O	28,688	300	350	400	500	5,500	
1892-S	115,500	240	260	300	425	2,500	
1893 . . . . 55	1,840,840	240	260	285	325	700	47,000
1893-CC	14,000	425	600	1,700	5,500	17,000	
1893-O	17,000	240	260	325	650	5,500	
1893-S	141,350	240	260	325	660	4,000	
1894 . . . . 43	2,470,735	240	260	285	325	700	47,000
1894-O	107,500	240	260	350	1,100	5,500	
1894-S	25,000	240	260	1,000	3,500	9,500	
1895 . . . . 56	567,770	240	260	285	300	700	47,000
1895-O	98,000	240	260	245	500	4,000	
1895-S	49,000	240	260	900	5,000	13,000	
1896 . . . . 78	76,270	240	260	285	325	800	46,000
1896-S	123,750	240	260	700	4,500	12,000	
1897 . . . . 69	1,000,090	240	260	285	325	900	46,000
1897-O	42,500	240	260	285	700	3,000	
1897-S	234,750	240	260	285	1,000	4,000	
1898 . . . . 67	812,130	240	260	285	350	700	46,000
1898-S	473,600	240	260	285	400	2,000	
1899 . . . . 86	1,262,219	240	260	285	325	700	44,000
1899-O	37,047	240	260	285	600	3,000	
1899-S	841,000	240	260	285	400	1,800	
1900 . . . . 120	293,840	240	260	285	350	600	40,000
1900-S	81,000	240	260	285	1,000	5,000	
1901 . . . . 85	1,718,740	240	260	285	325	600	40,000
1901-O	72,041	240	260	285	450	2,000	
1901-S	2,812,750	240	260	285	325	600	
1902 . . . . 113	82,400	240	260	285	350	1,200	40,000
1902-S	469,500	240	260	285	325	600	
1903 . . . . 96	125,830	240	260	285	325	1,100	40,000
1903-O	112,771	240	260	300	400	2,000	
1903-S	538,000	240	260	285	325	600	
1904 . . . . 108	161,930	240	260	285	400	900	40,000
1904-O	108,950	240	300	350	400	900	
1905 . . . . 86	200,992	240	260	285	325	900	40,000
1905-S	369,250	240	260	350	1,300	4,000	
1906 . . . . 77	165,420	240	260	285	325	900	40,000
1906-D	981,000	240	260	285	325	900	
1906-O	86,895	240	260	350	600	1,500	

	Mintage	VF-20	EF-40	AU-50	MS-60	MS-63	Proof-65
1906-S	457,000	240	260	300	500	2,500	
1907 .... 74	1,203,899	240	260	285	325	600	40,000
1907-D	1,030,000	240	260	285	325	825	
1907-S	210,500	240	260	300	800	2,500	

Indian Head Portrait (1907–1933)

	Mintage	VF-20	EF-40	AU-50	MS-60	MS-63	Proof-65
1907 with wire rim and periods before and after E PLURIBUS UNUM	500	—	—	$6,000	$9,000	$14,000	$45,000
1907 with rounded rim and periods	42	—	—	22,000	26,000	40,000	75,000
1907 with no periods	239,406	$380	$400	425	600	1,750	
1908 without IN GOD WE TRUST	33,500	380	425	500	800	2,500	
1908-D without motto	210,000	390	425	500	800	7,000	

Motto Added to Reverse (1908–1933)

	Mintage	Fine-12	EF-40	AU-50	MS-60	MS-63	Proof-65
1908 .... 116	341,370	$325	$400	$425	$500	$900	$33,000
1908-D	836,500	325	425	450	800	3,600	
1908-S	59,850	400	450	500	2,000	5,000	
1909 .... 74	184,789	325	400	400	600	1,200	45,000
1909-D	121,540	325	400	420	900	3,800	

	Mintage	Fine-12	EF-40	AU-50	MS-60	MS-63	Proof-65
1909-S	292,350	325	400	420	700	1,500	
1910 . . . . *204*	318,500	325	460	420	500	800	40,000
1910-D	2,356,640	325	460	420	500	800	
1910-S	811,000	325	400	440	900	3,800	
1911 . . . . . . *95*	505,500	325	400	420	500	800	35,000
1911-D	30,100	325	600	800	4,000	30,000	
1911-S	51,000	350	400	650	900	2,500	
1912 . . . . . . *83*	405,000	325	350	420	500	900	35,000
1912-S	300,000	325	400	450	1,000	2,500	
1913 . . . . . . *71*	442,000	325	350	420	500	800	36,000
1913-S	66,000	325	550	875	4,000	29,000	
1914 . . . . . . *50*	151,000	325	350	420	500	700	37,000
1914-D	343,500	325	350	420	500	1,100	
1914-S	208,000	325	350	450	700	5,000	
1915 . . . . . . *75*	351,000	325	350	420	500	1,000	40,000
1915-S	59,000	350	475	600	2,400	9,000	
1916-S	138,500	325	350	495	700	2,000	
1920-S	126,500	4,500	6,000	8,000	15,000	35,000	
1926	1,014,000	325	350	420	500	650	
1930-S	96,000	3,500	4,500	6,000	7,000	11,000	
1932	4,463,000	325	350	420	500	650	
1933	312,500	—	—	—	54,000	90,000	

DOUBLE EAGLES, OR $20 GOLD PIECES (1849–1933)

Coronet Portrait (1849–1907)

No Motto over Eagle (1849–1866)

	Mintage	VF-20	EF-40	AU-50	MS-60	MS-63	Proof-63
1849	1	(part of the U.S. Mint Collection)					
1850	1,170,261	$525	$600	$1,100	$3,300	$40,000	

	Mintage	VF-20	EF-40	AU-50	MS-60	MS-63	Proof-63
1850-O	141,000	650	1,100	3,500	16,000	40,000	
1851	2,087,155	525	550	750	3,000	18,000	
1851-O	315,000	600	700	1,400	15,000	40,000	
1852	2,053,026	525	550	750	3,000	14,000	
1852-O	190,000	550	700	1,500	14,000	35,000	
1853 combined total	1,261,326						
1853 regular date		500	550	800	5,000	25,000	
1853/2 overdate		650	1,000	3,000	30,000	—	
1853-O	71,000	650	850	2,500	20,000	45,000	
1854	757,899	525	600	800	4,300	25,000	
1854-O	3,250	13,000	30,000	57,000	110,000	—	
1854-S	141,468	575	625	900	3,000	8,000	
1855	364,666	575	675	925	4,000	35,000	
1855-O	8,000	2,500	5,000	14,500	50,000		
1855-S	879,675	575	625	950	6,000	22,000	
1856	329,878	575	625	800	4,000	37,000	
1856-O	2,250	15,000	28,000	57,000	120,000	350,000	
1856-S	1,189,750	575	625	750	3,700	20,000	
1857	439,375	600	675	800	3,200	25,000	
1857-O	30,000	950	1,600	3,800	15,000	40,000	
1857-S	970,500	525	600	700	3,200	20,000	
1858	211,714	550	700	1,500	4,500	28,000	
1858-O	35,250	1,000	1,600	4,000	16,000	40,000	
1858-S	846,710	525	650	1,000	8,000	25,000	
1859 ......*80*	43,517	900	2,000	4,000	25,000	60,000	
1859-O	9,100	3,000	6,200	15,000	35,000	125,000	
1859-S	636,445	525	650	1,000	2,500	11,000	
1860 ......*59*	577,611	525	650	750	3,500	16,000	
1860-O	6,600	2,500	5,500	13,000	35,000	125,000	
1860-S	544,950	525	650	900	5,000	125,000	
1861 combined total	2,976,387						
1861 with regular reverse ..*66*	500	550	650	2,100	7,500	—	
1861 with Paquet reverse (tall letters)		—	—	—	—	700,000*	
1861-O	17,741	1,300	3,500	6,500	18,000	40,000	
1861-S with regular reverse	748,750	525	650	1,100	5,000	30,000	
1861-S with Paquet reverse (tall letters)	19,250	6,000	10,000	25,000	75,000	—	
1862 ......*35*	92,098	700	1,300	3,800	11,000	35,000	
1862-S	854,173	525	650	1,600	15,000	35,000	
1863 ......*30*	142,760	525	650	1,600	10,000	35,000	
1863-S	966,570	525	650	1,400	5,000	27,000	
1864 ......*50*	204,235	525	650	1,400	10,000	30,000	$37,000
1864-S	793,660	525	650	1,700	7,000	25,000	

	Mintage	VF-20	EF-40	AU-50	MS-60	MS-63	Proof-63
1865 ....25..............	351,175	525	680	1,000	5,000	25,000	
1865-S	1,042,500	525	650	1,200	6,000	27,000	
1866-S	120,000	1,600	3,200	10,000	20,000	—	

* MS-67 specimen

Motto over Eagle (1866–1907)

	Mintage	VF-20	EF-40	AU-50	MS-60	MS-63	Proof-65
1866 ....30..............	698,745	$390	$425	$800	$4,500	$18,000	$110,000
1866-S	842,250	390	450	1,400	17,000	30,000	
1867 ....50..............	251,015	390	425	500	1,700	15,000	110,000
1867-S	920,750	390	425	950	12,500	18,500	
1868 ....25..............	98,575	390	450	1,200	11,000	18,500	115,000
1868-S	837,500	390	425	1,000	10,000	18,500	
1869 ....25..............	175,130	390	425	750	4,700	16,000	115,000
1869-S	686,750	390	425	750	4,500	17,000	
1870 ....35..............	155,150	390	450	1,000	6,000	20,000	110,000
1870-CC	3,789	40,000	75,000	120,000	—	—	
1870-S	982,000	390	425	675	5,000	20,000	
1871 ....30..............	80,120	390	525	1,100	4,150	17,000	110,000
1871-CC	17,387	2,000	4,500	10,000	26,500	—	
1871-S	928,000	390	425	575	3,000	12,500	
1872 ....30..............	251,850	390	425	600	2,000	15,000	110,000
1872-CC	26,900	975	1,500	3,000	18,500	40,000	
1872-S	780,000	395	425	500	2,000	18,000	
1873 combined total	1,709,800						
1873 closed 3 ....25		390	650	700	4,000	10,000	110,000
1873 open 3		390	425	475	750	6,000	
1873-CC	22,410	875	1,425	2,000	15,000	—	
1873-S	1,040,600	390	425	475	1,000	10,000	
1874 ....20..............	366,780	390	425	475	1,000	8,000	110,000
1874-CC	115,085	390	550	900	8,000	16,500	
1874-S	1,214,000	390	425	475	1,400	10,500	

	Mintage	VF-20	EF-40	AU-50	MS-60	MS-63	Proof-65
1875 .... 20	295,720	390	425	475	900	10,000	110,000
1875-CC	111,151	390	450	600	2,500	12,000	
1875-S	1,230,000	390	425	500	750	10,000	
1876 .... 45	583,860	390	425	500	750	9,000	90,000
1876-CC	138,441	425	525	500	3,000	15,000	
1876-S	1,597,000	390	425	475	750	8,000	

TWENTY DOLLARS Spelled Out (1877–1907)

	Mintage	VF-20	EF-40	AU-50	MS-60	MS-63	Proof-65
1877 .... 20	397,650	$425	$475	$500	$575	$2,000	$75,000
1877-CC	42,565	550	800	1,000	9,000	25,000	
1877-S	1,735,000	390	475	500	525	3,000	
1878 .... 20	543,625	390	475	500	525	2,500	70,000
1878-CC	13,180	700	1,500	3,000	8,000	—	
1878-S	1,739,000	390	425	500	750	10,000	
1879 .... 30	207,600	390	425	500	725	6,000	65,000
1879-CC	10,708	900	1,200	3,000	15,000	40,000	
1879-O	2,325	2,500	4,500	9,000	26,000	50,000	
1879-S	1,223,800	390	425	500	1,000	12,000	
1880 .... 36	51,420	390	425	550	2,500	15,800	65,000
1880-S	836,000	390	425	525	1,200	8,000	
1881 .... 61	2,199	3,000	7,000	14,000	40,000	75,000	65,000
1881-S	727,000	390	425	550	1,000	8,000	
1882 .... 59	571	6,000	15,000	28,000	60,000	90,000	70,000
1882-CC	39,140	500	600	875	6,500	22,000	
1882-S	1,125,000	390	425	525	700	18,000	
1883 (proof only)	92	—	—	—	—	—	90,000
1883-CC	59,962	425	600	1,000	5,000	20,000	
1883-S	1,189,000	390	425	480	500	4,000	
1884 (proof only)	71	—	—	—	—	—	90,000
1884-CC	81,139	450	600	700	3,000	18,500	
1884-S	916,000	390	425	500	600	2,500	
1885 .... 77	751	3,000	4,500	9,000	30,000	60,000	80,000
1885-CC	9,450	800	1,200	3,400	11,000	40,000	
1885-S	683,500	390	425	500	525	3,000	
1886 .... 106	1,000	4,600	10,000	20,000	35,000	75,000	70,000
1887 (proof only)	121	—	—	—	—	—	70,000
1887-S	283,000	390	425	475	575	5,000	
1888 .... 105	226,161	390	425	500	700	4,500	60,000
1888-S	859,600	390	425	500	525	3,000	
1889 .... 45	44,070	390	425	500	575	6,000	60,000
1889-CC	30,945	500	700	1,100	4,800	17,000	
1889-S	774,700	390	425	500	575	2,500	
1890 .... 55	75,940	390	425	500	590	3,000	60,000

	Mintage	VF-20	EF-40	AU-50	MS-60	MS-63	Proof-65
1890-CC	91,209	600	700	800	2,500	12,000	
1890-S	802,750	390	425	450	500	4,200	
1891 ....52...............	1,390	2,900	4,700	9,000	25,000	46,000	55,000
1891-CC	5,000	1,500	3,500	8,000	20,000	46,000	
1891-S	1,288,125	380	400	450	500	1,600	
1892 ....93...............	4,430	1,000	1,400	2,500	7,000	15,000	55,000
1892-CC	27,265	425	800	1,000	3,300	15,000	
1892-S	930,150	380	400	450	500	1,600	
1893 ....59...............	344,280	380	400	450	500	2,000	55,000
1893-CC	18,402	500	600	1,100	2,800	8,000	
1893-S	996,175	390	425	450	500	1,700	
1894 ....50...............	1,368,940	390	425	450	500	1,200	55,000
1894-S	1,048,550	390	425	450	500	1,200	
1895 ....51...............	1,114,605	390	425	450	500	900	52,000
1895-S	1,143,500	390	425	450	500	950	
1896 ....128..............	792,535	390	425	450	500	600	52,000
1896-S	1,403,925	390	425	450	500	1,400	
1897 ....86...............	1,383,175	390	425	450	500	900	52,000
1897-S	1,470,250	390	425	450	500	950	
1898 ....75...............	170,395	390	425	450	600	4,000	52,000
1898-S	2,575,175	390	425	450	500	950	
1899 ....84...............	1,669,300	390	425	450	500	900	52,000
1899-S	2,010,300	390	425	450	500	1,000	
1900 ....124..............	1,874,460	390	425	450	500	700	50,000
1900-S	2,459,500	390	425	450	500	1,100	
1901 ....96...............	111,430	390	425	450	500	675	50,000
1901-S	1,596,000	390	425	450	500	1,200	
1902 ....114..............	31,140	390	425	450	900	2,500	50,000
1902-S	1,753,625	390	425	450	500	1,200	
1903 ....158..............	287,270	390	425	450	500	600	50,000
1903-S	954,000	390	425	460	500	850	
1904 ....98...............	6,256,699	390	425	425	450	500	50,000
1904-S	5,134,175	390	425	450	500	575	
1905 ....92...............	58,919	390	425	450	1,300	17,000	50,000
1905-S	1,813,000	390	425	450	500	1,150	
1906 ....94...............	69,596	390	425	450	700	2,200	50,000
1906-D	620,250	390	425	450	600	1,200	
1906-S	2,065,750	390	425	450	600	1,200	
1907 ....78...............	1,451,786	390	425	450	500	600	50,000
1907-D	842,250	390	425	450	500	900	
1907-S	2,165,800	390	425	450	500	1,100	

Saint-Gaudens Portrait of Liberty (1907–1933)

	Mintage	AU-50	MS-60	MS-63	MS-64	MS-65	Proof-65
1907 ultra high relief, plain edge	1 known	—	—	—	—	—	$950,000
1907 ultra high relief, lettered edge (proof only)	24	—	—	—	—	—	800,000
1907 high relief with Roman-numerals date MCMVII, combined total	11,250						
1907 high relief with wire rim		$4,500	$7,000	$11,000	$16,500	$28,000	
1907 high relief with flat rim		4,500	7,000	11,000	16,500	28,000	
1907 with Arabic numerals	361,667	470	550	850	1,500	3,300	
1908 without IN GOD WE TRUST	4,271,551	470	500	650	700	1,000	
1908-D without motto	663,750	470	550	750	1,400	14,000	

Motto Added to Reverse (1908–1933)

	Mintage	AU-50	MS-60	MS-63	MS-64	MS-65	Proof-65
1908 .... *101*	156,258	$500	$600	$1,000	$4,000	$10,000	$30,000
1908-D	349,500	500	600	725	900	2,500	
1908-S	22,000	1,300	3,500	11,000	20,000	35,000	
1909 combined total	161,282						
1909 regular date *74*		570	850	2,500	7,000	58,000	40,000
1909/8 overdate		525	1,300	4,500	10,000	35,000	
1909-D	52,500	575	1,250	3,500	5,000	36,000	
1909-S	2,774,925	470	500	700	1,300	5,000	
1910 .... *167*	482,000	470	500	700	1,500	6,800	39,000
1910-D	429,000	470	500	700	900	2,500	
1910-S	2,128,250	470	500	800	1,800	10,000	
1911 .... *100*	197,250	470	500	1,000	3,000	11,000	35,000
1911-D	846,500	470	500	700	800	1,200	
1911-S	775,750	470	500	750	1,200	3,600	
1912 .... *74*	149,750	470	500	1,700	3,300	13,000	40,000
1913 .... *58*	168,780	470	500	2,200	5,500	22,000	40,000
1913-D	393,500	470	500	900	1,900	3,000	
1913-S	34,000	570	1,000	2,200	6,000	35,000	
1914 .... *70*	95,250	470	500	1,500	3,000	14,000	40,000
1914-D	453,000	470	500	700	1,000	2,100	
1914-S	1,498,000	470	500	675	700	2,000	
1915 .... *50*	152,000	470	500	1,600	3,300	11,000	43,500
1915-S	567,500	470	500	600	700	1,200	
1916-S	796,000	470	500	700	700	1,200	
1920	228,250	470	500	1,500	3,500	25,000	
1920-S	558,000	12,000	25,000	45,000	60,000	175,000	
1921	528,500	15,000	37,000	70,000	100,000	225,000	
1922	1,375,500	400	400	475	600	4,250	
1922-S	2,658,000	650	800	1,600	5,000	40,000	
1923	566,000	400	400	475	900	5,000	

	Mintage	AU-50	MS-60	MS-63	MS-64	MS-65	Proof-65
1923-D	1,702,250	400	400	475	600	850	
1924	4,323,500	400	400	475	500	800	
1924-D	3,049,500	1,300	3,000	4,500	15,000	55,000	
1924-S	2,927,500	1,100	2,200	5,000	14,000	35,000	
1925	2,831,750	400	400	475	500	800	
1925-D	2,938,500	1,000	2,700	7,000	20,000	58,000	
1925-S	3,776,500	975	5,500	26,000	40,000	70,000	
1926	816,750	400	400	475	500	800	
1926-D	481,000	2,400	8,000	26,000	40,000	75,000	
1926-S	2,041,500	1,300	2,000	2,500	5,500	35,000	
1927	2,946,750	400	400	475	500	800	
1927-D	180,000	200,000	275,000	375,000	450,000	650,000	
1927-S	3,107,000	5,000	12,000	26,000	40,000	90,000	
1928	8,816,000	400	400	475	500	800	
1929	1,779,750	7,000	9,000	14,000	21,000	40,000	
1930-S	74,000	13,000	18,000	36,000	45,000	78,000	
1931	2,938,250	11,000	15,000	25,000	33,000	50,000	
1931-D	106,500	10,000	12,000	18,000	30,000	65,000	
1932	1,101,750	9,000	11,000	17,000	27,000	45,000	
1933	445,500	(1 piece legal to own)				7,590,020	

COMMEMORATIVE COINS (1892–PRESENT)

Traditional Commemoratives (1892–1954)

	Number Minted	Number Melted	EF-40	MS-63	MS-65	Proof-63

COLUMBIAN EXPOSITION HALF DOLLARS

1892 . . . . . . *104*	949,896	None	$10.00	$85.00	$650	$7,500
1893 . . . . . . *3 reported*	4,052,104	2,501,700	10.00	80.00	675	15,000

ISABELLA QUARTER DOLLAR

1893 . . . . . . *20*	39,120	15,809	$190	$500	$3,000	$10,000

LAFAYETTE SILVER DOLLAR

1900 . . . . . . *1 known*	50,025	14,000	$190	$1,250	$7,000	$100,000

LOUISIANA PURCHASE EXPOSITION GOLD DOLLARS

Combined total	250,058	215,250				
1903 Jefferson . . . . *100* . . .			$300	$675	$2,500	$8,000
1903 McKinley . . . . *100* . . .			285	625	2,700	8,000

LEWIS AND CLARK EXPOSITION GOLD DOLLARS

1904 . . . . . . *about 7*	25,021	15,003	$400	$1,850	$8,000	$50,000
1905 . . . . . . *about 4*	35,037	25,000	400	2,100	16,000	65,000

PANAMA-PACIFIC EXPOSITION HALF DOLLAR

1915-S . . . . . *2 reported*	60,028	32,896	$145	$625	$2,300	$35,000

PANAMA-PACIFIC EXPOSITION GOLD DOLLAR

1915-S . . . . . *1 reported*	25,033	10,034	$275	$500	$2,400	$75,000

PANAMA-PACIFIC EXPOSITION QUARTER EAGLE ($2.50 GOLD PIECE)

	Minted	Melted	EF-40	MS-63	MS-65	Proof-63
1915-S .... *1 reported*	10,016	3,268	$1,050	$2,600	$5,300	$100,000

PANAMA-PACIFIC EXPOSITION $50 GOLD PIECES

	Minted	Melted	EF-40	MS-63	MS-65	Proof-63
1915-S round	1,510	1,027	$21,000	$38,500	$142,500	
1915-S octagonal	1,509	864	18,000	33,000	120,000	

MCKINLEY MEMORIAL GOLD DOLLARS

	Minted	Melted	EF-40	MS-63	MS-65	Proof-63
1916 ...... *at least 6*	20,020	10,049	$250	$650	$2,400	$30,000
1917 ...... *at least 5*	10,009	14	275	1,200	3,200	30,000

ILLINOIS CENTENNIAL HALF DOLLAR

	Minted	Melted	EF-40	MS-63	MS-65	Proof-63
1918 ...... *at least 2*	100,056	None	$60.00	$85.00	$425	$30,000

MAINE CENTENNIAL HALF DOLLAR

	Minted	Melted	EF-40	MS-63	MS-65	Proof-63
1920 ...... *1 known*	50,027	None	$60.00	$145	$450	$35,000

PILGRIM TERCENTENARY HALF DOLLARS

	Minted	Melted	EF-40	MS-63	MS-65	Proof-63
1920 ...... *2 reported*	200,110	48,000	$45.00	$70.00	$350	$30,000
1921 ...... *1 reported*	100,052	80,000	85.00	125	475	35,000

	Number Minted	Number Melted	EF-40	MS-63	MS-65	Proof-63
ALABAMA CENTENNIAL HALF DOLLARS						
1921 with 2 X 2 ......*I*	6,005	None	$130	$600	$2,250	$50,000
1921 without 2 X 2	64,038	5,000	65.00	450	2,250	
MISSOURI CENTENNIAL HALF DOLLARS						
1921 with 2 X 4 ......*I*	4,999	None	$240	$700	$5,500	$85,000
1921 without 2 X 4	45,028	29,600	160	600	5,600	
GRANT MEMORIAL HALF DOLLARS						
1922 with star ....*4 reported*	5,002	750	$410	$1,675	$5,500	$50,000
1922 without star ....*4 reported*	95,051	27,650	60.00	165	650	50,000
GRANT MEMORIAL GOLD DOLLARS						
1922 with star	5,016	None	$950	$1,500	$3,300	
1922 without star	5,000	None	925	1,500	3,300	
MONROE DOCTRINE CENTENNIAL HALF DOLLAR						
1923-S .....*2 reported*	274,076	None	$31.00	$105	$1,800	$50,000
HUGUENOT-WALLOON TERCENTENARY HALF DOLLAR						
1924 ......*I reported*	142,079	None	$60.00	$90.00	$450	$35,000
CALIFORNIA DIAMOND JUBILEE HALF DOLLAR						
1925-S ....*I reported*	150,199	63,606	$80.00	$220	$750	$50,000
FORT VANCOUVER CENTENNIAL HALF DOLLAR						
1925 ......*3 reported*	50,025	35,034	$180	$400	$1,000	$30,000
LEXINGTON-CONCORD SESQUICENTENNIAL HALF DOLLAR						
1925 ......*I reported*	162,098	86	$60.00	$90.00	$450	$35,000
STONE MOUNTAIN HALF DOLLAR						
1925 ......*I reported*	2,314,708	1,000,000	$35.00	$45.00	$185	$30,000
OREGON TRAIL MEMORIAL HALF DOLLARS						
1926 ......*2 known*	48,028	75	$75.00	$120	$185	$35,000
1926-S	100,055	17,000	75.00	120	185	
1928	50,028	44,000	135	160	300	
1933-D	5,250	242	225	280	375	
1934-D	7,006	None	115	185	275	
1936	10,006	None	105	135	195	
1936-S	5,006	None	120	175	260	
1937-D	12,008	None	90.00	220	185	
1938	6,006	None	190	220	240	
1938-D	6,005	None	190	220	240	
1938-S	6,006	None	145	200	240	

	Number Minted	Number Melted	EF-40	MS-63	MS-65	Proof-63
1939	3,004	None	300	450	650	
1939-D	3,004	None	300	450	650	
1939-S	3,005	None	300	450	650	

SESQUICENTENNIAL OF AMERICAN INDEPENDENCE HALF DOLLAR

1926 ...... 4 reported	1,000,524	859,408	$60.00	$165	$4,250	$50,000

SESQUICENTENNIAL OF AMERICAN INDEPENDENCE QUARTER EAGLE ($2.50 GOLD PIECE)

1926 ...... 2 reported	200,224	154,207	$250	$585	$3,500	$100,000

VERMONT SESQUICENTENNIAL HALF DOLLAR

1927 ...... 1 reported	40,033	11,892	$110	$180	$675	$30,000

HAWAIIAN SESQUICENTENNIAL HALF DOLLAR

1928 ...... 50	9,958	None	$775	$1,600	$4,000	$18,000

DANIEL BOONE BICENTENNIAL HALF DOLLARS

1934	10,007	None	$75.00	$85.00	$145	
1935 plain	10,010	None	75.00	80.00	140	
1935-D plain	5,005	None	75.00	80.00	140	
1935-S plain	5,005	None	75.00	100.00	140	
1935 with small 1934 on reverse	10,008	None	75.00	90.00	140	
1935-D with small 1934 on reverse	2,003	None	275	300	775	
1935-S with small 1934 on reverse	2,004	None	275	300	775	
1936	12,012	None	75.00	80.00	140	
1936-D	5,005	None	75.00	80.00	140	
1936-S	5,006	None	75.00	80.00	140	
1937 ...... 1 known proof	15,009	9,810	75.00	80.00	140	$25,000
1937-D .... 1 known proof	7,505	5,000	180	275	350	25,000
1937-S .... 1 known proof	5,005	2,500	180	275	350	25,000
1938	5,005	2,905	225	300	475	
1938-D	5,005	2,905	225	300	475	
1938-S	5,006	2,906	225	300	475	

MARYLAND TERCENTENARY HALF DOLLAR

1934 ...... 3 known	25,012	None	$105	$130	$275	$30,000

	Number Minted	Number Melted	EF-40	MS-63	MS-65	Proof-63
TEXAS INDEPENDENCE CENTENNIAL HALF DOLLARS						
1934	205,113	143,650	$70.00	$90.00	$160	
1935	10,008	12	70.00	90.00	160	
1935-D	10,007	None	70.00	90.00	160	
1935-S	10,008	None	70.00	90.00	160	
1936	10,008	1,097	70.00	90.00	160	
1936-D	10,007	968	70.00	90.00	160	
1936-S	10,008	943	70.00	90.00	160	
1937	8,005	1,434	80.00	100	210	
1937-D	8,006	1,401	80.00	100	210	
1937-S	8,007	1,370	80.00	100	210	
1938	5,005	1,225	150	280	350	
1938-D	5,005	1,230	150	280	350	
1938-S	5,006	1,192	150	280	350	

ARKANSAS CENTENNIAL HALF DOLLARS

1935 .... 1 reported	13,011	None	$65.00	$80.00	$260	$30,000
1935-D	5,505	None	65.00	85.00	260	
1935-S	5,506	None	65.00	85.00	260	
1936	10,010	350	65.00	80.00	260	
1936-D	10,010	350	65.00	80.00	260	
1936-S	10,012	350	65.00	80.00	260	
1937	5,505	None	70.00	90.00	230	
1937-D	5,505	None	70.00	95.00	230	
1937-S	5,506	None	70.00	95.00	300	
1938 .... 1 known proof	6,006	2,850	90.00	140	750	15,000
1938-D .... 1 known proof	6,005	2,850	90.00	140	750	15,000
1938-S .... 1 known proof	6,006	2,850	90.00	140	750	15,000
1939	2,104	None	100	225	900	
1939-D	2,104	None	100	225	900	
1939-S	2,105	None	100	225	900	

	Number Minted	Number Melted	EF-40	MS-63	MS-65	Proof-63

CONNECTICUT TERCENTENARY HALF DOLLAR

1935 ...... *about 6*	25,012	None	$160	$190	$400	$45,000

HUDSON, N.Y., SESQUICENTENNIAL HALF DOLLAR

1935 ...... *2 reported*	10,006	None	$380	$450	$1,150	$45,000

OLD SPANISH TRAIL HALF DOLLAR

1935 ...... *2 reported*	10,006	None	$625	$725	$925	$45,000

SAN DIEGO/CALIFORNIA-PACIFIC EXPOSITION HALF DOLLARS

1935-S ..... *2 reported*	250,130	180,000	$45.00	$65.00	$85.00	$20,000
1936-D	180,092	150,000	60.00	75.00	105	

ALBANY, N.Y., CHARTER HALF DOLLAR

1936	25,013	7,342	$190	$215	$300	

BRIDGEPORT, CONN., CENTENNIAL HALF DOLLAR

1936	25,015	None	$90.00	$100	$200	

CINCINNATI MUSIC CENTER HALF DOLLARS

1936	5,005	None	$195	$600	$350	
1936-D	5,005	None	195	600	325	
1936-S	5,006	None	195	750	475	

CLEVELAND CENTENNIAL/GREAT LAKES EXPOSITION HALF DOLLAR

1936	50,030	None	$50.00	$60.00	$220	

COLUMBIA, S.C., SESQUICENTENNIAL HALF DOLLARS

1936	9,007	None	$150	$180	$200	
1936-D	8,009	None	150	180	200	
1936-S	8,007	None	150	180	220	

DELAWARE TERCENTENARY HALF DOLLAR

1936	25,015	4,022	$140	$180	$325	

ELGIN, ILL., CENTENNIAL HALF DOLLAR

1936	25,014	5,000	$170	$195	$220	

GETTYSBURG BATTLE HALF DOLLAR

1936	50,028	23,100	$210	$240	$475	

LONG ISLAND TERCENTENARY HALF DOLLAR

1936	100,053	18,227	$50.00	$60.00	$300	

LYNCHBURG, VA., SESQUICENTENNIAL HALF DOLLAR

1936	20,013	None	$130	$160	$220	

COMMEMORATIVE COINS (1892–PRESENT)

	Number Minted	Number Melted	EF-40	MS-63	MS-65	Proof-63
NORFOLK, VA., TERCENTENARY HALF DOLLAR						
1936	25,013	8,077	$250	$300	$450	
PROVIDENCE, R.I., TERCENTENARY HALF DOLLARS						
1936	20,013	None	$60.00	$75.00	$200	
1936-D	15,010	None	60.00	80.00	200	
1936-S	15,011	None	60.00	80.00	200	
ROBINSON-ARKANSAS CENTENNIAL HALF DOLLAR						
1936	25,256	None	$65.00	$85.00	$190	
SAN FRANCISCO-OAKLAND BAY BRIDGE HALF DOLLAR						
1936-S	100,055	28,631	$70.00	$150	$225	
WISCONSIN TERRITORIAL CENTENNIAL HALF DOLLAR						
1936	25,015	None	$140	$160	$200	
YORK COUNTY, MAINE, TERCENTENARY HALF DOLLAR						
1936	25,015	None	$133	$110	$100	
ANTIETAM BATTLE HALF DOLLAR						
1937	50,028	32,000	$335	$385	$675	
ROANOKE ISLAND, N.C., HALF DOLLAR						
1937	49,080	21,000	$165	$185	$225	
NEW ROCHELLE, N.Y., HALF DOLLAR						
1938 ...... *about 10*	25,003	9,749	$225	$285	$300	$30,000
IOWA STATEHOOD CENTENNIAL HALF DOLLAR						
1946	100,057	None	$55.00	$67.00	$95.00	

BOOKER T. WASHINGTON HALF DOLLARS

	Number Minted	Number Melted	EF-40	MS-63	MS-65	Proof-63
1946	1,000,546	Unknown	$8.00	$13.00	$40.00	
1946-D	200,113	Unknown	8.00	13.00	40.00	
1946-S	500,279	Unknown	8.00	13.00	40.00	
1947	100,017	Unknown	8.00	20.00	80.00	
1947-D	100,017	Unknown	8.00	20.00	140	
1947-S	100,017	Unknown	8.00	20.00	80.00	
1948	20,005	12,000	15.00	30.00	60.00	
1948-D	20,005	12,000	15.00	30.00	60.00	
1948-S	20,005	12,000	15.00	30.00	60.00	
1949	12,004	6,000	20.00	60.00	90.00	
1949-D	12,004	6,000	20.00	60.00	90.00	
1949-S	12,004	6,000	20.00	60.00	90.00	
1950	12,004	6,000	18.00	30.00	60.00	
1950-D	12,004	6,000	18.00	30.00	60.00	
1950-S	512,091	Unknown	8.00	15.00	40.00	
1951	510,082	Unknown	8.00	35.00	50.00	
1951-D	12,004	5,000	15.00	35.00	60.00	
1951-S	12,004	5,000	15.00	35.00	60.00	

GEORGE WASHINGTON CARVER/BOOKER T. WASHINGTON HALF DOLLARS

	Number Minted	Number Melted	EF-40	MS-63	MS-65	Proof-63
1951	110,018*	Unknown	$8.00	$20.00	$175	
1951-D	10,004*	Unknown	15.00	25.00	100	
1951-S	10,004*	Unknown	15.00	25.00	60.00	
1952	2,006,292*	Unknown	8.00	15.00	30.00	
1952-D	8,006*	Unknown	15.00	25.00	140	
1952-S	8,006*	Unknown	15.00	25.00	60.00	
1953	8,003*	Unknown	10.00	20.00	100	
1953-D	8,003*	Unknown	10.00	20.00	125	
1953-S	108,020*	Unknown	8.00	20.00	60.00	
1954	12,006*	Unknown	8.00	20.00	90.00	
1954-D	12,006*	Unknown	10.00	20.00	95.00	
1954-S	122,024*	Unknown	8.00	20.00	60.00	

These are net mintages, after melting. The quantities actually minted and melted are unknown.

Modern Commemoratives (1982–Present)

(NOTE: For commemorative coins issued since 1982, the U.S. Mint has not disclosed the number actually minted and the number melted. The figures shown here are net mintages furnished by the Mint. The George Washington and Bill of Rights half dollars are of traditional 90-percent-silver composition. All other half dollars in the modern commemorative series are of copper-nickel clad composition, with no precious-metal content.)

	Net Mintage	MS-65	Proof-67

GEORGE WASHINGTON HALF DOLLAR

	Net Mintage	MS-65	Proof-67
1982-D uncirculated	2,210,458	$4.50	
1982-S proof	4,894,044	—	$4.50

LOS ANGELES OLYMPIC SILVER DOLLARS

	Net Mintage	MS-65	Proof-67
1983-P uncirculated	294,543	$9.00	
1983-D uncirculated	174,014	10.00	
1983-S uncirculated	174,014	10.00	
1983-S proof	1,577,025	—	$7.50
1984-P uncirculated	217,954	13.00	

	Net Mintage	MS-65	Proof-67
1984-D uncirculated	116,675	23.00	
1984-S uncirculated	116,675	23.00	
1984-S proof	1,801,210	—	$9.50

LOS ANGELES OLYMPIC EAGLES ($10 GOLD PIECES)

1984-P proof	33,309	—	$275
1984-D proof	34,533	—	250
1984-S proof	48,551	—	220
1984-W uncirculated	75,886	$220	
1984-W proof	381,085	—	200

STATUE OF LIBERTY HALF DOLLARS

1986-D uncirculated	928,008	$5.00	
1986-S proof	6,925,627	—	$5.00

STATUE OF LIBERTY SILVER DOLLARS

1986-P uncirculated	723,635	$11.50	
1986-S proof	6,414,638	—	$12.00

STATUE OF LIBERTY HALF EAGLES ($5 GOLD PIECES)

1986-W uncirculated	95,248	$110	
1986-W proof	404,013	—	$110

CONSTITUTION BICENTENNIAL SILVER DOLLARS

1987-P uncirculated	451,629	$7.50	
1987-S proof	2,747,116	—	$7.00

CONSTITUTION BICENTENNIAL HALF EAGLES ($5 GOLD PIECES)

1987-W uncirculated	214,225	$110	
1987-W proof	651,659	—	$110

1988 OLYMPIC SILVER DOLLARS

1988-D uncirculated	191,368	$10.00	
1988-S proof	1,359,366	—	$7.00

1988 OLYMPIC HALF EAGLES ($5 GOLD PIECES)

1988-W uncirculated	62,913	$120	
1988-W proof	281,465	—	$120

CONGRESS BICENTENNIAL HALF DOLLARS

1989-D uncirculated	163,753	$8.00	
1989-S proof	767,897	—	$5.00

CONGRESS BICENTENNIAL SILVER DOLLARS

1989-D uncirculated	135,203	$14.00	
1989-S proof	762,198	—	$11.00

	Net Mintage	MS-65	Proof-67

CONGRESS BICENTENNIAL HALF EAGLES ($5 GOLD PIECES)

	Net Mintage	MS-65	Proof-67
1989-W uncirculated	46,899	$125	
1989-W proof	*164,690*	—	$105

EISENHOWER CENTENNIAL SILVER DOLLARS

1990-W uncirculated	239,777	$10.00	
1990-P proof	*1,137,805*	—	$12.00

KOREAN WAR MEMORIAL SILVER DOLLARS

1991-D uncirculated	213,049	$15.00	
1991-P proof	*618,488*	—	$14.00

MOUNT RUSHMORE 50TH ANNIVERSARY HALF DOLLARS

1991-D uncirculated	172,754	$10.00	
1991-S proof	*753,257*	—	$10.00

MOUNT RUSHMORE 50TH ANNIVERSARY SILVER DOLLARS

1991-P uncirculated	133,139	$25.00	
1991-S proof	*738,419*	—	$21.00

MOUNT RUSHMORE 50TH ANNIVERSARY HALF EAGLES ($5 GOLD PIECES)

1991-W uncirculated	31,959	$125	
1991-W proof	*111,991*	—	$110

UNITED SERVICE ORGANIZATIONS (USO) SILVER DOLLARS

1991-D uncirculated	124,958	$15.00	
1991-S proof	*321,275*	—	$13.00

1992 OLYMPIC HALF DOLLARS

1992-P uncirculated	161,607	$5.00	
1992-S proof	*519,645*	—	$7.00

1992 OLYMPIC SILVER DOLLARS

1992-D uncirculated	187,552	$22	
1992-S proof	*504,505*	—	$25

1992 OLYMPIC HALF EAGLES ($5 GOLD PIECES)

1992-W uncirculated	27,732	$115	
1992-W proof	*77,313*	—	$115

1992 WHITE HOUSE SILVER DOLLARS

1992-D uncirculated	123,803	$25.00	
1992-W proof	*375,851*	—	$26.00

1992 COLUMBUS QUINCENTENARY HALF DOLLARS

1992-D uncirculated	135,702	$9.00	
1992-S proof	*390,154*	—	$9.00

	Net Mintage	MS-65	Proof-67
1992 COLUMBUS QUINCENTENARY SILVER DOLLARS			
1992-D uncirculated	106,949	$24.00	
1992-P proof	385,241	—	$23.00
1992 COLUMBUS QUINCENTENARY HALF EAGLES ($5 GOLD PIECES)			
1992-W uncirculated	24,329	$170	
1992-W proof	79,730	—	$180
1993 BILL OF RIGHTS HALF DOLLARS (SILVER)			
1993-W uncirculated	194,420	$12.00	
1993-S proof	585,821	—	$7.50
1993 BILL OF RIGHTS SILVER DOLLARS			
1993-D uncirculated	98,571	$18.00	
1993-S proof	534,007	—	$15.00
1993 BILL OF RIGHTS HALF EAGLES ($5 GOLD PIECES)			
1993-W uncirculated	23,455	$135	
1993-W proof	78,840	—	$115
1993 WORLD WAR II HALF DOLLARS			
1993-P uncirculated	197,072	$7.00	
1993-P proof	317,396	—	$9.00
1993 WORLD WAR II SILVER DOLLARS			
1993-D uncirculated	107,240	$24.50	
1993-W proof	342,041	—	$25.00
1993 WORLD WAR II HALF EAGLES ($5 GOLD PIECES)			
1993-W uncirculated	23,672	$160	
1993-W proof	67,026	—	$130
1994 WORLD CUP SOCCER HALF DOLLARS			
1994-D uncirculated	168,208	$7.25	
1994-P proof	609,354	—	$8.75
1994 WORLD CUP SOCCER SILVER DOLLARS			
1994-D uncirculated	81,524	$22.00	
1994-S proof	577,090	—	$25.00
1994 WORLD CUP HALF EAGLES ($5 GOLD PIECES)			
1994-W uncirculated	22,447	$135	
1994-W proof	89,614	—	$125
1994 THOMAS JEFFERSON 250TH ANNIVERSARY SILVER DOLLARS			
1994-P uncirculated	600,000	$27.00	
1994-S proof	600,000	—	$28.00

	Net Mintage	MS-65	Proof-67

1994 PRISONER OF WAR SILVER DOLLARS

	Net Mintage	MS-65	Proof-67
1994-W uncirculated	54,894	$45.00	
1994-P proof	224,350	—	$30.00

1994 VIETNAM VETERANS MEMORIAL SILVER DOLLARS

1994-W uncirculated	57,291	$40.00	
1994-P proof	227,573	—	$38.00

1994 WOMEN IN MILITARY SERVICE FOR AMERICA SILVER DOLLARS

1994-W uncirculated	53,571	$24.00	
1994-P proof	222,852	—	$25.00

1994 U.S. CAPITOL SILVER DOLLARS

1994-D uncirculated	68,332	$22.00	
1994-S proof	279,579	—	$18.00

1995 CIVIL WAR BATTLEFIELD HALF DOLLARS

1995-S uncirculated	119,303	$7.50	
1995-S proof	328,398	—	$7.50

1995 CIVIL WAR BATTLEFIELD SILVER DOLLARS

1995-P uncirculated	45,604	$22.00	
1995-S proof	328,569	—	$21.00

1995 CIVIL WAR BATTLEFIELD HALF EAGLES ($5 GOLD PIECES)

1995-W uncirculated	12,660	$260	
1995-W proof	55,010	—	$150

1995 OLYMPIC BASKETBALL HALF DOLLARS

1995-S uncirculated	171,001*	$9.00	
1995-S proof	169,655*	—	$10.00

1995 OLYMPIC GYMNAST SILVER DOLLARS

1995-D uncirculated	42,497*	$70.00	
1995-P proof	182,676*	—	$31.00

1995 OLYMPIC BLIND RUNNER SILVER DOLLARS

1995-D uncirculated	28,649*	$80.00	
1995-P proof	138,337*	—	$32.00

1995 OLYMPIC TORCH RUNNER GOLD HALF EAGLES ($5 GOLD PIECES)

1995-W uncirculated	14,675*	$185	
1995-W proof	57,442*	—	$170

	Net Mintage	MS-65	Proof-67

1995 SPECIAL OLYMPIC WORLD GAMES SILVER DOLLARS (PORTRAIT OF EUNICE KENNEDY SHRIVER)

	Net Mintage	MS-65	Proof-67
1995-W uncirculated	89,298	$22.00	
1995-P proof	*352,449*	—	$16.00

1995 OLYMPIC BASEBALL HALF DOLLARS

1995-S uncirculated	164,605*	$22.00	
1995-S proof	*118,087**	—	$13.00

1995 OLYMPIC TRACK AND FIELD SILVER DOLLARS

1995-D uncirculated	24,796*	$52.00	
1995-P proof	*136,935**	—	$28.00

1995 OLYMPIC CYCLING SILVER DOLLARS

1995-D uncirculated	19,662*	$80.00	
1995-P proof	*118,795**	—	$33.00

1995 OLYMPIC STADIUM GOLD HALF EAGLES ($5 GOLD PIECES)

1995-W uncirculated	10,579*	$180	
1995-W proof	*43,124**	—	$175

1996 NATIONAL COMMUNITY SERVICE SILVER DOLLARS

1996-S uncirculated	23,468	$250	
1996-S proof	*100,787*	—	$35.00

1996 OLYMPIC SWIMMING HALF DOLLARS

1996-S uncirculated	49,533*	$50.00	
1996-S proof	*114,315**	—	$12.50

1996 OLYMPIC SOCCER HALF DOLLARS

1996-S uncirculated	52,836*	$30.00	
1996-S proof	*122,412**	—	$60.00

1996 OLYMPIC TENNIS SILVER DOLLARS

1996-D uncirculated	15,983*	$125	
1996-P proof	*92,016**	—	$45.00

1996 OLYMPIC WHEELCHAIR ATHLETE SILVER DOLLARS

1996-D uncirculated	14,497*	$160	
1996-P proof	*84,280**	—	$40.00

1996 OLYMPIC ROWING SILVER DOLLARS

1996-D uncirculated	16,258*	$150	
1996-P proof	*151,890**	—	$35.00

1996 OLYMPIC HIGH JUMP SILVER DOLLARS

1996-D uncirculated	15,697*	$160	
1996-P proof	*124,502*	—	$35.00

	Net Mintage	MS-65	Proof-67
1996 OLYMPIC FLAG BEARER GOLD HALF EAGLES ($5 GOLD PIECES)			
1996-W uncirculated	9,174*	$250	
1996-W proof	32,886*	—	$260
1996 OLYMPIC CAULDRON GOLD HALF EAGLES ($5 GOLD PIECES)			
1996-W uncirculated	9,210*	$250	
1996-W proof	38,555*	—	$260
1996 SMITHSONIAN SESQUICENTENNIAL SILVER DOLLARS			
1996-D uncirculated	30,593*	$60.00	
1996-P proof	126,616*	—	$35.00
1996 SMITHSONIAN SESQUICENTENNIAL GOLD HALF EAGLES ($5 GOLD PIECES)			
1996-W uncirculated	8,948	$185	
1996-W proof	21,840	—	$200
1997 U.S. BOTANIC GARDEN SILVER DOLLARS			
1997-P uncirculated	57,272	$33.00	—
1997-P proof	264,528	—	$35.00
1997 FRANKLIN D. ROOSEVELT HALF EAGLES ($5 GOLD PIECES)			
1997-W uncirculated	11,805	$200	
1997-W proof	29,233	—	$200
1997 JACKIE ROBINSON SILVER DOLLARS			
1997-S uncirculated	27,170	$60.00	—
1997-W proof	98,297	—	$35.00
1997 JACKIE ROBINSON HALF EAGLES ($5 GOLD PIECES)			
1997-W uncirculated	4,594	$800	—
1997-W proof	21,760	—	$200
1997 NATIONAL LAW ENFORCEMENT SILVER DOLLARS			
1997-P uncirculated	28,575	$100	—
1997-P proof	110,428	—	$100
1998 BLACK REVOLUTIONARY WAR PATRIOTS SILVER DOLLARS			
1998-S uncirculated	37,210	$65.00	—
1998-S proof	75,070	—	$60.00
1998 ROBERT F. KENNEDY COMMEMORATIVE SILVER DOLLARS			
1998-S uncirculated	106,422	$33.00	—
1998-S proof	99,020	—	$35.00

* Through July 31, 1997

	Net Mintage	MS-65	Proof-67
1999 GEORGE WASHINGTON HALF EAGLES ($5 GOLD PIECES)			
1999-W uncirculated	22,508	$225	—
1999-W proof	41,688	—	$250
1999 DOLLEY MADISON SILVER DOLLARS			
1999-P uncirculated	89,203	$40.00	—
1999-P proof	224,495	—	$42.00
1999 YELLOWSTONE SILVER DOLLARS			
1999-P uncirculated	73,886	$40.00	—
1999-P proof	171,010	—	$40.00
2000 LIBRARY OF CONGRESS EAGLE ($10 BIMETALLIC: GOLD AND PLATINUM)			
2000 uncirculated	6,683*	$430	—
2000 proof	27,167*	—	$440
2000 LIBRARY OF CONGRESS SILVER DOLLARS			
2000 uncirculated	52,771*	$30.00	—
2000 proof	196,900*	—	$40.00
2001 LEIF ERICSON SILVER DOLLARS			
2001 uncirculated	28,150	$33.00	—
2001 proof	58,612	—	$43.00
2001 CAPITOL VISITOR CENTER HALF DOLLARS			
2001 uncirculated	(60,900)**	12.00	—
2001 proof	(77,100)**	—	15.00
2001 CAPITOL VISITOR CENTER SILVER DOLLARS			
2001 uncirculated	(35,400)**	40.00	—
2001 proof	(141,300)**	—	50.00
2001 CAPITOL VISITOR CENTER HALF EAGLES ($5 GOLD PIECES)			
2001 uncirculated	(5,700)**	600.00	—
2001 proof	(26,500)**	—	300.00
2001 AMERICAN BUFFALO SILVER DOLLARS			
2001 uncirculated	177,120	150.00	—
2001 proof	322,780	—	160.00
2002 WEST POINT SILVER DOLLARS			
2002 uncirculated		—	—
2002 proof		—	—
2002 OLYMPIC SILVER DOLLARS			
2002 uncirculated		—	—
2002 proof		—	—

	Net Mintage	MS-65	Proof-67
2002 OLYMPIC GOLD HALF EAGLES ($5 GOLD PIECES)			
2002 uncirculated	—	—	
2002 proof	—	—	

* *Through December 2000*
** *Through March 6, 2002*

AMERICAN EAGLE BULLION COINS
(1986–PRESENT)
$10 Platinum (⅟₁₀ Ounce)

	Mintage	MS-67	Proof-67
1997 uncirculated	70,250	$80.00	
1997-W proof	*37,260*	—	$100
1998 uncirculated	66,000	80.00	
1998-W proof	*19,919*	—	100
1999 uncirculated	40,000	80.00	
1999-W proof	*19,123*	—	100
2000 uncirculated	(28,000)*	80.00	
2000-W proof	*15,600*	—	100
2001 uncirculated	52,017	80.00	
2001-W proof	*12,193*	—	100
2002 uncirculated		80.00	
2002-W proof		—	100
2003 uncirculated		80.00	
2003-W proof		—	100

$25 Platinum (¼ Ounce)

	Mintage	MS-67	Proof-67
1997 uncirculated	27,100	$170	
1997 W proof	*18,726*	—	$200
1998 uncirculated	47,800	170	
1998-W proof	*14,919*	—	200
1999 uncirculated	31,800	170	
1999-W proof	*13,514*	—	200
2000 uncirculated	(19,400)*	170	
2000-W proof	*11,900*	—	200
2001 uncirculated	21,815	170	
2001-W proof	*8,858*	—	200
2002 uncirculated		170	
2002-W proof		—	200
2003 uncirculated		170	
2003-W proof		—	200

* *Through March 31, 2001*

$50 Platinum (½ Ounce)

	Mintage	MS-67	Proof-67
1997 uncirculated	20,500	$325	
1997-W proof	15,515	—	$400
1998 uncirculated	37,200	325	
1998-W proof	13,919	—	400
1999 uncirculated	28,200	325	
1999-W proof	11,098	—	400
2000 uncirculated	(18,800)*	325	
2000-W proof	11,000	—	400
2001 uncirculated	12,815	325	
2001-W proof	8,268	—	400
2002 uncirculated		325	
2002-W proof		—	400
2003 uncirculated		325	
2003-W proof		—	400

$100 Platinum (1 Ounce)

	Mintage	MS-67	Proof-67
1997 uncirculated	56,000	$650	
1997-W proof	21,000	—	$700
1998 uncirculated	138,500	650	
1998-W proof	14,203	—	700
1999 uncirculated	45,000	650	
1999-W proof	12,351	—	700
2000 uncirculated	(10,000)*	650	
2000-W proof	12,400	—	700
2001 uncirculated	14,070	650	
2001-W proof	8,990	—	700
2002 uncirculated		650	
2002-W proof		—	700
2003 uncirculated		650	
2003-W proof		—	700

* Through March 31, 2001

$5 Gold (⅒ Ounce)

	Mintage	MS-67	Proof-67
1986 (MCMLXXXVI) uncirculated	912,609	$50.00	
1987 (MCMLXXXVII) uncirculated	580,266	50.00	
1988 (MCMLXXXVIII) uncirculated	159,500	50.00	
1988-P (MCMLXXXVIII) proof	143,881	—	$65.00
1989 (MCMLXXXIX) uncirculated	264,790	50.00	
1989-P (MCMLXXXIX) proof	84,647	—	65.00

AMERICAN EAGLE BULLION COINS (1986–PRESENT)

	Mintage	MS-67	Proof-67
1990 (MCMXC) uncirculated	210,210	50.00	
1990-P (MCMXC) proof	99,349	—	72.50
1991 (MCMXCI) uncirculated	165,200	50.00	
1991-P (MCMXCI) proof	70,334	—	72.50
1992 uncirculated	209,300	50.00	
1992-P proof	64,874	—	72.50
1993 uncirculated	210,709	50.00	
1993-P proof	58,649	—	72.50
1994 uncirculated	206,380	50.00	
1994-W proof	62,794	—	72.50
1995 uncirculated	223,025	50.00	
1995-W proof	62,731	—	72.50
1996 uncirculated	425,000	50.00	
1996-W proof	55,964	—	72.50
1997 uncirculated	528,515	50.00	
1997-W proof	35,164	—	72.50
1998 uncirculated	1,445,000	50.00	
1998-W proof	39,706	—	72.50
1999 uncirculated	2,700,000	50.00	
1999-W proof	48,426	—	72.50
2000 uncirculated	(245,000)*	50.00	
2000-W proof	50,000	—	72.50
2001 uncirculated	269,147	50.00	
2001-W proof	37,547	—	72.50
2002 uncirculated		50.00	
2002-W proof		—	72.50
2003 uncirculated		50.00	
2003-W proof		—	72.50

$10 Gold (¼ Ounce)

	Mintage	MS-67	Proof-67
1986 (MCMLXXXVI) uncirculated	726,031	$125	
1987 (MCMLXXXVII) uncirculated	269,255	125	
1988 (MCMLXXXVIII) uncirculated	49,000	125	
1988-P (MCMLXXXVIII) proof	98,028	—	$140
1989 (MCMLXXXIX) uncirculated	81,789	125	
1989-P (MCMLXXXIX) proof	54,170	—	140
1990 (MCMXC) uncirculated	41,000	125	
1990-P (MCMXC) proof	62,674	—	145
1991 (MCMXCI) uncirculated	36,100	125	
1991-P (MCMXCI) proof	50,839	—	145
1992 uncirculated	59,546	125	
1992-P proof	46,269	—	145
1993 uncirculated	71,864	125	
1993-P proof	46,464	—	145

	Mintage	MS-67	Proof-67
1994 uncirculated	72,650	125	
1994-W proof	48,128	—	145
1995 uncirculated	83,752	125	
1995-W proof	47,553	—	145
1996 uncirculated	68,000	125	
1996-W proof	37,320	—	145
1997 uncirculated	108,805	125	
1997-W proof	29,984	—	145
1998 uncirculated	342,000	125	
1998-W proof	29,731	—	145
1999 uncirculated	560,000	125	
1999-W proof	34,416	—	145
2000 uncirculated	(64,000)*	125	
2000-W proof	36,000	—	145
2001 uncirculated	71,280	125	
2001-W proof	25,630	—	145
2002 uncirculated		125	
2002-W proof		—	145
2003 uncirculated		125	
2003-W proof		—	145

$25 Gold (½ Ounce)

	Mintage	MS-67	Proof-67
1986 (MCMLXXXVI) uncirculated	599,566	$250	
1987 (MCMLXXXVII) uncirculated	131,255	250	
1987-P (MCMLXXXVII) proof	143,398	—	$225
1988 (MCMLXXXVIII) uncirculated	45,000	250	
1988-P (MCMLXXXVIII) proof	76,528	—	225
1989 (MCMLXXXIX) uncirculated	44,829	250	
1989-P (MCMLXXXIX) proof	44,798	—	225
1990 (MCMXC) uncirculated	31,000	300	
1990-P (MCMXC) proof	51,636	—	225
1991 (MCMXCI) uncirculated	24,100	250	
1991-P (MCMXCI) proof	53,125	—	225
1992_P proof	54,404	250	
1992-P proof	40,976	—	225
1993 uncirculated	73,324	250	
1993-P proof	43,819	—	225
1994 uncirculated	62,400	250	
1994-W proof	44,595	—	275
1995 uncirculated	53,474	250	
1995-W proof	45,487	—	275
1996 uncirculated	42,000	250	
1996-W proof	34,375	—	275
1997 uncirculated	79,605	250	

AMERICAN EAGLE BULLION COINS (1986–PRESENT)

	Mintage	MS-67	Proof-67
1997-W proof	26,801	—	275
1998 uncirculated	182,000	250	
1998-W proof	25,550	—	275
1999 uncirculated	244,000	250	
1999-W proof	30,452	—	275
2000 uncirculated	(60,000)*	250	
2000-W proof	32,000	—	275
2001 uncirculated	48,047	250	
2001-W proof	23,261	—	275
2002 uncirculated		250	
2002-W proof		—	275
2003 uncirculated		250	
2003-W proof		—	275

* *Through March 31, 2001*

$50 Gold (1 Ounce)

	Mintage	MS-67	Proof-67
1986 (MCMLXXXVI) uncirculated	1,362,650	$400	
1986-W (MCMLXXXVI) proof	446,290	—	$410
1987 (MCMLXXXVII) uncirculated	1,045,500	400	
1987-W (MCMLXXXVII) proof	147,498	—	420
1988 (MCMLXXXVIII) uncirculated	465,000	400	
1988-W (MCMLXXXVIII) proof	87,133	—	430
1989 (MCMLXXXIX) uncirculated	415,790	400	
1989-W (MCMLXXXIX) proof	54,570	—	430
1990 (MCMXC) uncirculated	373,210	400	
1990-W (MCMXC) proof	62,401	—	430
1991 (MCMXCI) uncirculated	243,100	400	
1991-W (MCMXCI) proof	50,411	—	450
1992 uncirculated	275,000	400	
1992-W proof	44,826	—	450
1993 uncirculated	480,192	400	
1993-W proof	34,369	—	450
1994 uncirculated	221,663	400	
1994-W proof	46,741	—	550
1995 uncirculated	200,636	400	
1995-W proof	46,524	—	550
1996 uncirculated	194,500	400	
1996-W proof	35,680	—	550
1997 uncirculated	664,508	400	
1997-W proof	32,803	—	550
1998 uncirculated	1,518,500	400	
1998-W proof	26,047	—	550
1999 uncirculated	1,491,000	400	

	Mintage	MS-67	Proof-67
1999-W proof	31,446	—	550
2000 uncirculated	(94,000)*	400	
2000-W proof	33,000	—	550
2001 uncirculated	143,605	400	
2001-W proof	24,580	—	550
2002 uncirculated		400	
2002-W proof		—	550
2003 uncirculated		400	
2003-W proof		—	550

Proof Platinum Coin Sets

	Mintage	MS-67	Proof-67
1997 (all four platinum coins)			$2,000
1997 (three-coin set containing platinum, gold, and silver one-ounce Eagles)			1,600
1998 (all four platinum coins)			1,100
1998 (three-coin set containing platinum, gold, and silver one-ounce Eagles)			1,500
1999 (all four platinum coins)			1,300
1999 (three-coin set containing platinum, gold, and silver one-ounce Eagles)			1,600
2000 (all four platinum coins)			1,300
2000 (three-coin set containing platinum, gold, and silver one-ounce Eagles)			1,600
2001 (all four platinum coins)			1,300
2001 (three-coin set containing platinum, gold, and silver one-ounce Eagles)			1,600
2002 (all four platinum coins)			1,300
2002 (three-coin set containing platinum, gold and silver one-ounce eagles)			1,600
2003 (all four platinum coins)			1,300
2003 (three-coin set containing platinum, gold, and silver one-ounce eagles)			1,600

Proof Gold Coin Sets

	Mintage	MS-67	Proof-67
1987 ($50 and $25 coins only)			$650
1988 ($50 and $25 coins only)			850
1989 (all four coins)			850
1990 (all four coins)			850
1992 (all four coins)			850
1993 (all four coins)			850
1994 (all four coins)			1,050
1995 (all four coins)			1,050

	Mintage	MS-67	Proof-67
1995 (10th anniversary five-coin set, including silver eagle)			3,500
1996 (all four gold coins)			1,000
1997 (all four coins)			1,000
1998 (all four coins)			1,000
1999 (all four coins)			1,000
2000 (all four coins)			1,000
2001 (all four coins)			1,000
2002 (all four coins)			1,000
2003 (all four coins)			1,000

$1 Silver (1 Ounce)

	Mintage	MS-67	Proof-67
1986 uncirculated	5,393,005	$12.50	
1986-S proof	1,446,778	—	$20.00
1987 uncirculated	11,442,335	10.00	
1987-S proof	904,732	—	20.00
1988 uncirculated	5,004,500	11.00	
1988-S proof	557,370	—	40.00
1989 uncirculated	5,203,327	11.00	
1989-S proof	617,694	—	20.00
1990 uncirculated	5,840,210	11.00	
1990-S proof	695,510	—	24.00
1991 uncirculated	7,191,066	10.00	
1991 S proof	511,924	—	27.50
1992 uncirculated	5,540,068	10.00	
1992-S proof	498,543	—	24.00
1993 uncirculated	6,763,762	10.00	
1993-P proof	403,625	—	50.00
1994 uncirculated	4,227,319	10.00	
1994-P proof	355,531	—	45.00
1995 uncirculated	4,672,051	10.00	
1995-P proof	408,293	—	40.00
1995-W proof	30,110	—	2,500
1996 uncirculated	3,466,000	10.00	
1996-P proof	465,629	—	37.50
1997 uncirculated	4,295,004	10.00	
1997-P proof	434,682	—	24.00
1998 uncirculated	(4,270,000)	10.00	
1998-P proof	452,319	—	24.00
1999 uncirculated	(8,883,000)	10.00	
1999-P proof	549,769	—	24.00
2000 uncirculated	(9,133,000)*	10.00	
2000-P proof	600,000	—	24.00
2001 uncirculated	9,001,711	10.00	

	Mintage	MS-67	Proof-67
2001-W proof	746,154	—	24.00
2002 uncirculated		10.00	
2002-W proof		—	24.00
2003 uncirculated		10.00	
2003-W proof		—	24.00

* **Through March 31, 2001**

MODERN PROOF SETS (1950–PRESENT)

(NOTE: Since 1955, the United States Mint has packaged its annual proof sets in sealed holders. Proof sets made up of coins that have been removed from those holders and then reassembled may be worth substantially less than the prices listed here.)

	Number Sold	Issue Price	Market Value
1950	51,386	$2.10	$335
1951	57,500	2.10	250
1952	81,980	2.10	135
1953	128,800	2.10	100
1954	233,300	2.10	61.00
1955	378,200	2.10	52.00
1956	669,384	2.10	22.00
1957	1,247,952	2.10	11.00
1958	875,652	2.10	16.00
1959	1,149,291	2.10	13.00
1960 combined total	1,691,602	2.10	
1960 with small-date cent			16.00
1960 with large-date cent			8.00
1961	3,028,244	2.10	6.00
1962	3,218,019	2.10	6.50
1963	3,075,645	2.10	6.40
1964	3,950,762	2.10	6.50
1968-S	3,041,506	5.00	4.00
1969-S	2,934,631	5.00	3.50
1970-S combined total	2,632,810	5.00	
1970-S with small-date cent			80.00
1970-S with large-date cent			6.40
1970-S with no-S dime			575
1971-S combined total	3,220,733	5.00	
1971-S with regular nickel			3.00
1971-S with no-S nickel			800
1972-S	3,260,996	5.00	3.50

	Number Sold	Issue Price	Market Value
1973-S	2,760,339	7.00	4.00
1974-S	2,612,568	7.00	4.25
1975-S	2,845,450	7.00	5.50
1976-S	4,149,730	7.00	7.00
1977-S	3,251,152	9.00	5.00
1978-S	3,127,781	9.00	5.00
1979 combined total	3,677,175	9.00	
1979-S with clear S			56.00
1979-S with clogged S			5.50
1980-S	3,554,806	10.00	6.00
1981-S	4,063,083	11.00	6.50
1982-S	3,857,479	11.00	3.80
1983-S combined total	3,138,765	11.00	
1983-S with regular dime			5.00
1983-S with no-S dime			420
1983-S Prestige set	140,361	59.00	110
1984-S	2,748,430	11.00	8.50
1984-S Prestige set	316,680	59.00	60.00
1985-S	3,362,821	11.00	5.50
1986-S	2,411,180	11.00	15.00
1986-S Prestige set	599,317	48.50	55.00
1987-S	3,356,738	11.00	5.00
1987-S Prestige set	435,495	45.00	50.00
1988-S	3,031,287	11.00	8.00
1988 S Prestige set	231,661	45.00	60.00
1989-S	3,005,776	11.00	8.00
1989-S Prestige set	209,952	52.00	60.00
1990-S with regular cent	2,789,378	11.00	17.00
1990-S with no-S cent	3,555	11.00	2,900
1990-S Prestige set	506,126	46.00	47.50
1991-S	2,610,833	11.00	50.00
1991-S Prestige set	256,954	49.00	75.00
1992-S	2,675,618	12.50*	15.00
1992-S silver set	1,009,586	21.00*	25.00
1992-S Prestige set	183,285	56.00	70.00
1992-S Premier silver set	308,055	37.00	40.00
1993-S	2,337,819	12.50	15.00
1993-S silver set	589,712	21.00	30.00
1993-S Prestige set	232,063	57.00	70.00
1993-S Premier silver set	201,262	37.00	39.00
1994-S	2,260,631	12.50	15.00
1994-S silver set	628,439	21.00	55.00
1994-S Prestige set	175,670	56.00	70.00
1994-S Premier silver set	148,052	37.50	60.00
1995-S	2,019,828	12.50	125

	Number Sold	Issue Price	Market Value
1995-S silver set	541,121	21.00	150
1995-S Prestige set	106,128	61.00	125
1995-S Premier silver set	129,268	37.50	130
1996-S	2,085,216	12.50	13.00
1996-S silver set	623,268	21.00	75.00
1996-S Prestige set	65,000	57.00	275
1996-S Premier silver set	151,821	37.50	75.00
1997-S	1,975,000	12.50	50.00
1997-S silver set	598,560	21.00	150
1997-S Prestige set	80,000	48.00	250
1997-S Premier silver set	134,460	37.50	150
1998-S	2,965,503	12.50	28.00
1998-S silver set	878,996	21.00	55.00
1998-S Premier silver set	—	37.50	55.00
1999-S (full set)	(2,454,319)**	19.95	50.00
1999-S (partial set, quarter dollars only)	1,169,690	13.95	40.00
1999-S silver set	798,780	31.95	85.00
2000-S (full set)	(3,030,000)**	19.95	26.00
2000-S (partial set, quarter dollars only)	(962,800)**	13.95	19.00
2000-S silver set	(904,200)**	31.95	36.00
2001-S (full set)	(2,293,200)***	19.95	26.00
2001-S (partial set, quarter dollars only)	800,000	13.95	19.00
2001-S (silver set)	891,400	31.95	36.00
2002-S (full set)		19.95	—
2002-S (partial set, quarter dollars only)		13.95	—
2002-S (silver set)		31.95	—
2003-S (full set)		19.95	—
2003-S (partial set, quarter dollars only)		13.95	—
2003-S (silver set)		31.95	

* Some 1992-S proof sets were sold at an issue price of $11, then the price was raised to $12.50. Some 1992-S silver proof sets were sold at an issue price of $18.50, then the price was raised to $21.

** Through March 31, 2001

*** Through May 28, 2002

SPECIAL MINT SETS (1965–1967)

	Number Sold	Issue Price	Market Value
1965	2,360,000	$4.00	$4.50
1966	2,261,583	4.00	5.50
1967	1,863,344	4.00	7.50

TYPE COINS

Many collectors acquire U.S. coins by "type." This means they purchase just one specimen of a certain kind of coin—one Lincoln cent, for example, to represent the entire series of Lincoln cents. Because they are buying just one coin, they usually acquire a piece that is exceptionally attractive, one in a very high grade or level of preservation. But, to avoid paying a prohibitive premium, they select a date for which the mintage is fairly high—a so-called "common-date" coin. Coins acquired in this fashion are known as "type coins," and many buyers and sellers track the value of U.S. coins as a whole by following the performance of these "type coins."

The following chart was prepared by Heritage Rare Coin Galleries and was updated by Sal Germano. It provides a convenient look at U.S. type coins and their values. In using it, you will note such terms as "Liberty" and "Indian Head." These refer to elements of the coins' designs. For assistance in identifying these coins, refer to the illustrations accompanying the price listings in Chapter Four.

United States Coins by Type

	MS-60	MS-63	MS-65
HALF CENT (brown)	$170	$300	$1,000
LARGE CENT (brown)	$160	$225	$700
FLYING EAGLE CENT	$250	$600	$3,500
INDIAN CENT (brown)	$25	$40	$90
TWO-CENT PIECE (brown)	$75	$150	$450
THREE-CENT NICKEL	$85	$150	$650
THREE-CENT SILVER	$150	$275	$900
SHIELD NICKEL	$95	$175	$650

	MS-60	MS-63	MS-65
"V" OR LIBERTY NICKEL (NO CENTS)	$35	$75	$300
BUFFALO NICKEL	$20	$30	$50
CAPPED BUST HALF DIME	$275	$700	$2,500
LIBERTY SEATED HALF DIME	$115	$225	$1,200
CAPPED BUST DIME	$700	$1,500	$5,600
LIBERTY SEATED DIME	$130	$200	$1,000
BARBER DIME	$110	$150	$650
MERCURY DIME	$7	$12	$25
TWENTY-CENT PIECE	$450	$1,000	$5,000
CAPPED BUST QUARTER	$775	$2,500	$12,000
LIBERTY SEATED QUARTER	$235	$400	$1,600
BARBER QUARTER	$175	$300	$1,200
LIBERTY STANDING QUARTER	$100	$185	$450
CAPPED BUST HALF	$500	$1,400	$7,000
LIBERTY SEATED HALF	$350	$600	$3,200
BARBER HALF	$375	$750	$3,000
LIBERTY WALKING HALF	$30	$40	$100
LIBERTY SEATED DOLLAR	$1,000	$2,750	$18,000
MORGAN DOLLAR	$25	$30	$85
PEACE DOLLAR	$15	$25	$90
ONE DOLLAR GOLD PIECE	$275	$850	$1,800
$2.5 LIBERTY GOLD	$300	$700	$1,400
$2.5 INDIAN GOLD	$265	$800	$2,950
$3 GOLD	$1,750	$4,250	$10,500
$5 LIBERTY GOLD	$225	$550	$2,700

TYPE COINS

	MS-60	MS-63	MS-65
$5 INDIAN GOLD	$325	$1,100	$11,000
$10 LIBERTY GOLD	$250	$600	$3,000
$10 INDIAN GOLD	$390	$650	$3,000
$20 LIBERTY GOLD	$420	$600	$2,850
$20 ST. GAUDENS GOLD	$425	$500	$1,000

COIN PERIODICALS

COINage Magazine. Miller Magazines Inc., 4880 Market Street, Ventura, CA 93003. One-year subscription (12 monthly issues) $23, two-year subscription $36. Add $9 per year for all foreign countries, including Canada.

Coins Magazine. Krause Publications Inc., Iola, WI 54990. One-year subscription (12 monthly issues) $24.98, two-year subscription $46.98. Surface rate for other countries: $35.25, including Canada and Mexico. Air-mail subscriptions available; write for rates.

Coin World. Amos Press Inc., P.O. Box 150, Sidney, OH 45365. Six-month subscription (26 weekly issues) $15.97, one-year subscription $29.95. Outside the United States, add $40 per year. Air-mail subscriptions available; write for rates.

Numismatic News. Krause Publications Inc., Iola, WI 54990. Six-month subscription (26 weekly issues) $16.98 U.S., $53.98 foreign, including Canada and Mexico. One-year subscription $29.98 U.S., $102.98 foreign. Two-year subscription $56 U.S., $191.98 foreign. Special U.S. subscriptions available, including first- and second-class plain-wrapper delivery, regular delivery by United Parcel Service, and second-day and next-day delivery by United Parcel Service. Write for rates.

The Numismatist. American Numismatic Association, 818 North Cascade Avenue, Colorado Springs, CO 80903–3279. Published monthly and mailed to all members of the ANA without cost other than annual dues.

World Coin News. Krause Publications Inc., Iola, WI 54990. Six-month subscription (6 monthly issues) $12.98 U.S., $20.98 foreign, including Canada and Mexico. One-year subscription $22.98 U.S., $39.98 foreign. Two-year subscription $42.98 U.S., $74.98 foreign. Special U.S. subscriptions available, including first- and second-class plain-wrapper delivery and regular delivery by United Parcel Service. Write for rates.

COIN SPECIFICATIONS

HALF CENTS

Diameter: 23.5 millimeters (¹⁵⁄₁₆ of an inch)

Weight: 6.739 grams (0.238 ounce) in 1793–94 and part of 1795, 5.443 grams (0.192 ounce) thereafter

Composition: all-copper

Edge: Lettered (TWO HUNDRED FOR A DOLLAR) in 1793 and part of 1797, gripped in part of 1797, plain in all other cases

Designers: Joseph Wright (1793), Robert Scot (1794–1808), John Reich (1809–1836), Christian Gobrecht (1840–1857)

LARGE CENTS

Diameter: 25–28 millimeters (about 1 ¹⁄₁₆ inches) in 1793, 27–30 millimeters (about 1 1/8 inches) in 1794, 28–29 millimeters (about 1 ⅛ inches) thereafter

Weight: 13.478 grams (0.475 ounce) in 1793, 1794, and part of 1795, 10.886 grams (0.384 ounce) thereafter

Composition: All-copper

Edge: Vine and bars in part of 1793, lettered (ONE HUNDRED FOR A DOLLAR) in 1793–1994 and part of 1795, gripped in part of 1797, plain in all other cases

Designers: Henry Voight (1793 Chain and Wreath cents), Joseph Wright, Robert Scot, and John Smith Gardner (1793–1796

Liberty Cap), Robert Scot (1796–1807), John Reich (1808–1814), John Reich (1816–1835), Christian Gobrecht (1835–1857)

FLYING EAGLE CENTS

Diameter: 19 millimeters (¾ of an inch)
Weight: 4.666 grams (0.165 ounce)
Composition: 88 percent copper, 12 percent nickel
Edge: Plain
Designer: James B. Longacre

INDIAN HEAD CENTS

Diameter: 19 millimeters (¾ of an inch)
Weight: 4.666 grams (0.165 ounce) from 1859 to 1863 and part of 1864, 3.110 grams (0.110 ounce) in the rest of 1864 and thereafter
Composition: 88 percent copper, 12 percent nickel from 1859 to 1863 and part of 1864; 95 percent copper, 5 percent zinc and tin in the rest of 1864 and thereafter
Edge: Plain
Designer: James B. Longacre

LINCOLN CENTS

Diameter: 19 millimeter (¾ of an inch)
Weight: 3.110 grams (0.110 ounce) from 1909 to 1981 and part of 1982, except for 1943; 2.689 grams (0.095 ounce) in 1943; 2.5 grams (0.088 ounce) for part of 1982 and thereafter
Composition: 95 percent copper, 5 percent zinc and tin from 1909 to 1961 and part of 1962, except for 1943–1946; zinc-plated steel in 1943; 95 percent copper, 5 percent zinc in 1944–1946, 1963–1981 and parts of 1962 and 1982; 97.5 percent zinc, 2.5 percent copper (copper-plated zinc) for part of 1982 and thereafter
Edge: Plain

Designers: Victor D. Brenner (obverse from 1909 to date and reverse from 1909 to 1958), Frank Gasparro (reverse from 1959 to date)

TWO-CENT PIECES

Diameter: 23 millimeters (9/10 of an inch)
Weight: 6.221 grams (0.219 ounce)
Composition: 95 percent copper, 5 percent zinc and tin
Edge: Plain
Designer: James B. Longacre

SILVER THREE-CENT PIECES

Diameter: 14 millimeters (9/16 of an inch)
Weight: 0.802 grams (0.026 ounce) from 1851–1853, 0.746 grams (0.024 ounce) thereafter
Composition: 75 percent silver, 25 percent copper from 1851–1853; 90 percent silver, 10 percent copper thereafter
Edge: Plain
Designer: James B. Longacre

NICKEL THREE-CENT PIECES

Diameter: 17.9 millimeters (7/10 of an inch)
Weight: 1.944 grams (0.069 ounce)
Composition: 75 percent copper, 25 percent nickel
Edge: Plain
Designer: James B. Longacre

HALF DIMES

Diameter: 16.5 millimeters (about 2/3 of an inch) from 1792 to 1805, 15.5 millimeters (6/10 of an inch) thereafter
Weight: 1.348 grams (0.0434 ounce) from 1792 to 1836, 1.336 grams (0.04295 ounce) from 1837 to part of 1853, 1.244 grams (0.040 ounce) for part of 1853 and thereafter

Composition: 89.25 percent silver, 10.75 percent copper for 1792; 90 percent silver and 10 percent copper for 1794 and part of 1795; 89.25 percent silver, 10.75 percent copper for part of 1795 through 1836; 90 percent silver and 10 percent copper for 1837 and thereafter

Edge: Reeded

Designers: William Russell Birch (1792), Robert Scot (1794–1805)

SHIELD NICKELS

Diameter: 20.5 millimeters (¹³⁄₁₆ of an inch)

Weight: 5 grams (0.176 ounce)

Composition: 75 percent copper, 25 percent nickel

Edge: Plain

Designer: James B. Longacre

LIBERTY HEAD NICKELS

Diameter: 21.2 millimeters (⅚ of an inch)

Weight: 5 grams (0.176 ounce)

Composition: 75 percent copper, 25 percent nickel

Edge: Plain

Designer: Charles E. Barber

BUFFALO NICKELS

Diameter: 21.2 millimeters (⅚ of an inch)

Weight: 5 grams (0.176 ounce)

Composition: 75 percent copper, 25 percent nickel

Edge: Plain

Designer: James E. Fraser

JEFFERSON NICKELS

Diameter: 21.2 millimeters (⅚ of an inch)

Weight: 5 grams (0.176 ounce)

Composition: 75 percent copper, 25 percent nickel except for

1943–1945 and part of 1942; 56 percent copper, 35 percent silver and 9 percent manganese during those years
Edge: Plain
Designer: Felix Schlag

DRAPED BUST DIMES

Diameter: About 19 millimeters (²⁵⁄₃₂ of an inch)
Weight: 2.696 grams (0.087 ounce)
Composition: 89.25 percent silver, 10.75 percent copper
Edge: Reeded
Designer: Robert Scot

CAPPED BUST DIMES

Diameter: About 18.8 millimeters (¾ of an inch) from 1809 to 1827 and part of 1828; 18.5 millimeters (⁷⁄₁₀ of an inch) for part of 1828 and thereafter
Weight: 2.696 grams (0.087 ounce) from 1809 through 1836 and 2.696 grams (0.086 ounce) for 1837
Composition: 89.25 percent silver, 10.75 percent copper for 1809 to 1836; 90 percent silver and 10 percent copper for 1837 and 1838
Edge: Reeded
Designer: John Reich

SEATED LIBERTY DIMES

Diameter: 17.9 millimeters (⁷⁄₁₀ of an inch)
Weight: 2.673 grams (0.086 ounce) from 1837 to 1852 and part of 1853; 2.488 grams (0.080 ounce) for parts of 1853 and 1873 and from 1854 to 1872; 2.50 grams (0.084 ounce) from 1874 to 1891
Composition: 90 percent silver, 10 percent copper
Edge: Reeded
Designer: Christian Gobrecht

BARBER DIMES

Diameter: 17.9 millimeters (⅒ of an inch)
Weight: 2.50 grams (0.804 ounce)
Composition: 90 percent silver, 10 percent copper
Edge: Reeded
Designer: Charles E. Barber

"MERCURY" DIMES

Diameter: 17.9 millimeters (⅒ of an inch)
Weight: 2.50 grams (0.084 ounce)
Composition: 90 percent silver, 10 percent copper
Edge: Reeded
Designer: Adolph A. Weinman

ROOSEVELT DIMES

Diameter: 17.9 millimeters (⅒ of an inch)
Weight: 2.50 grams (0.084 ounce) from 1946 to 1964, 2.27 grams (0.080 ounce) from 1965 to date
Composition: 90 percent silver, 10 percent copper from 1946 to 1964; 75-percent-copper, 25-percent-nickel alloy bonded to pure copper core thereafter
Edge: Reeded
Designer: John R. Sinnock

TWENTY-CENT PIECES

Diameter: 22 millimeters (⅞ of an inch)
Weight: 5 grams (0.161 ounce)
Composition: 90 percent silver, 10 percent copper
Edge: Plain
Designer: William Barber

DRAPED BUST QUARTER DOLLARS

Diameter: About 27.5 millimeters (1 ½ inches)
Weight: 6.739 grams (0.217 ounce)
Composition: 89.25 percent silver, 10.75 percent copper
Edge: Reeded
Designer: Robert Scot

CAPPED BUST QUARTER DOLLARS

Diameter: 27 millimeters (1 ¼ inches) from 1815 to 1828, 24.3 millimeter (19/20 of an inch) from 1831 to 1838
Weight: 6.739 grams (0.217 ounce) from 1815 through 1836 and 6.68 grams (0.215 ounce) for 1837 and 1838
Composition: 89.25 percent silver, 10.75 percent copper for 1815 to 1836; 90 percent silver and 10 percent copper for 1837 through 1838
Edge: Reeded
Designer: John Reich

SEATED LIBERTY QUARTER DOLLARS

Diameter: 24.3 millimeters (¹⁹⁄₂₀ of an inch)
Weight: 6.68 grams (0.215 ounce) from 1838 to 1852 and part of 1853; 6.221 grams (0.2 ounce) from 1854 to 1872 and part of 1873; 6.25 grams (0.201 ounce) in part of 1873 and from 1874 to 1891
Composition: 90 percent silver, 10 percent copper
Edge: Reeded
Designer: Christian Gobrecht

BARBER QUARTER DOLLARS

Diameter: 24.3 millimeters (¹⁹⁄₂₀ of an inch)
Weight: 6.25 grams (0.201 ounce)
Composition: 90 percent silver, 10 percent copper
Edge: Reeded
Designer: Charles E. Barber

STANDING LIBERTY QUARTER DOLLARS

Diameter: 24.3 millimeters (¹⁹⁄₂₀ of an inch)
Weight: 6.25 grams (0.201 ounce)
Composition: 90 percent silver, 10 percent copper
Edge: Reeded
Designer: Hermon A. MacNeil

WASHINGTON QUARTER DOLLARS

Diameter: 24.3 millimeters (¹⁹⁄₂₀ of an inch)
Weight: 6.25 grams (0.201 ounce) from 1932 to 1964; 5.670 grams (0.200 ounce) from 1965 to date
Composition: 90 percent silver, 10 percent copper from 1932 to 1964; 75-percent-copper, 25-percent-nickel alloy bonded to pure copper core thereafter
Edge: Reeded
Designer: John Flanagan
Note: The State quarter dollars of 1999 have the same specifications (except for the designer) as the Washington quarters of 1965–1998

FLOWING HAIR HALF DOLLARS

Diameter: About 32.5 millimeters (1 ₃₂⁄... of an inch)
Weight: 13.48 grams (0.433 ounce)
Composition: 90 percent silver and 10 percent copper for 1794 and 1795
Edge: Lettered (FIFTY CENTS OR HALF A DOLLAR)
Designer: Robert Scot

DRAPED BUST HALF DOLLARS

Diameter: 32.5 millimeters (1 ₃₂⁄... of an inch)
Weight: 13.48 grams (0.433 ounce)
Composition: 89.25 percent silver, 10.75 percent copper
Edge: Lettered (FIFTY CENTS OR HALF A DOLLAR)
Designer: Robert Scot

CAPPED BUST HALF DOLLARS

Diameter: 32.5 millimeters (1 ⅝ of an inch)
Weight: 13.48 grams (0.433 ounce)
Composition: 89.25 percent silver, 10.75 percent copper
Edge: Lettered (FIFTY CENTS OR HALF A DOLLAR)
Designer: John Reich

CAPPED BUST HALF DOLLARS (REEDED EDGE)

Diameter: 30.6 millimeters (1 ⁷⁄₁₀ of an inch)
Weight: 13.48 grams (0.433 ounces) for 1836, 13.36 grams (0.430 ounce) thereafter
Composition: 89.25 percent silver, 10.75 percent copper for 1836; 90 percent silver and 10 percent copper 1837 through 1839
Edge: Reeded
Designer: Christian Gobrecht (after John Reich)

SEATED LIBERTY HALF DOLLARS

Diameter: 30.6 millimeters (1 ⁷⁄₁₀ of an inch)
Weight: 13.36 grams (0.430 ounce) from 1839 to 1852 and part of 1853; 12.44 grams (0.4 ounce) in part of 1853 and 1873 and from 1854 to 1872; 12.5 grams (0.402 ounce) in part of 1873 and from 1874 to 1891
Composition: 90 percent silver, 10 percent copper
Edge: Reeded
Designer: Christian Gobrecht

BARBER HALF DOLLARS

Diameter: 30.6 millimeters (1 ⁷⁄₁₀ of an inch)
Weight: 12.5 grams (0.402 ounce)
Composition: 90 percent silver, 10 percent copper
Edge: Reeded
Designer: Charles E. Barber

WALKING LIBERTY HALF DOLLARS

Diameter: 30.6 millimeters (1 %o of an inch)
Weight: 12.5 grams (0.402 ounce)
Composition: 90 percent silver, 10 percent copper
Edge: Reeded
Designer: Adolph A. Weinman

FRANKLIN HALF DOLLARS

Diameter: 30.6 millimeters (1 %o of an inch)
Weight: 12.5 grams (0.402 ounce)
Composition: 90 percent silver, 10 percent copper
Edge: Reeded
Designer: John R. Sinnock

KENNEDY HALF DOLLARS

Diameter: 30.6 millimeters (1 %o of an inch)
Weight: 12.5 grams (0.402 ounce) in 1964; 11.5 grams (0.370 ounce) from 1965 to 1970; 11.34 grams (0.400 ounce) from 1971 to date
Composition: 90 percent silver, 10 percent copper in 1964; 40 percent silver from 1965 to 1970 (80-percent-silver, 20-percent-copper alloy bonded to a 20.9-percent-silver, 79.1-percent-copper core); 75-percent-copper, 25-percent-nickel alloy bonded to pure copper core from 1971 to date
Edge: Reeded
Designers: Gilroy Roberts (obverse) and Frank Gasparro (reverse)

FLOWING HAIR SILVER DOLLARS

Diameter: About 39 to 40 millimeters (1 %6 inches)
Weight: 26.96 grams (0.867 ounce)
Composition: 90 percent silver, 10 percent copper
Edge: Lettered (HUNDRED CENTS ONE DOLLAR OR UNIT)
Designer: Robert Scot

DRAPED BUST SILVER DOLLARS

Diameter: 39.5 millimeters (1 ⅝ inches)
Weight: 26.96 grams (0.867 ounce)
Composition: 89.25 percent silver, 10.75 percent copper
Edge: Lettered (HUNDRED CENTS ONE DOLLAR OR UNIT)
Designer: Robert Scot

GOBRECHT SILVER DOLLARS

Diameter: 39.5 millimeters (1 ⅝ inches)
Weight: Issue of 1836, 26.96 grams (0.867 ounce); issue of 1836 (struck in 1837) and 1838–1839, 26.73 grams (0.859 ounce)
Composition: 416 grain standard, 1836 only: 89.25 percent silver, 10.75 percent copper; 412.5 grain standard, 1836 (coined in 1837) and 1838–1839, 90 percent silver, 10 percent copper
Edge: Plain in 1836, reeded in 1839
Designer: Christian Gobrecht

SEATED LIBERTY SILVER DOLLARS

Diameter: 38.1 millimeters (1 ½ inches)
Weight: 26.73 grams (0.859 ounce)
Composition: 90 percent silver, 10 percent copper
Edge: Reeded
Designer: Christian Gobrecht

MORGAN SILVER DOLLARS

Diameter: 38.1 millimeters (1 ½ inches)
Weight: 26.73 grams (0.859 ounce)
Composition: 90 percent silver, 10 percent copper
Edge: Reeded
Designer: George T. Morgan

PEACE SILVER DOLLARS

Diameter: 38.1 millimeters (1 ½ inches)
Weight: 26.73 grams (0.859 ounce)
Composition: 90 percent silver, 10 percent copper
Edge: Reeded
Designer: Anthony de Francisci

TRADE DOLLARS

Diameter: 38.1 millimeters (1 ½ inches)
Weight: 27.216 grams (0.875 ounce)
Composition: 90 percent silver, 10 percent copper
Edge: Reeded
Designer: William Barber

EISENHOWER DOLLARS

Diameter: 38.1 millimeters (1 ½ inches)
Weight: 22.68 grams (0.800 ounce)
Composition: 75-percent-copper, 25-percent-nickel alloy bonded to pure copper core
Edge: Reeded
Designer: Frank Gasparro

ANTHONY DOLLARS

Diameter: 26.5 millimeters (1 ⁵⁄₁₀ inch)
Weight: 8.1 grams (0.286 ounce)
Composition: 75-percent-copper, 25-percent-nickel alloy bonded to pure copper core
Edge: Reeded
Designer: Frank Gasparro

SACAGAWEA DOLLARS

Diameter: 26.5 millimeters (1 ⁵⁄₁₀ inches)
Weight: 8.1 grams (0.286 ounce)

Composition: 50 percent copper (core); clad layers are 4 percent nickel, 77 percent copper, 12 percent zinc, 7 percent manganese. Net alloy is 6 percent zinc, 3.5 percent manganese, 2 percent nickel, and 88.5 percent copper

Edge: Plain

Designers: Glenna Goodacre (obverse) and Thomas D. Rogers, Sr. (reverse)

GOLD DOLLARS

Diameter: 13 millimeters (½ inch) from 1849 to 1853 and part of 1854; 14.86 millimeters (⁹⁄₁₀ of an inch) for part of 1854 and thereafter

Weight: 1.672 grams (0.054 ounce)

Composition: 90 percent gold, 10 percent copper and silver

Edge: Reeded

Designer: James B. Longacre

CAPPED BUST FACING RIGHT QUARTER EAGLES ($2.50 GOLD PIECES)

Diameter: About 20 millimeters (⁹⁄₁₀ of an inch)

Weight: 4.374 grams (0.141 ounce)

Composition: 91.67 percent gold, 8.33 percent copper and silver

Edge: Reeded

Designer: Robert Scot

CAPPED BUST FACING LEFT QUARTER EAGLES

Diameter: About 20 millimeters (⁹⁄₁₀ of an inch)

Weight: 4.374 grams (0.141 ounce)

Composition: 91.67 percent gold, 8.33 percent copper and silver

Edge: Reeded

Designer: John Reich

CAPPED HEAD QUARTER EAGLES

Diameter: 18.5 millimeters (¾ inch) from 1821 to 1827, 18.2 millimeters (⁷⁄₁₀ inch) from 1829 to 1834

Weight: 4.374 grams (0.141 ounce)

Composition: 91.67 percent gold, 8.33 percent copper and silver

Edge: Reeded

Designer: Robert Scot and John Reich

CLASSIC HEAD QUARTER EAGLES

Diameter: 18.2 millimeters (⁷⁄₁₀ of an inch)

Weight: 4.18 grams (0.134 ounce)

Composition: 89.92 percent gold, 10.08 percent copper and silver from 1834 to 1836; 90 percent gold, 10 percent copper and silver from 1837 to 1839

Edge: Reeded

Designer: William Kneass

CORONET QUARTER EAGLES

Diameter: 18.2 millimeters (⁷⁄₁₀ of an inch)

Weight: 4.18 grams (0.134 ounce)

Composition: 90 percent gold, 10 percent copper

Edge: Reeded

Designer: Christian Gobrecht

INDIAN HEAD QUARTER EAGLES

Diameter: 18 millimeters (⁷⁄₁₀ of an inch)

Weight: 4.18 grams (0.134 ounce)

Composition: 90 percent gold, 10 percent copper

Edge: Reeded

Designer: Bela Lyon Pratt

$3 GOLD PIECES

Diameter: 20.5 millimeters (⁹⁄₁₀ of an inch)
Weight: 5.015 grams (0.161 ounce)
Composition: 90 percent gold, 10 percent copper
Edge: Reeded
Designer: James B. Longacre

STELLAS ($4 GOLD PIECES)

Diameter: 22 millimeters (⅞ of an inch)
Weight: 7 grams (0.225 ounce)
Composition: 85.71 percent gold, 4.29 percent silver, 10 percent copper
Edge: Reeded
Designers: Charles E. Barber and George T. Morgan

CAPPED BUST HALF EAGLES ($5 GOLD PIECES)

Diameter: 25 millimeters (1 inch)
Weight: 8.748 grams (0.281 ounce)
Composition: 91.67 percent gold, 8.33 percent copper and silver
Edge: Reeded
Designer: Robert Scot

CAPPED DRAPED BUST FACING LEFT HALF EAGLES

Diameter: 25 millimeters (1 inch)
Weight: 8.748 grams (0.281 ounce)
Composition: 91.67 percent gold, 8.33 percent copper and silver
Edge: Reeded
Designer: John Reich

CAPPED HEAD HALF EAGLES

Diameter: 25 millimeters (1 inch) from 1813 to 1828 and part of 1829; 23.8 millimeters (¹⁵⁄₁₆ of an inch) for part of 1829 and thereafter

Weight: 8.748 grams (0.281 ounce)

Composition: 91.67 percent gold, 8.33 percent copper and silver

Edge: Reeded

Designer: John Reich

CLASSIC HEAD HALF EAGLES

Diameter: 22.5 millimeters (⅞ of an inch)

Weight: 8.36 grams (0.269 ounce)

Composition: 89.92 percent gold, 10.08 percent copper from 1834 to 1836; 90 percent gold, 10 percent copper and silver in 1837 and 1838

Edge: Reeded

Designer: William Kneass

CORONET HALF EAGLES

Diameter: 22.5 millimeters (⅞ of an inch) in 1839 and part of 1840; 21.6 millimeters (¹⁷⁄₂₀ of an inch) for part of 1840 and thereafter

Weight: 8.36 grams (0.269 ounce)

Composition: 90 percent gold, 10 percent copper

Edge: Reeded

Designer: Christian Gobrecht

INDIAN HEAD HALF EAGLES

Diameter: 21.6 millimeters (¹⁷⁄₂₀ of an inch)

Weight: 8.36 grams (0.269 ounce)

Composition: 90 percent gold, 10 percent copper

Edge: Reeded

Designer: Bela Lyon Pratt

CAPPED BUST EAGLES ($10 GOLD PIECES)

Diameter: 33 millimeters (1³⁄₁₀ inches)
Weight: 17.496 grams (0.563 ounce)
Composition: 91.67 percent gold, 8.33 percent copper and silver
Edge: Reeded
Designer: Robert Scot

CORONET EAGLES

Diameter: 27 millimeters (1 ¹⁄₁₆ inches)
Weight: 16.718 grams (0.538 ounce)
Composition: 90 percent gold, 10 percent copper and silver from 1838 to 1872 and part of 1873; 90 percent gold, 10 percent copper for part of 1873 and thereafter
Designer: Christian Gobrecht

INDIAN HEAD EAGLES

Diameter: 27 millimeters (1 ¹⁄₁₆ inches)
Weight: 16.718 grams (0.538 ounce)
Composition: 90 percent gold, 10 percent copper
Edge: Starred (46 raised stars from 1907 to 1911, 48 raised stars thereafter; each star represents one of the states in the Union, and two new states—New Mexico and Arizona—joined the Union in 1912)
Designer: Augustus Saint Gaudens

LIBERTY HEAD DOUBLE EAGLES ($20 GOLD PIECES)

Diameter: 34.2 millimeters (1 ⅜ inches)
Weight: 33.436 grams (1.075 ounce)
Composition: 90 percent gold, 10 percent copper and silver from 1849 to 1872 and part of 1873; 90 percent gold, 10 percent copper for part of 1873 and thereafter
Edge: Reeded
Designer: James B. Longacre

SAINT-GAUDENS DOUBLE EAGLES
($20 GOLD PIECES)

Diameter: 34.2 millimeters (1 ⅜ inches)
Weight: 33.436 grams (1.075 ounce)
Composition: 90 percent gold, 10 percent copper
Edge: Lettered (E PLURIBUS UNUM, with stars dividing the words)
Designer: Augustus Saint-Gaudens
*NOTE: The weight in ounces is given in avoirdupois for base metals
and troy standard for gold and silver*

WHERE TO LOOK FOR MINT MARKS

Mint marks appear in a number of different locations on U.S. coins. Today, the standard location on regular-issue coins—the five coins made for use in commerce—is the obverse, or "heads" side. In earlier times, however, most coins carried these letters on the reverse.

Following is a list of where to look for mint marks on various U.S. coins:

- **Lincoln cents (1909–present)**—on the obverse, below the date.

- **Indian Head cents (1908 and 1909 only)**—on the reverse, below the wreath.

- **Jefferson nickels (1938–1964)**—on the reverse, to the right of Monticello, except on part-silver war nickels of 1942–1945; there, a large mint mark appears above Monticello.

- **Jefferson nickels (1968–present)**—on the obverse, below the date.

- **Buffalo nickels (1913–1938)**—on the reverse, below the words FIVE CENTS.

- **Liberty Head nickels (1912 only)**—on the reverse, to the left of the word CENTS.

WHERE TO LOOK FOR MINT MARKS

- **Roosevelt dimes (1946–1964)**—on the reverse, to the left of the torch's base.

- **Roosevelt dimes (1968–present)**—on the obverse, above the date.

- **"Mercury" dimes (1916–1945)**—on the reverse, to the left of the fasces.

- **Barber dimes (1892–1916)**—on the reverse, below the wreath.

- **Washington quarters (1932–1964)**—on the reverse, below the wreath.

- **Washington quarters (1968–present)**—on the obverse, to the right of George Washington's pigtail.

- **Standing Liberty quarters (1916–1930)**—on the obverse, to the left of the date.

- **Barber quarters (1892–1916)**—on the reverse, below the eagle.

- **Kennedy half dollars (1964)**—on the reverse, to the left of the eagle's tail feathers.

- **Kennedy half dollars (1968–present)**—on the obverse, below John F. Kennedy's neck.

- **Walking Liberty half dollars (1916–1917)**—on the obverse, below IN GOD WE TRUST.

- **Walking Liberty half dollars (1917–1947)**—on the reverse, above and to the left of HALF DOLLAR. (Half dollars dated 1917 come in both mint-mark varieties.)

- **Barber half dollars (1892–1915)**—on the reverse, below the wreath.

- **Anthony dollars (1979–1981)**—on the obverse, above Susan B. Anthony's right shoulder.

- **Eisenhower dollars (1971–1978)**—on the obverse, below Dwight D. Eisenhower's neck.

• **Peace silver dollars (1921–1935)**—on the reverse, below the word ONE.

• **Morgan silver dollars (1878–1921)**—on the reverse, below the wreath.

• **Saint-Gaudens double eagles (1907–1933)**—on the obverse, above the date.

• **Liberty Head $20 double eagles**—on the reverse, below the eagle.

SCOTT A. TRAVERS ranks as one of the most influential coin dealers in the world. He is the former vice president (1997–1999) of the American Numismatic Association, and his name is familiar to readers everywhere as the author of five bestselling books on coins: *How to Make Money in Coins Right Now, The Coin Collector's Survival Manual, One-Minute Coin Expert, Travers' Rare Coin Investment Strategy,* and *The Investor's Guide to Coin Trading.* All of them have won awards from the prestigious Numismatic Literary Guild (NLG). In 2002, NLG awarded him its highest bestowable honor, the lifetime achievement Clemy. His investment guide, *Scott Travers' Top 88 Coins Over $100,* has been called "the most important list of coin recommendations ever written" by *COINage* magazine. He is a contributing editor to *COINage* magazine and a regular contributor to other numismatic periodicals. His opinions as an expert are often sought by publications such as *Barron's, Business Week,* and *The Wall Street Journal,* and he has served as a coin valuation consultant to the Federal Trade Commission. A frequent guest on radio and television programs, Scott Travers has won awards and gained an impressive reputation not only as a coin expert but also as a forceful consumer advocate for the coin-buying public. He has coordinated the liquidation of numerous important coin collections. He is president of Scott Travers Rare Coin Galleries, Inc., in New York City.

American Numismatic Association
Application for Membership

☐ **Yes,** I want to be a part of America's Coin Club. I will receive the association's award winning month'y journal, *The Numismatist;* access to the world's largest Numismatic library, discounts on numismatic books and dozens of other exclusive member benefits. ST4

Name _____

Address _____

C/S/Z _____

☐ **Enclosed is $33 for a 1 yr. membership**
I herewith make application for membership in the American Numismatic Association, subject to the bylaws of the Association. I also agree to abide by the Code of Ethics adopted by the Association.
Signature _____

American Numismatic Association
818 N. Cascade Avenue
Colorado Springs, CO 80903-3279
1-800-367-9723

Chartered by Congress in 1912 to promote the hobby and science of numismatics.